Standards
and Assessment

THE CORE OF QUALITY INSTRUCTION

Standards and Assessment

THE CORE
OF QUALITY INSTRUCTION

LISA ALMEIDA, LAURA BENSON, JAN CHRISTINSON,
BRANDON DOUBEK, LYNN HOWARD, LOAN MASCORRO, THOMASINA PIERCY,
GABRIEL RSHAID, STEPHEN VENTURA, MARYANN WIGGS

EDITED BY LAURA BESSER

LEAD+
LEARN
PRESS

ENGLEWOOD, COLORADO

The Leadership and Learning Center
317 Inverness Way South, Suite 150
Englewood, Colorado 80112
Phone 1.866.399.6019 | Fax 303.504.9417
www.LeadandLearn.com

Published by Lead + Learn Press, a division of Advanced Learning Centers, Inc.

Lead + Learn Press also publishes books in a variety of electronic formats. Some content that appears in print may not be available in electronic books.

Library of Congress Cataloging-in-Publication Data

Standards and assessment : the core of quality instruction / Lisa Almeida ... [et al.].
   p. cm.
   Includes index.
   ISBN 978-1-935588-03-0 (alk. paper)
   1. Academic achievement—United States—Testing. 2. Education—United States—
Evaluation. I. Almeida, Lisa.
   LB3051.S788 2011
   371.26'20973--dc22
                                       2011011379

ISBN 978-1-935588-03-0

Printed in the United States of America

15 14 13 12 11   01 02 03 04 05 06 07

Contents

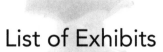

List of Exhibits

About the Authors

Lisa Almeida is the Director of Certification and a Distinguished Professional Development Associate with The Leadership and Learning Center. As a Distinguished Professional Development Associate, Lisa continually works with clients and their certified instructors. She supports much of The Center's core content that includes, but is not limited to, Engaging Classroom Assessments: The Making Standards Work Series, Decision Making for Results and Data Teams, Five Easy Steps to a Balanced Math Program, Common Formative Assessments, certification courses, and implementation support.

Laura Benson is a Professional Development Associate with The Leadership and Learning Center. Laura brings more than 30 years of teaching to her work as a teacher educator and literacy consultant. Her work in professional development began during the first years of her teaching career when she was asked to develop a writers' workshop lab classroom for colleagues. Laura's demonstrations of writing instruction and evaluation grew into staff development efforts devoted to reading instruction and integrating literacy instruction and content-area learning.

Jan Christinson is a Professional Development Associate with The Leadership and Learning Center. He conducts seminars based on two publications he co-authored: *Five Easy Steps to a Balanced Math Program* and *Student Generated Rubrics: An Assessment Model to Help All Students Succeed*. Jan's primary goal is to improve classroom instruction and thereby improve student learning. With 32 years of experience as an elementary and middle school classroom teacher, Jan brings a wide and varied range of educational experiences to his presentations.

Brandon Doubek is a Professional Development Associate with The Leadership and Learning Center who brings more than 20 years of experience to his work as a leader, teacher educator, professor, instructional strategy consultant, and researcher. He has provided seminars and follow-up site visits for Common Formative Assessments, Engaging Classroom Assessments, Data Teams, Decision Making for Results, Advanced Data-Driven Decision Making, Powerful Strategies for Effective Teaching, Writing to Learn, Response to Intervention, Differentiated Instruction, and Daily Disciplines of Leadership. He is known for engaging participants and students through humor and breaking down complex ideas into manageable pieces of information that can easily be implemented.

Lynn Howard is a Professional Development Associate with The Leadership and Learning Center. She worked in the Charlotte-Mecklenburg Schools system for more than 30 years as a middle grades science teacher, coordinator of the gifted program, and regional assistant superintendent. Lynn has conducted extensive staff development around the country and has brought a wealth of experience to districts and schools. Lynn is the author of *Ready for Anything: Supporting New Teachers for Success* and *Five Easy Steps to a Balanced Science Program (Primary, Upper Elementary and Middle School,* and *Secondary)*. Lynn holds a bachelor's degree in biology and master's degrees in earth science and education from the University of North Carolina at Charlotte. She has also earned Academy Certification from the National Staff Development Council and endorsements in Gifted and Talented. And as someone who has survived being locked in an outhouse miles from civilization, she brings an adventurous approach to the real-life strategies for teaching and learning.

Loan Mascorro is a Professional Development Associate with The Leadership and Learning Center. She was a classroom teacher and an administrator in an urban school district, where she successfully implemented the Data Teams process to use the practices of monitoring and feedback to enable student achievement based on common formative assessment results. Loan has worked with students from diverse backgrounds with differing learning needs, including English language learners and students receiving Special Education services. Her expertise in instruction, data analysis, standards, and assessment results in high-quality professional learning for educators. Loan enthusiastically provides professional development support by utilizing best practices and powerful research-based strategies in her approach to helping educators increase learning for all students in measurable ways.

Thomasina D. Piercy is a Professional Development Associate with The Leadership and Learning Center. She earned her degree in curriculum and instruction with a focus on reading from the University of Maryland. As a principal and a teacher, she taught graduate writing and reading courses to educators from various states in the East Coast region. Thommie's research received the Reading Research Award from the State of Maryland International Reading Association Council. She was honored with the Bailer Award from McDaniel College for her distinguished career in education, and she was the recipient of the Court Appointed Special Advocate Children's Hero Award. As a teacher, she was named one of five expert teachers by the Maryland State Department of Education.

Gabriel Rshaid is a Professional Development Associate with The Leadership and Learning Center. He has been an educator for more than 20 years, having taught various subjects at the elementary and high school levels. For the last 12 years, he has been a K–12 principal in independent schools while remaining active in the classroom. His passion for learning and growing up with technological developments have taken him on a journey to think about education in the context of how these changes can improve the learning process. The experience has, in turn, led him to present at numerous venues on the topic of twenty-first-century education and the future of learning.

Stephen Ventura is a Professional Development Associate with The Leadership and Learning Center. He is a highly motivational and knowledgeable speaker who approaches high-stakes data collection and decision making armed with practical, research-based strategies. He is a former elementary, middle school, and high school teacher. His administrative experiences encompass those of assistant principal, principal, director, and superintendent.

Maryann D. Wiggs is a Professional Development Associate with The Leadership and Learning Center. With more than four decades of experience in education, Maryann brings an abundance of expertise and wisdom to her presentations, ensuring that teachers and administrators gain practical strategies for enhancing instructional performance. As the former Assistant Superintendent of Curriculum and Instruction and Executive Director of Learning Services in two Colorado school districts, Maryann has been instrumental in orchestrating the alignment of all aspects of the leaders' and teachers' work to improve the quality of instruction in the classroom, including alignment of standards, assessment, curriculum, instruction, interventions, supervision, and evaluation. Maryann is a former speech pathologist, special and general education teacher, behavior consultant, and teacher leader, having served learners at the elementary, middle, high school, and college levels.

Foreword

LARRY AINSWORTH

Standards and assessment truly are at the very core of quality instruction. Here is why: The central purpose of assessment is to *inform instructional decision making.* Standards provide the *what,* instruction provides the *how,* and assessment results indicate *next steps* the educator needs to take to meet the diverse learning needs of students as they strive day-to-day to understand those standards.

The high-stakes assessments administered annually in every state are, for the most part, based directly upon state standards. To prepare students to succeed on state assessments, educators rightly focus their instruction on state standards and then regularly administer in-school formative assessments aligned to the concepts, skills, and rigor of those standards. They design these formative assessments to reflect the formats, question types, and academic language students are likely to encounter on summative, external tests. If the participating educators will then analyze the results of these formative assessments in order to make accurate inferences about what their students currently know and are able to do—and then adjust instruction accordingly—they are indeed using assessment results to "drive" instruction.

The historic adoption of the Common Core State Standards (CCSS) in English language arts and mathematics by nearly every state in the United States and the District of Columbia puts the bright spotlight on standards—and corresponding assessments—as never before. Even though the national assessments aligned to the CCSS will not be ready for administration until the 2014/15 school year, school districts in adopting states need to begin *now* to prepare educators and students for these more rigorous standards and matching assessments. Providing *quality instruction* is the only logical way educators can prepare their students to show—through a body of in-school assessment evidence—that students have indeed learned these new standards.

In the following pages, my colleagues at The Leadership and Learning Center present important ideas for your professional consideration as you continue striving to effectively implement powerful standards, instruction, and assessment practices for improving student achievement. The insights and recommendations of these writers are applicable not only to the CCSS in English language arts and mathematics but to the existing standards in all other content areas as well. Here is a preview of what these authors have to share:

In Chapter 1, Getting to Know the Common Core State Standards, **Maryann Wiggs**—one of the Center's acknowledged experts on the subject of the new national standards—presents an informative overview of the CCSS. She rightly urges educators and leaders not to go it alone in their efforts to mine the depths of these new, more rigorous standards: "As an educational community, the CCSSI (Common Core State Standards Initiative) provides a marvelous opportunity to form collaborative partnerships across time zones to leverage the strenuous work of implementing our 'shared' standards. There is power in harnessing our collective capacity as we build networks to engage in the shared work of designing high-quality, rigorous curricular units of study, robust performance assessment tasks, and aligned instructional and technology resource materials."

In Chapter 2, The Power of Performance Assessments, **Lisa Almeida** draws upon decades of respected research to emphasize the inestimable value of students' active involvement in performance tasks. She advocates relevant and engaging learning that enables students to genuinely construct their own understanding of the standards in focus: "Meaningful learning is experiential; hands-on equates to 'minds-on' and is heavily infused with critical reasoning. Authentic performance assessment involves observing students 'doing' experiences in meaningful contexts."

Jan Christinson, unquestionably one of the nation's foremost experts in mathematics instruction and assessment methods, presents the first of five steps in his Balanced Math Program aimed at "building" mathematically powerful students. He explains in Chapter 3 how daily student self-assessment—a formative process coupled with feedback and reflection—provides benefits to students and teachers alike: "Math Review puts the students into the assessment equation, where they belong, and provides the necessary support for them to deal with their misconceptions and to develop confidence in their ability to do math."

"A conceptual approach to learning science allows students to deepen scientific understanding by connecting science concepts to science meaning," writes **Lynn Howard** in Chapter 4, Connecting Science Standards and Assessments. Presenting a conceptual unit design approach to the teaching of science, Lynn provides a framework that "allows educators to truly understand the structure and processes embedded in their state science standards. This progression of recognizing how standards and assessments are correlated builds professional and collaborative learning communities in which science teaching and learning is making a difference for students."

Loan Mascorro explains in Chapter 5 how common formative assessments can be used effectively with English language learners: "Authentic assessment, rooted in the simplicity of knowing a student's name and acknowledging his background, language level, and cultural history, allows the educator to develop common formative assessments for learning. . . . [U]sing intentionally created formative assessments with all students [helps] to determine their current level of understanding of an academic area while crafting access to social and instructional understanding."

In Chapter 6, **Brandon Doubek** discusses the importance of carrying out a task within its optimum context: "The case for understanding contexts of standards and assessments is not only critical to teaching and learning but is also at the heart of the levels at which instruction, curriculum, and assessment are interpreted. So often the planning stage of instruction begins with teachers looking at a textbook and choosing chapters from a book or some other materials to deliver instruction, rather than starting with the target curriculum standard to determine what is delivered to students."

In Chapter 7, **Laura Benson** compares the valuable aid that maps provide the world traveler to the help educators get from assessments when used as maps en route to a standards destination. She writes: "Formative assessments help us determine where our students are individually in their journey toward a specific literacy standard. By knowing every student as an individual reader, writer, learner, and thinker with our use of formative methodology, we are better able to craft standards-focused instruction so that it fulfills genuine student needs in response to their strengths, curiosity, and current stages of development."

Thommie Piercy discusses in Chapter 8 the critical need for educators to become well versed in *disciplinary literacy* in order to help students truly comprehend the increasingly complex reading texts that accompany the CCSS. "Students need to hit the ground running in middle and high school, being equipped with the informational knowledge and text know-how required to read complex texts with understanding. . . . The disciplinary literacy model described in this chapter is an instructional framework with discipline-specific processes for deep understanding of complex texts."

In Chapter 9, **Stephen Ventura** makes a compelling case for taking on one of the most problematic issues in the standards reform movement: effective grading practices. He poses a provocative question to set the stage for a lucid and persuasive argument in favor of changing our grading system to improve student achievement and motivation: "Why do so many educators believe that awarding a grade of zero will motivate students? I hope to sensitively challenge readers by suggesting that grades are largely influenced by personal judgment and that the same student with the same work can receive wildly different feedback based on the grading policies of the teacher."

Finally, in Chapter 10, **Gabriel Rshaid** asks us to look beyond the traditional model of education and assessment to help educators learn how to assess the twenty-first-century learner in the information age. He writes: "Assessment has largely been geared to evaluate how much learning occurred during the formal schooling years, and not to [determining] how learners have developed skills that enable them to transcend their learning experience in school throughout the rest of their lives. If lifelong learning is the global objective, then both assessment and related standards must reflect this goal and attempt to measure whether learners have acquired the desired skills."

Collectively the ideas presented in this volume will do much to advance our ever-growing understanding of how educators and leaders can effectively design, implement, monitor, and sustain intentionally aligned best practices founded upon the bedrock of education: standards, assessment, curriculum, and instruction.

The Hope and Promise of the Common Core

This informational chapter provides an overview of the Common Core State Standards (CCSS). Maryann Wiggs helps us see that by increasing the rigor of teaching and learning using the CCSS, we will increase the quality of education in all of our schools. She guides us through the design and organization of both the English language arts and mathematics CCSS. While encouraging us to fully explore the standards documents, she provides a synopsis of each. Learning about the CCSS and translating those into classroom experiences are two very different practices. Maryann provides a framework for planning, implementing, and monitoring the CCSS in schools. She reminds us that while changing our traditional use of standards may be challenging, the benefits are numerous. Read on to learn more about how to make the CCSS work for teachers and increase the learning opportunities for students.

CHAPTER ONE

Getting to Know the
Common Core State Standards

MARYANN D. WIGGS

*These Standards are not intended to be new names for old ways of
doing business. They are a call to take the next step. It is time for
states to work together to build on lessons learned from two decades
of standards based reforms. It is time to recognize that standards are
not just promises to our children, but promises we intend to keep.*

CCSSI (2010f, p. 5)

Along with thoughtful study of the content of the Common Core State Standards
(CCSS) and accompanying appendices, this chapter provides a synopsis of some of the
design and organizational features of the standards that are important to keep in mind
when developing an informed, multiyear implementation plan. To access all CCSS documents and available resources, visit www.corestandards.org.

The Hope and the Promise of the
Common Core State Standards

Noble Intentions

The Common Core State Standards Initiative (CCSSI), coordinated by the National
Governors Association Center for Best Practices (NGA Center) and the Council of Chief
State School Officers (CCSSO), released the Common Core State Standards (CCSS) for
English language arts (ELA) and mathematics in June 2010. The widespread support of
both sets of common core academic standards, as evidenced by the voluntary adoption
of the CCSS by the majority of states across the country, represents an unprecedented
opportunity for economies of scale toward improving the quality of education for our
nation's youth.

The K–12 CCSS incorporate the strengths and lessons learned from current state standards and then further scale up grade-level expectations by benchmarking against the rigorous standards of high-performing countries. Informed by evidence and research, the CCSS documents define *what students should know and be able to do* at every level of schooling in ELA and mathematics to ensure preparedness upon graduation from high school to succeed in college and careers in a shifting global economy and society (CCSSI, 2010a).

It is the hope and the promise of the CCSSI that we come together as a nation to address the disparity in achievement gaps exhibited across the country, thus increasing equitable access for many more students to transition from high school to college and the workforce prepared to succeed. The development of these focused, specific, and rigorous common academic standards is the cornerstone of an interconnected accountability structure to improve higher levels of learning and achievement for all students, not just some students. Indeed, if we are to fully realize this vision, then leaders at all levels must galvanize efforts to translate the standards into actions that are equally focused and explicit in improving the quality of instruction in classrooms across the United States.

Reaching the Summit Together

A map provides its user with perspective of the terrain to be navigated and, when consulted throughout a journey, serves to orient the traveler. Similarly, the general overview provided in this chapter on becoming familiar with the CCSS provides perspective on the infrastructure and learning progressions within the standards. It is, however, no substitute for actually digging into and conducting a careful reading of the entire standards documents and accompanying appendices. Better yet, don't go it alone. Indeed, working together, the authors, validating committees, supporters, and organizers of the CCSSI accomplished together what no one individual or organization could, or should, have created alone. They are to be commended for an exemplary product.

Navigating the terrain of understanding the CCSS is merely the starting point for the arduous journey of implementing the standards within the context of diverse educational settings. It will take sharing the load and sticking together to ensure that all students reach the summit of what is possible for their future. As an educational community, the CCSSI provides a marvelous opportunity to form collaborative partnerships across time zones to leverage the strenuous work of implementing our "shared" standards. There is power in harnessing our collective capacity as we build networks to engage in the shared work of designing high-quality, rigorous curriculum units of study, robust performance assessment tasks, and aligned instructional and technology resource materials. There is equal power in reaching mutual decisions about putting aside what does not work and what we know contributes to diffusion of effort.

As you solidify your understanding of the CCSS, consider the distance your school or district must travel to achieve our nation's shared goals. The Systemic Alignment Action Plan document provides a framework for planning, implementing, and monitoring the Common Core that is provided near the end of this chapter. The Systemic Alignment Action Plan framework will help the user gain perspective of the terrain to be navigated when implementing the CCSS and, when consulted throughout the journey, will serve to orient the user on the progress attained.

Understanding Core State Standards for English Language Arts and Literacy in History/Social Studies, Science, and Technical Subjects

The Big Picture

To fully appreciate the design and organization of the K–12 English language arts standards it is important to understand the special role of the four sets of strand-specific college and career readiness (CCR) anchor standards. There are a total of 32 CCR anchor standards divided into four literacy strands. The reading strand has 10 CCR anchor standards, the writing strand has 10, the speaking and listening strand has six, and the language strand has six. Each set of anchor standards defines broad literacy expectations for CCR. The CCR anchor standards serve as the "North Star" for each literacy strand, providing clear orientation as students advance on the path toward CCR.

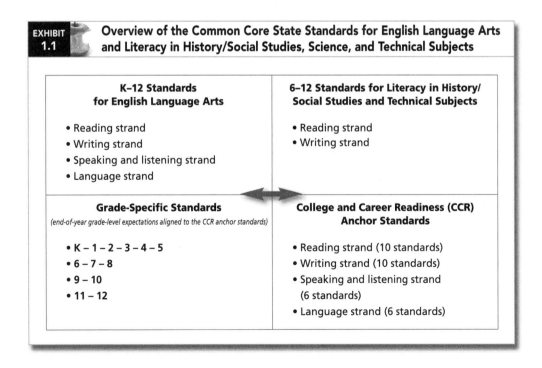

EXHIBIT 1.1   Overview of the Common Core State Standards for English Language Arts and Literacy in History/Social Studies, Science, and Technical Subjects

K–12 Standards for English Language Arts	6–12 Standards for Literacy in History/ Social Studies and Technical Subjects
• Reading strand • Writing strand • Speaking and listening strand • Language strand	• Reading strand • Writing strand
Grade-Specific Standards *(end-of-year grade-level expectations aligned to the CCR anchor standards)* • K – 1 – 2 – 3 – 4 – 5 • 6 – 7 – 8 • 9 – 10 • 11 – 12	**College and Career Readiness (CCR) Anchor Standards** • Reading strand (10 standards) • Writing strand (10 standards) • Speaking and listening strand (6 standards) • Language strand (6 standards)

As noted in Exhibit 1.1, there is a direct, one-to-one correspondence between each grade-specific standard and a CCR anchor standard. Grade-specific standards define end-of-year expectations in each of the four literacy strands. The standards are based on a mastery model of learning whereby students are expected to demonstrate proficiency in each year's grade-specific standard and further advance knowledge and skills as they progress through the grades (CCSSI, 2010b, p. 8).

EXHIBIT 1.2   Organization of the English Language Arts Standards

Section I: Standards for ELA and Literacy in History/Social Studies, Science, and Technical Subjects K–5

- Reading standards for literature K–5 (RL)
- Reading standards for informational text K–5 (RI)

- Reading standards: foundational skills K–5 (RF)

- Writing standards K–5 (writing [W])

- Speaking and listening standards K–5 (SL)

- Language standards K–5 (L)

Section II: Standards for English Language Arts 6–12

- Reading standards for literature 6–12 (RL)
- Reading standards for informational text 6–12 (RI)

- Writing standards 6–12 (W)

- Speaking and listening standards 6–12 (SL)

- Language standards 6–12 (L)

Section III: Standards for Literacy in History/Social Studies, Science, and Technical Subjects 6–12

- Reading standards for literacy in history/social studies 6–12 (RH)

- Reading standards for literacy in science and technical subjects 6–12 (RST)

- Writing standards for literacy in history/social studies, science, and technical subjects 6–12 (WHST)

Appendix A provides supplementary material on reading exemplars and foundational skills, definitions of writing, the role of speaking and listening, an overview of progressive language skills, a glossary of terms, and a detailed discussion on text complexity. Contains 43 pages.

Appendix B provides numerous sample texts illustrating the complexity, quality, and range of reading appropriate for various grade levels with accompanying sample performance tasks. The standards intentionally do not offer a reading list, as school districts and states must decide on curriculum. Contains 183 pages.

Appendix C provides annotated samples demonstrating at least adequate performance in student writing at various grade levels. Contains 107 pages.

Design and Organization

The standards document for K–12 English language arts (ELA) and literacy in history/social studies, science, and technical subjects is divided into three main sections with three appendices. Exhibit 1.2 illustrates how each section is organized around K–5 literacy content; 6–12 literacy content; and a separate section for 6–12 standards for literacy in history/social studies, science, and technical subjects. The reading strand is further divided into K–5 reading standards for foundational skills, K–12 reading standards for literature, and K–12 reading standards for informational text. The three appendices are critical reading for bringing the standards to life in the classroom. The appendices provide exemplars of student performance tasks and, more importantly, descriptors for understanding the level of rigor and application intended by the grade-specific standards.

Grade-Specific Standards and the Spiral Effect

Among the most salient accomplishments in design considerations of the ELA standards document are the learning pathways that a student follows as he or she advances from one grade-specific standard to the next, leading to proficiency in each CCR anchor standard. While the anchor standards taken together serve to provide focus on what matters most for CCR in the area of ELA, coherence is accomplished by the explicit articulation of knowledge and skills along the learning progressions. The specificity of the content within the learning progressions makes visible and clear the expectations for student learning (CCSSI, 2010a). In other words, the grade-specific standards clearly define competence at every level of schooling.

The "spiral effect" is a useful metaphor for further understanding how the learning progressions are structured to provide support for many more students to both access and accelerate through the learning pathways.

Consider the following definitions from the Merriam-Webster online dictionary (http://www.merriam-webster.com/).

Spiral when used as an *adjective:*
- winding around a center or pole and gradually receding from or approaching it
- of or relating to the advancement to higher levels through a series of cyclical movements

Spiral when used as a *noun:*
- the path of a point in a plane moving around a central point while continuously receding from or approaching it
- a continuous spreading and accelerating increase or decrease

The spiral effect metaphor relates to the ascending level of difficulty embedded in the content of each grade-specific standard as it approaches the CCR anchor standard.

EXHIBIT 1.3	Grade-Specific Standards and the "Spiral Effect"— Writing Standard 7 Example

This example illustrates how skills and concepts for end-of-year, grade-specific expectations for a given standard are both reinforced and expanded as students advance through the grades. The result is a "spiral effect" whereby students repeatedly practice mastered competencies from the year prior in the context of new competencies being "added" each year as the standard increases in complexity and sophistication. New skills and concepts added to each grade level from the year prior are noted in **bold**.

W.CCR.7	**CCR Writing Anchor Standard 7:** **Conduct short as well as more sustained research projects based on focused questions, demonstrating understanding of the subject under investigation.**
W.11-12.7 Grade 11–12 students:	Conduct short as well as more sustained research projects to answer a question (including a self-generated question) or solve a problem; narrow or broaden the inquiry when appropriate; synthesize multiple sources on the subject, demonstrating understanding of the subject under investigation.
W.9-10.7 Grade 9–10 students:	Conduct short **as well as more sustained research projects** to answer a question (including a self-generated question) **or solve a problem; narrow or broaden the inquiry when appropriate; synthesize multiple sources on the subject, demonstrating understanding of the subject under investigation.**
W.8.7 Grade 8 students:	Conduct short research projects to answer a question (**including a self-generated question**), drawing on several sources and generating additional related, focused questions **that allow for multiple avenues of exploration.**
W.7.7 Grade 7 students:	Conduct short research projects to answer a question, drawing on several sources and **generating additional related, focused questions for further research and investigation.**
W.6.7 Grade 6 students:	Conduct short research projects **to answer a question, drawing on several sources and refocusing the inquiry when appropriate.**
W.5.7 Grade 5 students:	Conduct short research projects that **use several sources** to build knowledge through investigation of different aspects of a topic.
W.4.7 Grade 4 students:	Conduct short research projects that build knowledge **through investigation of different aspects of** a topic.
W.3.7 Grade 3 students:	**Conduct short research projects that build knowledge about a topic.**
W.2.7 Grade 2 students:	Participate in shared research and writing projects (e.g., **read a number of books on a single topic to produce a report; record science observations**).
W.1.7 Grade 1 students:	Participate in shared research and writing projects (e.g., explore a number of **"how to" books on a given topic and use them to write a sequence of instructions**).
W.K.7 Kindergarten students:	**Participate in shared research and writing projects (e.g., explore a number of books by a favorite author and express opinions about them).**

Source: Adapted from CCSS ELA, 2010b, pgs. 19, 21, 44, 46

The CCR standards serve as the central point or significant learning expectation toward which all grade-specific standards aspire. As students move along the plane of a particular learning trajectory they study the same expectation each year at ever-increasing increments of complexity and sophistication. The gradual cycling through repeated exposure to iterations of the same concepts and processes each year breaks complex learning expectations into manageable teaching and learning targets. Exhibit 1.3 illustrates how concepts and skills for a given standard are both reinforced and expanded as students advance through the grades.

Synopsis of the Reading Strand

The reading standards for literature and informational text are composed of nine standards focused on reading comprehension and one standard focused on the range and level of text complexity. The nine reading comprehension standards are further broken down into specific standards around the themes of *key ideas and details, craft and structure,* and *integration of knowledge and ideas.* Standard 10 defines a grade-by-grade "staircase" of increasing text complexity that progresses from early reading to the CCR level (CCSSI, 2010b, p. 8).

The standards demand that the quality and the volume of what students read expand in order for students to become proficient at higher levels of thinking and reading comprehension. Guidance is provided regarding the breadth and depth of required reading content that paint a portrait of a literate citizen that should include, but not be limited to, classic and contemporary literature, myths and poems, dramas, stories from diverse cultures, U.S. founding documents, and American literature. Two appendices serve as companion documents for the CCSS ELA reading standards. Appendix A provides a complete discussion regarding why text complexity matters and explains a three-part model for measuring text complexity. Appendix B, featured in Exhibit 1.4, provides both text exemplars and sample performance tasks to illustrate the complexity, quality, and range of student reading and application at various grade levels. While the titles presented in Appendix B provide useful examples, all decisions regarding selection of high-quality literature and informational texts reside with each individual school and district (CCSSI, 2010c, 2010d).

Throughout the standards tremendous emphasis is placed on students' ability to closely read and interact with increasingly challenging literature and informational text. While the K–5 reading standards represent a balance between literature and informational text, there is a shift when students reach the 6–12 reading standards toward greater focus on literary nonfiction. Aligned with the National Assessment of Educational Process (NAEP) Reading Framework, the CCSS ELA standards indicate that by senior year in high school 70 percent of the sum of student reading across the grade should be informational text (CCSSI, 2010b, p. 5). At all levels students are expected to actively

EXHIBIT 1.4 Appendix B: 6–8 Text Exemplars and Student Performance Tasks

Text exemplars are provided as examples *only* to illustrate the complexity, quality, and range of student reading at various grade levels.	Sample performance tasks are provided to further illustrate the application of the standards to texts of sufficient complexity, quality and range.
Stories Cooper, Susan. *The Dark Is Rising* Twain, Mark. *The Adventures of Tom Sawyer* Taylor, Mildred D. *Roll of Thunder, Hear My Cry* Sutcliff, Rosemary. *Black Ships before Troy: The Story of the Iliad* **Drama** Fletcher, Louise. *Sorry, Wrong Number* Goodrich, Frances, and Albert Hackett. *The Diary of Anne Frank: A Play* **Poetry** Hughes, Langston. "I, Too, Sing America" Neruda, Pablo. "The Book of Questions" Whitman, Walt. "O Captain! My Captain!" **Informational Text** Adams, John. "Letter on Thomas Jefferson" Lord, Walter. *A Night to Remember* Douglass, Frederick. *Narrative of the Life of Frederick Douglass an American Slave, Written by Himself* Churchill, Winston, "Blood, Toil, Tears and Sweat: Address to Parliament on May 13th, 1940" Petry, Ann. *Harriet Tubman: Conductor on the Underground Railroad* **Source:** CCSSI, 2010d , pp. 8, 9.	**Sample Performance Task** Students compare and contrast Laurence Yep's fictional portrayal of Chinese immigrants in turn-of-the-twentieth-century San Francisco in *Dragonwings* to historical accounts of the same period (using material detailing the 1906 San Francisco earthquake) in order to glean a deeper *understanding of how authors use or alter historical sources* to create a sense of *time and place* as well as make fictional characters lifelike and real. [RL.7.9] Students analyze how the playwright Louise Fletcher *uses particular elements* of drama (e.g., setting and dialogue) to create dramatic tension in the play *Sorry, Wrong Number*. [RL.7.3] Students *trace* the line of *argument* in Winston Churchill's "Blood, Toil, Tears and Sweat" address to Parliament and *evaluate* his *specific claims* and opinions *in the text, distinguishing* which *claims* are *supported by* facts, *reasons, and evidence*, and which *are not*. [RI.6.8] **Source:** CCSSI, 2010d, pp. 89, 93.

engage in making within-text and between-text connections while using analytical thinking skills to synthesize textual evidence (TCRWP, 2010).

Synopsis of the Reading Standards for Literacy in History/Social Studies, Science, and Technical Subjects

The reading standards for literacy in history/social studies, science, and technical subjects follow the exact same pattern as that of the reading standards for literature and informational text. Thus, the design and organization of the standards support literacy instruction as a shared responsibility within the school. This integrated approach to literacy promotes relevant, real-world application of students' reading skills as they analyze, evaluate, and differentiate primary and secondary sources in history and decipher information from scientific diagrams to effectively communicate information and understanding of key concepts and ideas in science and technical subjects. The reading standards for literacy in history/social studies, science, and technical subjects are designed to seamlessly complement content-area literacy (CCSSI, 2010b, p. 4).

Examine the following three reading standards for literacy in science and technical subjects for grades 6 through 8 (CCSSI, 2010b, p. 62), and note how these standards work to mutually reinforce literacy as a shared responsibility across content areas.

> **[RST.6-8.1]** Cite specific textual evidence to support analysis of science and technical texts.

> **[RST.6-8.8.]** Distinguish among facts, reasoned judgment based on research findings, and speculation in a text.

> **[RST.6-8.9.]** Compare and contrast the information gained from experiments, simulations, video, or multimedia sources with that gained from reading a text on the same topic.

Synopsis of the Writing Strand

The first nine writing standards are designed around the three themes of *text types and purposes, production and distribution of writing,* and *research to build and present knowledge.* Writing standard 10 addresses the range of writing over short and extended time frames. Appendix A of the CCSS for ELA both defines and brings clarity to the rationale for inclusion of the three types of writing showcased in the writing standards. Appendix C of the ELA standards serves to support the writing standards by providing extensive samples of student writing that convey an understanding of adequate performance levels in writing arguments, information/explanatory texts, and narratives across various grades. Annotations following each writing piece provide further insight into the intent of the standards with regard to what is considered proficient writing at various grade levels (CCSSI, 2010e).

One hallmark of the writing standards is the deliberate shift toward a focus on nonfiction writing as evidenced by the emphasis on arguments and informative text types. In the early grades, students begin opinion writing that gradually moves toward demonstrating command of composing arguments based on substantive claims, sound reasoning, and relevant evidence. The writing standards are based on the NAEP Writing Framework expecting 80 percent of student writing throughout high school to be on argument and informative/explanatory text, mirroring what matters most for readiness in meeting the demands of college and real-world application (CCSSI, 2010b, p. 5). Another aspect of nonfiction writing emphasized in the standards is the ability for students to conduct research that results in both short and more substantial formal writing projects. The importance of research blended into the standards as a whole is reflective of the need for students to be able to gather, comprehend, evaluate, synthesize, and report on information and ideas quickly and efficiently to answer questions or solve problems (CCSSI, 2010b, p. 4). It is an expectation that students will incorporate technology and digital media in a manner that best supports communicative intent.

Throughout the literacy standards tremendous value is placed on growing analytical thinkers and critical consumers and providing tools and structures for students to express their voice orally and in writing. In the following example of a grade 8 writing standard, note the level of cognitive demand and rigor and the integration of the reading, writing, and language standards.

> [**W.8.1.**] Write arguments to support claims with clear reasons and relevant experiences (CCSSI, 2010b, p. 42).
> a. Introduce claim(s), acknowledge and distinguish the claim(s) from alternative or opposing claims, and organize the reasons and evidence logically.
> b. Support claim(s) with logical reasoning and relevant evidence, using accurate, credible sources and demonstrating an understanding of the topic or text.
> c. Use words, phrases, and clauses to create cohesion and clarify the relationships among claim(s), counterclaims, reasons, and evidence.
> d. Establish and maintain a formal style.
> e. Provide a concluding statement or section that follows from and supports the argument presented.

Synopsis of the Writing Standards for Literacy in History/Social Studies, Science, and Technical Subjects

The standards insist that instruction in reading, writing, speaking, listening, and language be a shared responsibility within the school (CCSSI, 2010b, p. 4). Thus, the design and organization of the ELA standards promote writing across disciplines while increasing the rigor within content-area literacy. The K–5 literacy standards for history/social studies, science, and technical subjects are embedded within the K–5 content strands. Writing standards for these areas in grades 6 through 12 are aligned with the 10 CCR writing anchor standards and complement both the CCSS ELA writing standards and subject-area content (CCSSI, 2010b, p. 33).

Examine Exhibit 1.5 alongside Exhibit 1.3 with regard to the shared expectations for writing standard 7. Consider the many opportunities for the ELA educator and content-specific educators to work together in mutually reinforcing ways to advance proficiency in conducting, writing about, or speaking about student research.

EXHIBIT 1.5	Grade-Specific Standards and the "Spiral Effect"—Writing Standard 7 Example: Writing Standards for Literacy in History/Social Studies, Science, and Technical Subjects 6–12

This example illustrates how skills and concepts for end-of-year, grade-specific expectations for a given standard are both reinforced and expanded as students advance through the grades. The result is a "spiral effect" whereby students repeatedly practice mastered competencies from the year prior in the context of new competencies being "added" each year as the standard increases in complexity and sophistication. New or more sophisticated skills and concepts added to each grade level from the year prior are noted in **bold**.

W.CCR.7	**CCR Writing Anchor Standard 7:** **Conduct short as well as more sustained research projects based on focused questions, demonstrating understanding of the subject under investigation.** =
WHST.11-12.7 **Grade 11–12 students:**	Conduct short as well as more sustained research projects to answer a question (including a self-generated question) or solve a problem; narrow or broaden the inquiry when appropriate; synthesize multiple sources on the subject, demonstrating understanding of the subject under investigation.
WHST.9-10.7 **Grade 9-10 students:**	Conduct short **as well as more sustained research projects** to answer a question (including a self-generated question) **or solve a problem; narrow or broaden the inquiry when appropriate; synthesize multiple sources on the subject, demonstrating understanding of the subject under investigation.** +
WHST.6-8.7 **Grade 6-8 students:**	Conduct short research projects to answer a question (**including a self-generated question**), drawing on several sources and generating additional related, focused questions **that allow for multiple avenues of exploration.** +

Source: Adapted from CCSSI, 2010b, p. 64.

Synopsis of the Speaking and Listening Strand

The six speaking and listening standards are equally distributed around the two themes of *comprehension and collaboration* and *presentation of knowledge and ideas.* Both themes reinforce twenty-first-century skills in establishing the importance of effective oral communication and collaborative discussion to build understanding and solve problems. Along the speaking and listening learning pathways it is expected that students will have multiple opportunities to grow and expand their expertise in leading and participating in collaborative conversations where increasingly complex information and ideas are shared and negotiated. Specific attention is given in the standards to the ability to present evidence and to effectively participate in discussion, whether in one-on-one, small-group, or whole-class settings. Student proficiency in using media and visual display of information to enhance understanding of presentations is embedded within the speaking and listening standards (CCSSI, 2010b, p. 22).

Compare the criteria for proficiency in collaborative communication in the following grade 8 standard example with your own experience participating in a committee meeting, department meeting, or community forum.

> [**SL.8.1**] Engage effectively in a range of collaborative discussions (one-on-one, in groups, and teacher-led) with diverse partners on grade 8 topics, texts, and issues, building on others' ideas and expressing their own clearly (CCSSI, 2010b, p. 49).
>
> a. Come to discussions prepared, having read or researched material under study; explicitly draw on that preparation by referring to evidence on the topic, text, or issue to probe and reflect on ideas under discussion.
>
> b. Follow rules for collegial discussions and decision-making, track progress toward specific goals and deadlines, and define individual roles as needed.
>
> c. Pose questions that connect the ideas of several speakers and respond to others' questions and comments with relevant evidence, observations, and ideas.
>
> d. Acknowledge new information expressed by others, and, when warranted, qualify or justify their own views in light of the evidence presented.

Synopsis of the Language Strand

While the ELA standards organize the language standards in their own strand, these standards are intended to be embedded across the strands of reading, writing, and speaking and listening. The six language standards are organized around the themes of *conventions of standard English*, *knowledge of language*, and *vocabulary acquisition and use*. Thus, the standards emphasize the importance of using formal English in writing and speaking (CCSSI, 2010b, p. 21).

As evidenced in the grade 8 standard example that follows, students are expected to demonstrate increasing independence in navigating unknown words important to comprehension and expression.

> [**L.8.4.**] Determine or clarify the meaning of unknown and multiple-meaning words and phrases based on *grade 8 reading and content*, choosing flexibly from a range of strategies (CCSSI, 2010b, p. 53).
>
> a. Use context (e.g., the overall meaning of a sentence or paragraph; a word's position or function in a sentence) as a clue to the meaning of a word or phrase.
>
> b. Use common, grade-appropriate Greek and Latin affixes and roots as clues to the meaning of a word (e.g., precede, recede, secede).
>
> c. Consult general and specialized reference materials (e.g., dictionaries, glos-

saries, thesauruses), both print and digital, to find the pronunciation of a word or determine or clarify its precise meaning or its part of speech.

    d. Verify the preliminary determination of the meaning of a word or phrase (e.g., by checking the inferred meaning in context or in a dictionary).

An Integrated Model of Literacy

Consider the following two statements from the introduction to the ELA standards:

> The Standards insist that instruction in reading, writing, speaking, listening, and language be a shared responsibility within the school. (CCSSI, 2010b, p. 4)

> While the Standards delineate specific expectations in reading, writing, speaking, listening, and language, each standard need not be a separate focus for instruction

---

EXHIBIT 1.6

Grade 8 Student Performance Task Illustration

Students examine claims of products used in advertising, analyze the language used in such claims, design and conduct scientific experiments to test claims, effectively summarize the evidence from their findings in a lab report, and present results for peer review prior to communicating, in writing, the results of their evidence to the product developer.

[RST.6-8.3] Follow precisely a multistep procedure when carrying out experiments, taking measurements, or performing technical tasks.	**[WHST.6-8.1]** Write arguments focused on discipline-specific content.
[RST.6-8.7] Integrate quantitative or technical information expressed in words in a text with a version of that information expressed visually (e.g., in a flowchart, diagram, model, graph or table).	**[W.8.2]** Write informative/explanatory texts to examine a topic and convey ideas, concepts, and information through the selection, organization, and analysis of relevant content.
[RST.6-8.8] Distinguish among facts, reasoned judgment based on research findings, and speculation in a text.	**[W.8.7]** Conduct short research projects to answer a question (including a self-generated question), drawing on several sources and generating additional related, focused questions that allow for multiple avenues of exploration.
[SL.8.3] Delineate a speaker's argument and specific claims, evaluating the soundness of the reasoning and relevance and sufficiency of the evidence and identifying when irrelevant evidence is introduced.	**[L.8.6]** Acquire and use accurately grade-specific general academic and domain-specific words and phrases; gather vocabulary knowledge when considering a word or phrase important to comprehension or expression.

Source: CCSSI, 2010b, pp. 42, 44, 49, 53, 82, 64.

and assessment. Often, several standards can be addressed by a single rich task. (CCSSI, 2010b, p. 5)

As we solidify understanding about the design and organization of the ELA standards, it is clear that repeated exposure to big, important themes is woven throughout grade levels and content areas. Thus, the reading, writing, speaking and listening, and language strands work together in mutually reinforcing ways. Exhibit 1.6 demonstrates a few of the possible ways to integrate multiple literacy standards within one rich task.

Understanding the Common Core State Standards for Mathematics

The Big Picture

Maintaining a true line for preparing students for CCR, the infrastructure of the CCSS for mathematics (CCSSM), however, differs from the infrastructure of the CCSS for ELA. The CCSSM utilize a format that best fulfills the function in communicating intent of the standards while fostering focus and coherence along learning progressions in K–12 mathematics. Throughout the document, the CCSSM place an emphasis on mathematical practices and spotlight equal attention on developing understanding of core concepts and fluency with procedural skills. The CCSSM are written to assume mastery, in any given year, of the preceding year's standards (CCSSI, 2010f, p. 3).

The CCSSM document is organized into three distinct sections outlining the standards of mathematical practices, standards for mathematical content for K–8, and standards for mathematical content for high school. A glossary and a few tables toward the end of the document provide further clarification of terminology. Appendix A provides an extensive overview of units of study incorporating the high school mathematics standards as they are played out in two model pathways for either a traditional or integrated high school course sequence (CCSSI, 2010g).

Exhibit 1.7 presents an overview of the CCSSM structure.

Design and Organization

One hallmark of the CCSSM is the learning pathways along which a student must travel to be college and career ready, as well as the embedded design feature of continually returning to prior learning at ever-increasing levels of complexity. The development of the mathematics standards began with research-based learning progressions detailing what is known today about how students' mathematical knowledge, skill, and understanding develop over time (CCSSI, 2010f, p. 4.).

EXHIBIT 1.7

Overview of the Structure of the Common Core State Standards for Mathematics

K–8	High School
Grade	Conceptual Category
Domain	Domain
Cluster	Cluster
Standards	Standards

Synopsis of the Standards for Mathematical Practice

The standards for mathematical practice are described as the "habits of mind" to be developed in students of mathematics. The set of eight guiding principles portrays the dispositions of a proficient math student persevering with engagement of the standards for mathematical content as they grow in mathematical competence. Therefore, the standards for mathematical practice, outlined in Exhibit 1.8, are expected to be embedded in mathematics instruction throughout K–12. Instructional notes provide descriptors of mathematically proficient students exhibiting each of the eight mathematical practice standards (CCSSI, 2010f, pp. 6, 7, 8).

EXHIBIT 1.8

Standards for Mathematical Practice

1. Make sense of problems and persevere in solving them.
2. Reason abstractly and quantitatively.
3. Construct viable arguments and critique the reasoning of others.
4. Model with mathematics.
5. Use appropriate tools strategically.
6. Attend to precision.
7. Look for and make use of structure.
8. Look for and express regularity in repeated reasoning.

Synopsis of Standards for Mathematical Content (K–8)

The K–8 standards for mathematical content are organized in *domains*, *clusters*, and *standards* within each grade level. The preamble for each grade level begins with explicit descriptors of focal points for instructional time. Focus, clarity, and specificity are key features of the standards for mathematical content, and no more than four critical areas of study are emphasized in any given grade level. Following the preamble, an overview page succinctly outlines each domain and cluster for a given grade. Grade-specific standards are then organized within clusters.

- *Domains* are larger groups of related standards. Standards from different domains may sometimes be closely related.
- *Clusters*, within the domains, are groups of related standards. Standards from different clusters may sometimes be closely related, because mathematics is a connected subject.
- *Standards*, within the clusters, define *what students should know and be able to do* at each grade level. (CCSSI, 2010f, p. 5)

Exhibit 1.9 provides an overview of the K–5 domains.

EXHIBIT 1.9 **Overview of K–5 Domains**

Grade K	Grade 1	Grade 2	Grade 3	Grade 4	Grade 5
Counting and Cardinality					
Operations and Algebraic Thinking	Operations and Algebraic Thinking	Operations and Algebraic Thinking	Operations and Algebraic Thinking	Operations and Algebraic Thinking	Operations and Algebraic Thinking
Number and Operations in Base Ten	Number and Operations in Base Ten	Number and Operations in Base Ten	Number and Operations in Base Ten and Fractions	Number and Operations in Base Ten and Fractions	Number and Operations in Base Ten and Fractions
Measurement and Data	Measurement and Data	Measurement and Data	Measurement and Data	Measurement and Data	Measurement and Data
Geometry	Geometry	Geometry	Geometry	Geometry	Geometry

EXHIBIT 1.10	Learning Progression for Understanding Place Value K–5

This example illustrates how skills and concepts for end-of-year, grade-specific expectations for a given standard are both reinforced and expanded as students advance through the grades. Notice how students repeatedly encounter mastered competencies from the year prior in the context of new competencies being "added" each year as the standard increases in complexity and sophistication. New skills and concepts added to each grade level from the year prior are noted in **bold.**

Domain: Number and Operations in Base Ten [NBT]	
Grade 5 **[5.NBT]** p. 35	Cluster: *Understand the place value system.*
	Standard 1. Recognize that in a multi-digit number, **a digit in one place represents** ten times what it represents in the place to its right and **1/10 of what it represents in the place to its left**.
	Standard 3b. Compare two decimals to thousandths based on meanings of the digits in each place using >, +, and < symbols to record the results of the comparisons.
	Standard 4. Use place value understanding to **round decimals to any place**.
Grade 4 **[4.NBT]** p. 29	Cluster: *Generalize place value understanding for multi-digit whole numbers.*
	Standard 1. Recognize that in a multi-digit whole number, a digit in one place represents ten times what it represents in the place to its right.
	Standard 2. Read and write multi-digit whole numbers using base-ten numerals, number names, and expanded form. **Compare two multi-digit numbers** based on meanings of the digits in each place using >, +, and < symbols to record the results of the comparisons.
	Standard 3. Use place value understanding to **round multi-digit whole numbers to any place**.
Grade 3 **[3.NBT]** p. 24	Cluster: *Use place value understanding and properties of operations to perform multi-digit arithmetic.*
	Standard 1. Use place value understanding to **round whole numbers to the nearest 10 or 100**.
Grade 2 **[2.NBT]** p. 19	Cluster: *Understand place value.*
	Standard 1: Understand that the three digits of a **three-digit number** represent amounts of **hundreds**, tens, and ones. Understand the following special cases: a. **100 can be thought of as a bundle of ten tens—called a "hundred."** b. **The numbers 100, 200, 300, 400, 500, 600, 700, 800, 900 refer to one, two, three, four, five, six, seven, eight, or nine hundreds (and 0 tens** and 0 ones).
	Standard 3: Read and write numbers to 1000 using base-ten numerals, number names, and **expanded form.**
	Standard 4: **Compare two three-digit numbers** based on meanings of the **hundreds**, tens, and ones digits, using >, +, and < to record the results of the comparisons.
Grade 1 **[1.NBT]** p. 15–16	Cluster: *Understand place value.*
	Standard 2: Understand that the two digits of a two-digit number represent amounts of tens and ones. Understand the following special cases: a. **10 can be thought of as a bundle of ten ones—called a "ten."** b. The numbers from 11 to 19 are composed of a ten and one, two, three, four, five, six, seven, eight, or nine ones. c. **The numbers 10, 20, 30, 40, 50, 60, 70, 80, 90 refer to one, two, three, four, five, six, seven, eight, or nine tens (and 0 ones).**
	Standard 3: Compare two two-digit numbers based on meanings of the tens and ones digits, recording the results of comparisons with the symbols >, +, and <.
Grade K **[K.NBT]** p. 12	Cluster: *Work with numbers 11–19 to gain foundations in place value.*
	Standard 1: Compose and decompose numbers from 11 to 19 into ten ones and further ones, and record each composition or decomposition by a drawing or equation; understand that these numbers are composed of ten ones and one, two, three four, five, six, seven, eight, or nine ones.

Source: Adapted from CCSSI (2010f).

In K–5 students gain a solid foundation in whole numbers, addition, subtraction, multiplication, division, fractions, and decimals—which taken together provide students with a strong foundation for learning and applying more demanding math concepts, procedures, and applications (Achieve, 2010). Exhibit 1.10 illustrates how the thread for "understanding place value" spirals along a K–5 learning progression while increasing in complexity from grade to grade.

In grades 6 through 8, students continue to build upon the strong foundation in grades K–5 through hands-on learning in geometry, algebra, probability, and statistics. The standards for grades 7 and 8 include significantly more algebra and geometry content. Indeed, an abrupt shift in some of the domains takes place from elementary to the middle level. The standards are more aggressive in establishing a timeline for particular concepts, such as establishing basic algebraic proficiency as a universal objective for all students by eighth grade (Confrey & Krupa, 2010). Exhibit 1.11 provides an overview of domains for grades 6 through 8.

EXHIBIT 1.11   Overview of 6–8 Domains

Grade 6	Grade 7	Grade 8
Ratios and Proportional Relationships	Ratios and Proportional Relationships	Functions
The Number System	The Number System	The Number System
Expressions and Equations	Expressions and Equations	Expressions and Equations
Geometry	Geometry	Geometry
Statistics and Probability	Statistics and Probability	Statistics and Probability

Synopsis of Standards for High School (9–12) Mathematical Content

High school standards for mathematical content are listed in conceptual categories, rather than grade levels or courses, as illustrated in Exhibit 1.12. Conceptual categories, taken together, paint a portrait of the mathematics students must master in order to be college and career ready. The five conceptual categories are *number and quantity, algebra, functions, geometry,* and *statistics and probability. Modeling* standards are distributed within the five major categories and are notated in the standards document with a "star" symbol. Standards notated with a "plus" symbol within the standards document

---

EXHIBIT 1.12   **Overview of High School Conceptual Categories**

Number and quantity
Algebra
Functions
Modeling
Geometry
Statistics and probability

---

are beyond the CCR level but are necessary for advanced mathematics courses, such as calculus, discrete mathematics, and advanced statistics. Standards with a "plus" are also found in courses expected for all students (CCSSI, 2010f, p. 57).

An introduction is provided in CCSSM for each of the five conceptual categories that further define the intent and level of application expected of students mastering the standards. Using a similar pattern to organization of the K–8 standards, an overview page follows the introduction for each conceptual category, followed by domains, clusters, and standards.

- *Conceptual categories*: overarching ideas that describe strands of content 9–12
- *Domains/clusters*: groups of standards that describe coherent aspects of the content category
- *Standards:* define what students should know and be able to do

The standards for high school mathematics call on students to practice applying mathematical ways of thinking to real-world issues and challenges and emphasize mathematical modeling. The standards are extremely clear on what is important. High school mathematics standards require students to develop a depth of understanding and ability to apply mathematics to novel situations, as college students and employees regularly are called to do (CCSSI 2010a).

Decisions regarding mathematics course sequence rest with individual schools and districts. Although it is a critical component of implementing the standards, course sequence is not mandated by the standards. Exhibit 1.13 demonstrates how two model pathways arrange the content of the standards in both a traditional and an integrated course sequence found in Appendix A of CCSSM (Achieve, 2010).

EXHIBIT 1.13	Appendix A: High School Mathematics Course Pathways	

Traditional Pathway	Integrated Pathway
Algebra II	Mathematics III
Geometry	Mathematics II
High School Algebra I	Mathematics I
Pathway A: Consists of two algebra courses and a geometry course, with some data, probability, and statistics infused throughout each.	**Pathway B:** Typically seen internationally, consists of a sequence of three courses, each of which treats aspects of algebra, geometry and data, probability, and statistics.

Systemic Alignment Action Plan

The whole world is watching as we provide more complex instruction, covering a wider range of skills, to an increasingly diverse group of students. It is not these challenges that will define our generation of teachers, however—but our response.

White, *Extraordinary Teachers* (2009, p. 13)

The Systemic Alignment Action Plan provides a framework for schools and districts to use when working systemically to implement the CCSS. It is designed on the premise that standards and assessments are the core of quality instruction. Thus, all planning, implementing, and monitoring decisions are aligned with a singular, focused purpose. Central to the success of implementation effectiveness is the presence of establishing a compelling vision, setting a clear direction, and orchestrating the phase-in of critical components in manageable increments.

The 14 components of the Systemic Alignment Action Plan framework work synergistically in the context of an aligned reform effort. To achieve maximum effect, the system in which the CCSS are embedded must commit to a singular, focused initiative around which all other practices revolve. A laser-like focus on student learning is the core of the CCSS. As indicated earlier in this chapter, the Systemic Alignment Action

Plan framework is designed to be a work in progress and will help the user gain perspective of the terrain to be navigated when implementing the CCSS and, when consulted throughout the journey, will serve to orient the user on the progress achieved.

As your CCSS Implementation Team conducts an accurate assessment of the current status of your school or district in relation to full implementation of the standards, begin by taking stock of what will and will not change. The following questions can be used to guide reflection:

- What are similarities and differences in your current expectations for students with those of the CCSS?
- What specific impact will the CCSS have on lesson planning, assessment, and teaching practices in your school or district?
- What is the impact on Professional Learning Communities, Data Teams, and/or cross-school or cross-department collaboration?
- What are the implications for professional development?

See also Exhibit 1.14 for the Systemic Alignment Action Plan framework.

Challenges and Opportunities

Education has the power to change an entire nation.

The Leadership and Learning Service Team Project,
Zambia (2010)

Centering Force

Standards are the centering force for schooling. Taken together, standards and assessments are the core of quality instruction. Elegant in their simplicity, standards are the *"what" kids should know and be able to do,* and assessments are the *"how" we know they know it.* According to the Thomas B. Fordham Institute (Finn & Petrilli, 2010, p. 2), "Fortunately, the Common Core turned out to be a commendable product, a significant improvement in academic expectations and clarity for the vast majority of states." How school plays out in terms of grade-level groupings, course design, curriculum maps, report cards, intervention systems, and accountability systems is all benchmarked on the hope and the promise that we get the standards right in the first place. The Fordham Institute (Finn & Petrilli, 2010, p. 2) further notes, "Standards describe the destination that schools and students are supposed to reach, but by themselves have little power to effect change. Much else needs to happen to successfully journey toward that destination." The "much else" that needs to happen is the close alignment of the *written, taught, tested, and attained* curriculum. The remaining chapters in this book shift attention toward the power of assessments in determining attainment of the standards.

EXHIBIT 1.14 Systemic Alignment Action Plan for the Common Core State Standards

District/School:

PLANNING	Initiative	6 Months	1 Year	18 Months	2 Years	30 Months	3 Years
Transition Inquiry Process	**Multiyear action planning process:** • Organize a CCSSI Transition Implementation Team • Create timelines for key deliverables • Establish incremental goals						
Communication	**Strategic communication plan for staff, students, parents, the community:** • Ensure clear, consistent messaging • Engage all stakeholders • Develop a solid understanding of CCSSI • Provide access to available resources • Publish the road map for implementation						
Distribute the Leadership	**Create a unified vision:** • Gain commitment • Protect the focus • Persist in holding to key deliverables • Sustain the momentum • Nurture collaborative efforts						
Curriculum Audit and Gap Analysis	**Cross-walks between state/local standards and CCSSI:** • Identify consistencies and gaps • Share what stays the same and what will change • Develop curriculum maps						
Initiative Inventory	**Alignment of implemented initiatives with CCSSI:** • Identify district-/school-wide initiatives • Compare level of rigor with CCSSI • Weed the garden • Develop action plan to align rigor						
Learning Context	**Implications for rethinking:** • Staffing patterns • School schedules • Course design and model pathways • Graduation requirements • Instructional materials and resources • Technology • Structures for collaboration						

EXHIBIT 1.14

Systemic Alignment Action Plan for the Common Core State Standards (continued)

IMPLEMENTATION	Initiative	6 Months	1 Year	18 Months	2 Years	30 Months	3 Years
Professional Development	**Needs assessment to identify top priorities and key goals for CCSSI.** **Sample topics:** • Depth in content expertise • Discipline-specific literacy • Creation of exemplars for grade-level expectations and progressions • Increase in nonfiction writing across the curriculum • Increase in levels of rigor and thinking skills • Differentiation of the instruction • Understanding of assessment literacy • Creation of performance assessments						
Design Curricular Units	**Build the foundation:** • Prioritize standards • Align priority and supporting standards • Prepare a pacing calendar • Construct the unit-planning organizer **Design the unit of study:** • "Unwrap" the standards • Create unit assessments (pre/post and progress monitoring checks) • Plan for instruction, daily and weekly						
Quality Instruction	**Standards-based instructional practices:** • Focus on clearly defined standards • Use power strategies for effective teaching • Design engaging learning experiences • Conduct frequent, short-cycle assessments						
Access and Acceleration	**Create structures for success:** • Design structures and strategies for access and acceleration for all sub-groups, including English language learners, individualized education program students, and gifted students • Organize interventions to meet diverse needs						
Assessment Inventory	**Assessment alignment:** • Ensure alignment of current assessments with the CCSS, noting consistencies and gaps • Design common formative assessments, including performance-based assessments and tasks aligned to the CCSS • Prepare for the next generation of assessments • Consider implications for online assessments • Understand status and growth metrics						

EXHIBIT 1.14

Systemic Alignment Action Plan for the Common Core State Standards (continued)

MONITORING	Initiative	6 Months	1 Year	18 Months	2 Years	30 Months	3 Years
Effective Feedback	**Feedback for continuous improvement:** • Become proficient at using effective instructional feedback strategies that advance learning for students • Align effective grading practices • Implement Professional Learning Communities/Data Teams to monitor progress and respond to the effectiveness of instruction						
Accountability	**Incorporate new measures into a holistic accountability system:** • Monitor what is valued • Examine cause data (adult actions) and effect data (student results) • Act on the evidence • Celebrate successes						
Systemic Alignment	**Ensure CCSSI alignment with:** • State, district, and school policies • Personnel performance supervision and evaluation policies and practices • Identify funding sources • Employ systemic focus of time, effort, resources						

Challenges

Indeed, the CCSS provide a clear road map of the learning pathways a student must follow in English and mathematics for him or her to be sufficiently prepared for college and the workforce. The standards do not, however, provide the full range of skills and learning a student will need to be college and career ready. Nor do the standards address all that can or should to be taught in our schools. The decisions about how teachers instruct and what instructional resources are selected are deferred to schools, districts, and/or states (CCSSI, 2010b, p. 4).

The CCSS represents a finite set of standards to be learned, and once mastered, there are endless possibilities for students to engage in advanced studies. While the design and organizational features of the CCSS contribute to access and acceleration for all students, clearly student learning does not always subscribe to such a precise linear time frame based on grade placement. Therefore, we stand on the threshold of implementing the challenging work ahead to articulate the structures for success that will be required for all students, including those performing well below grade level, English language learners receiving intervention supports, and students with special needs.

Opportunities

Informed participation is a prerequisite for collective action, and humanity prospers when people work together for the common good. Such a great and noble vision is attainable. It is attainable in environments that foster teamwork, collegial partnerships, and collaboration with the broader community, all working together to give children first call on our time and energy. The CCSSI is both a challenge and an opportunity to come together, as a nation, and change for the better what is possible, what is expected, and what should exist for our children.

References

Achieve, Inc. (2010, June). Understanding the Common Core State Standards [PowerPoint presentation]. Retrieved from http://www.achieve.org/achievingcommoncore

Common Core State Standards Initiative (CCSSI). (2010a, June). Common Core State Standards webinar [PowerPoint presentation]. Retrieved from http://www.corestandards.org

Common Core State Standards Initiative (CCSSI). (2010b, June). *Common Core State Standards for English language arts & literacy in history/social studies, science, and technical subjects* [PDF document]. Retrieved from http://www.corestandards.org/assets/CCSSI_ELA%20Standards.pdf

Common Core State Standards Initiative (CCSSI). (2010c, June). *Common Core State Standards for English language arts & literacy in history/social studies, science, and technical subjects: Appendix A* [PDF document]. Retrieved from http://www.corestandards.org/assets/Appendix_A.pdf

Common Core State Standards Initiative (CCSSI). (2010d, June). *Common Core State Standards for English language arts & literacy in history/social studies, science, and technical subjects: Appendix B* [PDF document]. Retrieved from http://www.corestandards.org/assets/Appendix_B.pdf

Common Core State Standards Initiative (CCSSI). (2010e, June). *Common Core State Standards for English language arts & literacy in history/social studies, science, and technical subjects: Appendix C* [PDF document]. Retrieved from http://www.corestandards.org/assets/Appendix_C.pdf

Common Core State Standards Initiative (CCSSI). (2010f, June). *Common Core State Standards for mathematics* [PDF document]. Retrieved from http://www.corestandards.org/assets/CCSSI_Math%20Standards.pdf

Common Core State Standards Initiative (CCSSI). (2010g, June). *Common Core State Standards for mathematics: Appendix A* [PDF document]. Retrieved from http://www.corestandards.org/assets/CCSSI_Mathematics_Appendix_A.pdf

Confrey, J., & Krupa E. (2010). *Curriculum design, development, and implementation in an era of Common Core State Standards.* Arlington, VA: Center for the Study of Mathematics Curriculum.

Finn, C. E., Jr., & Petrilli, M. J. (2010, October). *Now what? Imperatives and options for Common Core implementation and governance* [PDF document]. Retrieved from http://www.edexcellence.net/publications-issues/publications/now-what-imperatives-and.html

Teachers College Reading & Writing Project (TCRWP). (2010, September). Spotlight article: Common Core Standards alignment update. Retrieved from http://readingandwritingproject.com/news/common-core-standards-alignment-update.html

Impacting Learning with Standards and Assessment

This section will help frame assessment in the eyes of students. Many of the students in our schools still see the word "assessment" as synonymous with "test," "quiz," and "exam." Very few of today's students would say that assessment is a tool teachers use to provide feedback on their learning.

The authors in this section discuss important concepts related to using assessment as a feedback tool. They have also recommended several practical strategies that will help teachers use assessment as a powerful instructional tool.

If the fundamental purpose of a performance assessment is to improve student learning, then why aren't teachers leveraging these valuable learning experiences in the classroom? With the emphasis on large-scale tests and increasing student achievement on those tests, most often we don't have the time nor do we see the benefits. Lisa Almeida highlights the numerous benefits of performance assessments: they are conducive to authentic learning, highly motivational to students, energizing, and collaborative, just to name a few. She helps us to see that performance assessments empower both the teacher and the student. Lisa guides us through the process of using assessments as a tool to engage students in a standards-based learning experience.

Jan Christinson skillfully shows us the benefits of formative assessments in mathematics and shows us how to engage students in the assessment process. He walks us through the Math Review process in a clear, logical, and interesting way. In this practical approach, students are engaged in meaningful conversation and rigorous problem solving. Jan illustrates the importance of self-awareness, metacognition, and reflection in a math assessment. You will never see Math Review as a traditional activity again after reading this chapter; you will instead use it as a method of formative assessment and a tool for providing feedback to students.

Similar to Jan's insight regarding the Math Review process, Lynn Howard introduces us to the "conceptual unit," an approach and a process that will help students deepen their understanding of scientific concepts. While this process may at first appear as an instructional technique, we quickly learn that it is more of a standards and assessment framework. She uses this structure when approaching the methodology of teaching science standards. Her practical approach can help any teacher create standards-based science assessments that promote student learning in a rigorous and meaningful way.

Loan Mascorro endearingly allows us to see assessment through the eyes of an English language learner. Her personal experiences help us to see the critical role of standards-based assessments for ELL students. Loan reminds us that in order for high levels of learning to occur, standards, assessment, and instruction need to be inseparable processes. This approach must be systematic and thoughtful if we are to help prepare English language learners for success.

CHAPTER TWO

The Power of
Performance Assessments

LISA ALMEIDA

What you will do matters. All you need is to do it.
JUDY GRAHN

The research on using performance assessments for instructional and formative deci-sions is significant, but the history of the practice of performance assessments is incon-sistent. Even with the pressures to produce "twenty-first-century learners," the definition of that term's performance assessments is fuzzy, its adoption is also inconsistent, and the prognosis for future use is questionable. Tony Wagner, the Harvard University–based education expert and author of *The Global Achievement Gap: Why Even Our Best Schools Don't Teach the New Survival Skills Our Children Need—and What We Can Do about It,* explains that students need three basic skills if they want to thrive in a knowledge-based economy: the ability to think critically and problem solve, the ability to communicate effectively, and the ability to collaborate (Friedman, 2010). Performance assessments, when properly designed and implemented, challenge students with multiple engaging opportunities to meet the personal and professional demands of today's world.

Research on Performance Assessments

Meaningful learning is experiential; hands-on equates to "minds-on" and is heavily infused with critical reasoning. Authentic performance assessment involves observing students "doing" experiences in meaningful contexts. An abundance of research is avail-able as a result of many performance assessment observations. "Authentic Assessment: It Really Works" was an action research project that focused on increasing retention of information through the use of alternative methods of instruction. The study focused on elementary students in a suburban area that had experienced a decline in standard-ized test scores. A review of test items soon became the focus for teachers, which resulted in knowledge-level learning for students. Teachers reviewed literature that provided solution strategies including, but not limited to, performance tasks, investigations, learning logs, and reflections. Evidence indicated that the use of authentic assessments enhanced retention and created more independence. It also assisted students in developing their own learning and improved the transfer of knowledge across content areas. Moreover, this data revealed that authentic performance assessments helped students perform well on standardized tests and were a powerful tool for lifelong learning (Engel, Pulley, & Rybinski, 2003).

"Keeping the Focus on the Child: Supporting and Reporting on Teaching and Learning with a Classroom-Based Performance Assessment System" describes the findings of a large-scale, classroom-based performance assessment of literacy for primary grades. The study finds the assessment instrument to be reliable and valid. Follow-up studies of the assessment's use point to its positive impact on teachers' practices and on school and district policies. Furthermore, findings suggest that classroom-based performance assessments can provide viable accountability, as well as an instructional tool to capture a range of students' abilities in a range of formats. The study concludes that the use of such an assessment has the potential to enhance teachers' knowledge about literacy and their ability to effectively support students' learning (Falk, Moirs, & Ort, 2007).

Results from "Development of Authentic Assessments for the Middle School Classroom" provide evidence that differentiated authentic assessments can quantify information about student learning as well as inform the instructional process. The study is unique because it also measured inter-rater reliability using student responses to the assessment in classrooms in two states. The authors explain the rationale for implementing authentic assessments in the middle school. For example, it is vital that middle school students learn in an environment that consists of small communities, cooperative learning, and flexible grouping, which complement the basic principles of performance assessments. It is abnormal for a student to complete a task independently because it is a small-group process that carries individual accountability. The results of this study begin to present evidence that these assessments can be developed to provide consistent information about student learning, especially on academic learning standards. The authors point out that often the focus of teaching is on high-stakes assessments and the focus of classroom instruction is on test preparation. The focus should be on helping students gain understanding through the construction of their own knowledge and making interconnections among facts and concepts within and across disciplines. The differentiated authentic assessments used what the authors refer to as "contemporary instructional methods used in today's classrooms": writing across the curriculum, hands-on approaches, problem solving and reasoning emphases, and cooperative learning (Brighton, Callahan, Moon, & Robinson, 2005, p. 129).

One of the ultimate research studies on the power of performance assessments lasted seven years. It focuses on the impact performance assessments have on the nation's second largest school district, Los Angeles Unified School District. The most important finding is the project's success in scaling up empirically tested assessment design models and scoring procedures to a district assessment involving more than 300,000 students per year. This finding raises the possibility that high-quality, learning-centered assessment may again be a practical option for large-scale assessment and accountability. The research article is very comprehensive, addressing how a large teaching staff learns to use relevant principles to evaluate student work and guide instruction. This article is one of a series that highlights the seven-year project. The authors believe that the culmination of work related to "Scaling Up, Scaling Down: Seven Years of Performance Assessment Development in the Nation's Second Largest School District" will stand as a useful example of strategies for scaling up research-tested assessment development models and for validating performance assessments for instructional improvement and accountability purposes (Baker, Niemi, & Sylvester, 2007).

If one still needs convincing of the power of performance assessments to empower students and teachers, *Visible Learning: A Synthesis of over 800 Meta-analyses Relating to Achievement,* by John Hattie (2009), captures numerous strategies that fit "hand to glove" with authentic performance assessments. Hattie, the author and researcher, highlights the power of feedback and its 0.73 effect size—recall that an effect size of 1.0 is considered "perfect." He implores teachers to always have their students reflect on three questions:

1. Where am I going?

2. How am I going?

3. Where do I need to go next?

Hattie's major argument is that "when teaching and learning is visible, there is a greater likelihood of students reaching higher levels of achievement." Teaching and learning are visible when performance assessments are implemented. The teacher shares the goal, the Priority Standard(s), the Essential Questions, and the scoring guides, all critical components of an effective performance assessment. Students should be expected to provide in-depth answers to Hattie's three questions. Hattie states, "It involves an accomplished teacher who knows a range of learning strategies to build on the students' surface, deep knowing and understanding, and conceptual understanding." Creating and executing a performance assessment requires higher-level thinking from the practitioner. That is why it is critical that teachers work on the work with colleagues instead of in isolation. The collective wisdom of the team is much more powerful than the wisdom of one. Additionally, "the teacher needs to provide direction and redirection in terms of the content being understood and thus maximize the power of feedback, and to have the skill to get out of the way when learning is progressing towards the success criteria" (Hattie, 2009, p. 38).

The teacher plays two critical roles during the implementation phase of performance assessments. First and foremost, the role of "teacher as activator" dominates the instructional period. The teacher as activator involves many effective strategies, such as feedback ($d = 0.74$), metacognition strategies ($d = 0.67$), cooperative versus individualistic learning ($d = 0.59$), direct instruction ($d = 0.59$), and mastery learning ($d = 0.57$) (Hattie, 2009, p. 243). Once students finish task one, they begin to work on different tasks at different times. This approach results in the teacher transitioning to "teacher as facilitator." The teacher as facilitator plans to use effective strategies, such as small-group learning ($d = 0.49$), including cooperative learning ($d = 0.59$), worked examples ($d = 0.57$), and questioning ($d = 0.46$) (Hattie, 2009, pp. 243, 297–298). It is not uncommon to find a teacher working with a small group of students who need additional instructional support to reach proficiency on a subsequent task. For example, a teacher has a few students who are revising work to reach proficiency on task two while other students are working in cooperative groups on task three and perhaps task four. It may be hard to actually find the teacher when the classroom comes alive during performance assessment work time.

Real-Life Scenarios

Testimonials to teaching and learning "coming alive" are frequently revealed when performance assessments are systematically implemented. Jo Peters, principal of Lew Wallace Elementary School in Albuquerque, New Mexico, shares how performance assessments have energized her students:

> I wanted to let you know that I was in Javonna's room this morning (she's doing the performance assessment on uniforms) and what I saw was awesome! Students were very much involved. I got interviewed by two of them as those two are on task two already. It took most kids a while to make proficient on task one, and when I was in there Darrien finally did. He announced it to the class when he went to mark the Data Wall; we all cheered! Next time you come to Lew Wallace, you will have to go into her class!! (J. Peters, personal communication, January 2007)

Daniel Delao, a first-grade teacher at Lew Wallace, shares how performance assessment collaboration with his principal has affected his instructional planning and assessment implementation:

> Listen, I just wanted to share the positive and truly inspiring work we did with Engaging Classroom Assessments (ECA) and performance assessments this year. First, Jo (the principal) and I actually collaborated on a new performance assessment based on non-standard and standard units of measurement for first grade. This assessment was actually quite evolved because

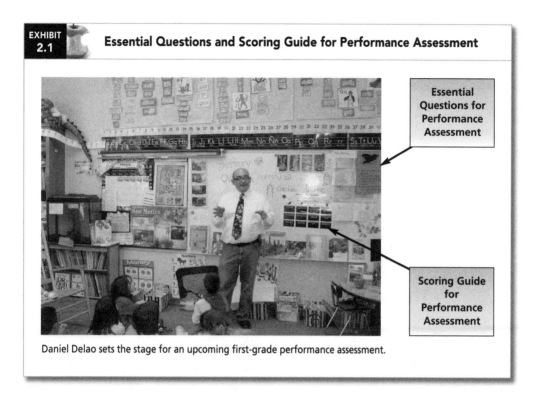

EXHIBIT 2.1   **Essential Questions and Scoring Guide for Performance Assessment**

Essential Questions for Performance Assessment

Scoring Guide for Performance Assessment

Daniel Delao sets the stage for an upcoming first-grade performance assessment.

it was the most kid-friendly performance assessment ever. It was easy to read and easy to organize. We made it so efficient in that tasks and rubrics were back to back and laminated. The rubrics were never more than 1 or 2 sentences. We really wanted an easy to follow, portable performance assessments [sic]. We put the task cards on a key ring. It worked! Students were easily able to follow along and self-guide themselves through all four tasks.

In fact, students were always checking in with me throughout the day and asking, "When can I get to task 2?" "When can we work on our tasks?" And, when we did work on our performance assessments . . . wow! Students wanted to go for the gold (exemplary). They would say, "I want to do the criteria to get to exemplary." I mean, the performance assessment was so well defined, so clear to them that they could recite the criteria for each marker on the rubric. (D. Delao, personal communication, June 12, 2010)

Defining Performance Assessment

In *Making Standards Work: How to Implement Standards-Based Assessments in the Classroom, School, and District*, author Doug Reeves builds a strong case for creating and implementing performance assessments. Performance assessments require higher-level thinking skills and, therefore, a demonstration of knowledge, skills, and understanding

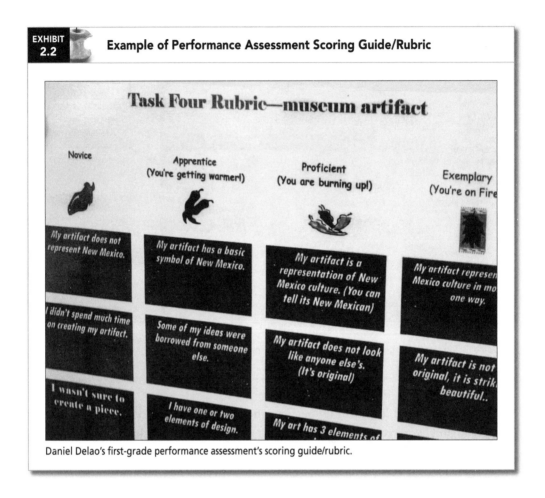

EXHIBIT 2.2   Example of Performance Assessment Scoring Guide/Rubric

Task Four Rubric—museum artifact

Novice

Apprentice
(You're getting warmer!)

Proficient
(You are burning up!)

Exemplary
(You're on Fire)

My artifact does not represent New Mexico.

My artifact has a basic symbol of New Mexico.

My artifact is a representation of New Mexico culture. (You can tell its New Mexican)

My artifact represen Mexico culture in mo one way.

I didn't spend much time on creating my artifact.

Some of my ideas were borrowed from someone else.

My artifact does not look like anyone else's. (It's original)

My artifact is not original, it is strik beautiful..

I wasn't sure to create a piece.

I have one or two elements of design.

My art has 3 elements of

Daniel Delao's first-grade performance assessment's scoring guide/rubric.

by the student. Students are expected to apply and analyze new information with respect to a given real-life situation versus rote memorization of a fixed body of facts (Reeves, 2003, p. 117). Educators must realize that the performance assessment development process "is far more than the creation of a test. It is the essence of teaching and learning. By asking the right questions, combining factual knowledge with deep understanding, and providing multiple opportunities for success after detailed feedback and coaching, assessments can be transformed from fearful evaluations into constructive learning experiences" (p. 123). Moreover, Reeves states the fundamental purpose of performance assessment is the improvement of student learning, not the rendering of an evaluation. One can add that performance assessments are used as formative assessment versus summative assessment.

In *Student-Involved Assessments for Learning*, assessment expert Rick Stiggins (2005) states that performance assessments enable teachers to watch students solve problems and infer reasoning proficiency, observe and evaluate skills as they are being performed, and assess the attributes of created products. James Popham (2003) elaborates on the definition by acknowledging that performance tests always present a task to students—and the more the student assessment task resembles the tasks to be performed by people in real life, the more likely it is that the test will be labeled a performance assessment. Additionally, he echoes the importance of measuring a student's mastery of a high-level, sometimes quite sophisticated skill through the use of very elaborate constructed-response items and a rubric.

According to standards and assessment expert Larry Ainsworth (2010, p. 161), authentic performance assessments have the following impacts on teaching and learning:

> In terms of *instruction,* it enables educators to teach the Priority Standards and supporting standards through inquiry and problem solving within the context of the performance task they are about to assign to students.

> In terms of *learning,* students have the opportunity to engage in incremental learning experiences—learning progressions—that are designed to help them make their own connections to the standards in focus while developing both conceptual understanding (concepts) and procedural understanding (skills).

> In terms of *curriculum,* performance tasks provide the "what" educators will use to give their students truly engaging learning experiences.

> In terms of *assessment,* performance tasks provide multiple benefits—performance tasks provide educators with a "window" into student understanding, giving them the formative diagnostic data they need to monitor and adjust instruction for different students.

A Deeper Look at the Performance Assessment Model

Educators need to consider all the critical components when creating and/or using a performance assessment. Whether the work consists of starting from scratch or tweaking a published assessment, it needs to be done with a collaborative team. A great deal of focused dialogue on standards, instruction, and assessment occurs during the development of a performance assessment. In addition, as with many skills, the more often educators create or use a performance assessment, the more efficient their work on assessments will become. A common concern is the time it takes to create a single performance assessment. However, it can be thought of as a unit lesson plan "on steroids" that aligns to the Priority Standards and supporting standards, encompasses differentiated instruction, and provides immediate and specific feedback to students and teachers. Practitioners in South Dakota support this notion, sharing with the author that

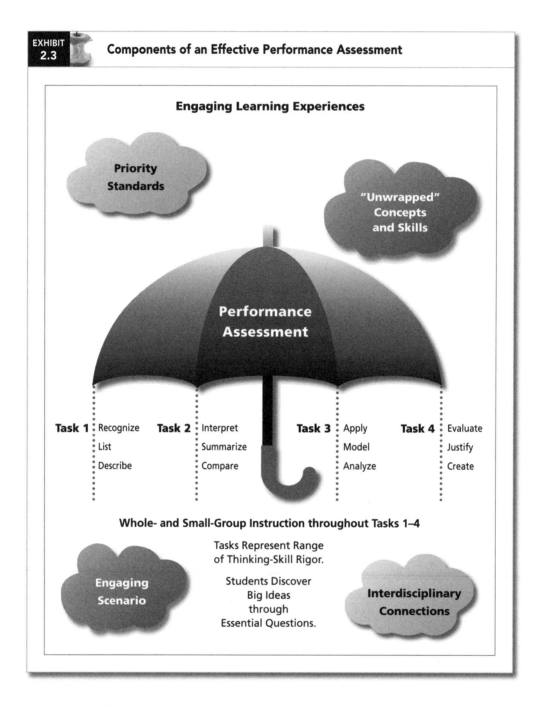

EXHIBIT 2.3 Components of an Effective Performance Assessment

Engaging Learning Experiences

Priority Standards

"Unwrapped" Concepts and Skills

Performance Assessment

Task 1 Recognize / List / Describe   **Task 2** Interpret / Summarize / Compare   **Task 3** Apply / Model / Analyze   **Task 4** Evaluate / Justify / Create

Whole- and Small-Group Instruction throughout Tasks 1–4

Tasks Represent Range of Thinking-Skill Rigor.

Students Discover Big Ideas through Essential Questions.

Engaging Scenario

Interdisciplinary Connections

creating a performance assessment takes a lot of time upfront, but it saves them invaluable time during the school year.

Exhibit 2.4 illustrates 10 steps to designing a performance assessment. These steps align with the graphic shown in Exhibit 2.3.

EXHIBIT 2.4	10 Steps to Designing a Performance Assessment

Building the Foundation, Steps 1–5

Step 1: Select the assessment topic.

Step 2: Identify matching Priority Standards and supporting standards.

Step 3: "Unwrap" the matching standards and create a graphic organizer to effectively identify key concepts and skills that the assessment needs to address.

Step 4: Determine the Big Ideas that students arrive at by the completion of the tasks; the Big Ideas are the answers to the Essential Questions.

Step 5: Write Essential Questions that invite students into the learning and assessment process and the tasks. The questions should engage learners and ideally have a real-life connection. Each Essential Question should have a Big Idea that matches it, that is, the answer to the question.

Step 6: Design performance tasks. Four tasks are the average for a performance assessment. If all the concepts and skills are thoroughly addressed after three tasks, it is unnecessary to create a "filler" task. There should be a minimum of three tasks to provide students with ample learning opportunities and provide teachers with a preponderance of evidence that indicates mastery occurred.

Step 7: Develop performance tasks once your "road map" is completed. It is highly recommended that the group map out where it wants the students to go between task one and task four. It is very easy, especially with more than one thinker involved in the development, to get side-tracked and detour from the end result. Keeping the desired end in mind helps keep many on the right path.

Step 8: Identify interdisciplinary standards that are apparent throughout the assessment. More than likely, there are language arts, writing, career readiness, and/or problem-solving connections. Be mindful that inter-disciplinary standards are not the focus of the tasks; however, it behooves teachers and students to make the cross-curricular connections.

Designing the Assessment, Steps 6–10

Step 9: Create an engaging scenario by making an explicit link to the real world. The tasks are "what" the students are doing. The engaging scenario communicates "why" the students have to complete the tasks and the assessment. An effective scenario contains a real-life situation, a challenge, an external audience (versus the teacher), a specific role the students take on throughout the tasks, and a final product or perfor-mance as evidence of learning.

Step 10: Develop scoring guides (rubrics) for each task that are user friendly for all stakeholders. Teachers administer the scoring guide before each task. Some choose to provide students with all the tasks and accompanying scoring guides at the beginning of the assessment, whereas others distribute the next task and scoring guide as the student(s) successfully completes the prior task. How the teacher decides to organize and disseminate materials typically depends on what is developmentally appropriate for the students.

Connections to Common Core State Standards

Performance assessments and the Common Core State Standards (CCSS) go together like wine and cheese, margaritas and happy hour, or milk and cookies: The characteristics of the CCSS harmonize with the principles of performance assessments. Consider the following key points of the standards that support the consistent use of authentic assessments:

- Students learn at more rigorous levels by including rigorous content and application of knowledge through high-order skills.
- Teachers' instruction is aimed toward more rigorous outcomes.
- Emphasis is placed on interdisciplinary literacy and critical thinking.
- The design structure supports English language learners, students with individual education plans, and other sub-groups to accelerate access to levels; therefore, CCSS is complementary to differentiation.
- There is an expectation of interdisciplinary connections with math and English language arts to science and social studies.
- The CCSS are evidence based.

Furthermore, the upcoming 2014/15 national assessments will measure the teaching and learning of the CCSS and will emphasize *performance assessments* and critical thinking. Similar to authentic performance assessments, the national assessments will focus on critical thinking and informational writing in all content areas. It is imperative that districts plan for systematic implementation of performance assessments as formative assessments (i.e., each grade level and course collaboratively implement performance assessments on a quarterly basis with coaching and feedback provided by district Engaging Classroom Assessments certified instructors) that will provide timely feedback to teachers and students. The formative performance assessments will afford data on whether the instruction, as well as the learning, is on the right track to the summative national assessments. The strategic data allow stakeholders to make a "predictive value" as to how students are likely to perform on the next assessment (Ainsworth & Viegut, 2006). Therefore, practitioners are able to make midcourse adjustments to ensure conceptual understanding by the summative assessment.

The CCSS in mathematics support the use of performance assessments in many ways. For example, there are fewer standards at each grade level. Performance assessments should assess the Priority Standards. Popham (2003, pp. 102–103) recommends "reserving performance assessments for only the most significant of your high-priority curricular aims." The standards are more complex regarding what students should learn at a conceptual level. Therefore, complex tasks are required to provide students with multiple opportunities to demonstrate proficiency. The high school standards specifically ask students to practice applying mathematical ways of thinking to real-world issues and challenges. Hence, the performance assessment's engaging scenario (Step 9 in Exhibit 2.4) explicitly links what they are being asked to complete to real-life situations.

Perhaps the most critical element of an effective standards-based performance assessment is the development of the engaging scenario; the opportunities are limitless (Reeves, 2003). Additionally, the assessment's Essential Questions (Step 5) should aim to make real-life connections to entice the learners to find the answers—the Big Ideas. In addition, the standards set a rigorous definition of college and career readiness as they expect high school students to develop a depth of understanding and have the ability to apply mathematics to novel situations, as in life.

The reading CCSS expect students to build knowledge, gain insights, explore possibilities, and broaden their perspectives through reading a diverse array of classic and contemporary literature. Additionally, the students engage with challenging informational texts in a range of subjects. The writing standards require the ability to write logical arguments based on substantive claims, sound reasoning, and relevant evidence with opinion writing, which is a basic form of argument. The opinion writing begins in the earliest grades. All these characteristics enhance a performance assessment. It is hard to find any performance assessment that does not have a connection to English language arts, if that discipline is not the focus area. Think about how powerful the performance assessment and the four performance tasks will be when combined with strategic development to include these engaging language arts standards with other disciplines.

The writing CCSS can be embedded into any performance assessments. Exhibit 2.3 indicates including nonfiction writing throughout the assessment. The writing standards specifically call for students to have the ability to write logical arguments based on substantive claims, sound reasoning, and relevant evidence; hence, research focuses on short, focused projects similar to work scenarios. They also emphasize that students present findings in a written analysis.

It is common for teachers to embed speaking and listening into one or two tasks. Many will design task four to be a culminating project that requires students to connect the prior tasks' learning and present some type of evidence of learning. The speaking and listening CCSS require students to gain, evaluate, and present increasingly complex information, ideas, and evidence through listening and speaking, as well as through media. Additionally, a critical focus of these standards calls for students to engage in academic discussions in small-group and whole-class settings. Students demonstrate their speaking and listening understanding by participating in formal presentations and informal discussions where they collaborate to answer questions, build understanding, and solve problems.

The standards prepare students for real-life experience in college and in twenty-first-century careers. The English language arts CCSS are every assessment designer's dream if the assessment is performance based. What other assessment format *effectively* measures evidence-based, higher-level thinking standards? As with any project-based learning and assessment, teachers determine proficiency for each task and communicate it to students. Therefore, all teaching and learning efforts aim for the same target.

Exhibit 2.5 shows the English language arts key points, and Exhibit 2.6 provides the key points for mathematics.

EXHIBIT 2.5	Key Points in English Language Arts

Reading	• The standards establish a "staircase" of increasing complexity in what students must be able to read so that all students are ready for the demands of college- and career-level reading no later than the end of high school. The standards also require the progressive development of reading comprehension so that students advancing through the grades are able to gain more from whatever they read. • Through reading a diverse array of classic and contemporary literature as well as challenging informational texts in a range of subjects, students are expected to build knowledge, gain insights, explore possibilities, and broaden their perspective. Because the standards are building blocks for successful classrooms, but recognize that teachers, school districts and states need to decide on appropriate curriculum, they intentionally do not offer a reading list. Instead, they offer numerous sample texts to help teachers prepare for the school year and allow parents and students to know what to expect at the beginning of the year. • The standards mandate certain critical types of content for all students, including classic myths and stories from around the world, foundational U.S. documents, seminal works of American literature, and the writings of Shakespeare. The standards appropriately defer the many remaining decisions about what and how to teach to states, districts, and schools.
Writing	• The ability to write logical arguments based on substantive claims, sound reasoning, and relevant evidence is a cornerstone of the writing standards, with opinion writing—a basic form of argument—extending down into the earliest grades. • Research—both short, focused projects (such as those commonly required in the workplace) and longer term in depth research —is emphasized throughout the standards but most prominently in the writing strand since a written analysis and presentation of findings is so often critical. • Annotated samples of student writing accompany the standards and help establish adequate performance levels in writing arguments, informational/explanatory texts, and narratives in the various grades.
Speaking and Listening	• The standards require that students gain, evaluate, and present increasingly complex information, ideas, and evidence through listening and speaking as well as through media. • An important focus of the speaking and listening standards is academic discussion in one-on-one, small-group, and whole-class settings. Formal presentations are one important way such talk occurs, but so is the more informal discussion that takes place as students collaborate to answer questions, build understanding, and solve problems.
Language	• The standards expect that students will grow their vocabularies through a mix of conversations, direct instruction, and reading. The standards will help students determine word meanings, appreciate the nuances of words, and steadily expand their repertoire of words and phrases. • The standards help prepare students for real life experience at college and in twenty-first-century careers. The standards recognize that students must be able to use formal English in their writing and speaking but that they must also be able to make informed, skillful choices among the many ways to express themselves through language. • Vocabulary and conventions are treated in their own strand not because skills in these areas should be handled in isolation but because their use extends across reading, writing, speaking, and listening.
Media and Technology	• Just as media and technology are integrated in school and life in the twenty-first century, skills related to media use (both critical analysis and production of media) are integrated throughout the standards.

Source: CCSSI (2010a).

| EXHIBIT 2.6 | **Key Points in Mathematics** |

- The K–5 standards provide students with a *solid foundation in whole numbers, addition, subtraction, multiplication, division, fractions and decimals*—which help young students build the foundation to successfully apply more demanding math concepts and procedures, and move into applications.

- In kindergarten, the standards follow successful international models and recommendations from the National Research Council's Early Math Panel report, by focusing kindergarten work on the number core: learning how numbers correspond to quantities, and learning how to put numbers together and take them apart (the beginnings of addition and subtraction).

- The K–5 standards build on the best state standards to provide detailed guidance to teachers on how to navigate their way through knotty topics such as *fractions, negative numbers, and geometry*, and do so by maintaining a continuous progression from grade to grade.

- The standards stress not only procedural skill but also conceptual understanding, to make sure students are learning and absorbing the critical information they need to succeed at higher levels - rather than the current practices by which many students learn enough to get by on the next test, but forget it shortly thereafter, only to review again the following year.

- Having built a strong foundation K–5, students can do hands on learning in geometry, algebra and probability and statistics. Students who have completed 7th grade and mastered the content and skills through the 7th grade will be *well-prepared for algebra* in grade 8.

- The middle school standards are robust and provide a coherent and rich *preparation for high school mathematics*.

- The high school standards call on students to *practice applying mathematical ways of thinking to real world issues and challenges*; they prepare students to think and reason mathematically.

- The high school standards set a *rigorous definition of college and career readiness*, by helping students develop a depth of understanding and ability to apply mathematics to novel situations, as college students and employees regularly do.

- The high school standards *emphasize mathematical modeling*, the use of mathematics and statistics to analyze empirical situations, understand them better, and improve decisions. For example, the draft standards state: "Modeling links classroom mathematics and statistics to everyday life, work, and decision-making. It is the process of choosing and using appropriate mathematics and statistics to analyze empirical situations, to understand them better, and to improve decisions. Quantities and their relationships in physical, economic, public policy, social and everyday situations can be modeled using mathematical and statistical methods. When making mathematical models, technology is valuable for varying assumptions, exploring consequences, and comparing predictions with data."

Source: CCSSI (2010b).

Real-Life Engaging Scenarios

Ali Nava, another teacher from Lew Wallace Elementary School, shares how performance assessments support her first graders in mastering measurement, a Priority Standard. Additionally, she indicates, the assessments help to create a standards-based classroom where the children can articulate the importance of academic standards, their work toward achieving proficiency, and the all-around excitement of teaching and learning in Ms. Nava's classroom.

One of the best parts was that we tied in good children's literature to the performance assessment. In fact, Jo [Peters, Lew Wallace principal] came in and read a relevant children's book to the class as part of the Engaging Scenario and brought her own bear to share! It was priceless! Jo had the students in rapt attention. We hooked them with the Engaging Scenario. My students were engaged every day we worked on our performance assessment. And with a post test, a district end-of-the-year post test mind you, the majority did great on measurement!

Over the past few years, the other first grade teacher and I had been approached by many kindergarten parents with inquiries about our particular teaching styles and classrooms. This year, we decided to hold a Kindergarten Open House, and invite curious parents to attend the informational session about our classrooms. During this event, my current first grade students provided presentations on why standards are important, and discussed two performance assessments, one on measurement and the other on New Mexico facts to illustrate how we use and collect data.

I am very eager to perfect my use of performance assessments, and included my performance assessment data as an integral part of my dossier that was submitted for Level II Licensure. It would be so awesome if you could come to Lew Wallace to observe all of the exemplary teaching techniques that are being done by me and other teachers in the school.

Performance Assessments Rock!!! (A. Nava, personal communication, June 13, 2010)

The practitioners and instructional leaders at Lew Wallace Elementary School need not be reminded of how critical it is to engage students. In *The Art and Science of Teaching*, Marzano (2007) reminds educators of the basic generalization that learners must actively engage in the processing of information and that the teaching and learning process involves interaction among the teacher, the students, and the content. Performance assessments are such a powerful tool for teaching and learning. Learn more about the use of performance assessments and create an action plan for implementation, whether your state adopts the CCSS or not. Consider a pilot approach to implementation as a safe way to get started, learn from others, and perfect the instruction and assessment tool. We have too much to lose as educators to not embrace performance assessments. Students' expectations of their education continue to rise, and effective performance assessment will be crucial to meeting them.

You have to leave the city of your comfort and go into the wilderness of your intuition. What you'll discover will be wonderful. What you'll discover is yourself.

ALAN ALDA

References

Ainsworth, L. (2010). *Rigorous curriculum design: How to create curricular units of study that align to standards, instruction, and assessment.* Englewood, CO: Lead + Learn Press.

Ainsworth, L., & Viegut, D. J. (2006). *Common formative assessments: How to connect standards-based instruction and assessment.* Thousand Oaks, CA: Corwin Press.

Baker, E., Niemi, D., & Sylvester, R. (2007). Scaling up, scaling down: Seven years of performance assessment development in the nation's second largest school district. *Educational Assessment, 12*(3/4), 195–214.

Brighton, C., Callahan, C., Moon, T., & Robinson, A. (2005). Development of authentic assessments for the middle school classroom. *The Journal of Secondary Gifted Education, 16*(2/3), 119–133.

Common Core State Standards Initiative (CCSSI). (2010a). Key points in English language arts. Retrieved from http://www.corestandards.org/about-the-standards/key-points-in-english-language-arts

Common Core State Standards Initiative (CCSSI). (2010b). Key points in mathematics. Retrieved from http://www.corestandards.org/about-the-standards/key-points-in-mathematics

Engel, M., Pulley, R., & Rybinski, A. (2003). *Authentic assessment: It really works* (master's action research project). Saint Xavier University, Chicago, IL.

Falk, B., Moirs, K., & Ort, S. (2007). Keeping the focus on the child: Supporting and reporting on teaching and learning with a classroom-based performance assessment system. *Educational Assessment, 12*(1), 47–75.

Friedman, T. L. (2010, November 21). Teaching for America. *The New York Times,* p. WK8.

Hattie, J. (2009). *Visible learning: A synthesis of over 800 meta-analyses relating to achievement.* New York, NY: Routledge.

Marzano, R. (2007). *The art and science of teaching.* Alexandria, VA: Association for Supervision and Curriculum Development.

Popham, J. (2003). *Test better, teach better: The instructional role of assessment.* Alexandria, VA: Association for Supervision and Curriculum Development.

Reeves, D. (2003). *Makings standards work: How to implement standards-based assessments in the classroom, school, and district* (3rd ed.). Englewood, CO: Advanced Learning Press.

Stiggins, R. (2005). *Student-involved assessments for learning* (4th ed.). Upper Saddle River, NJ: Prentice-Hall.

Wagner, T. (2008). *The global achievement gap: Why even our best schools don't teach the new survival skills our children need—and what we can do about it.* New York, NY: Basic Books.

CHAPTER THREE

The Power of Frequent Assessment in Mathematics

JAN CHRISTINSON

Many issues surround the learning of mathematics that can make it a very difficult experience for many students. Math concepts build on each other and are very dependent on foundational skills; students develop misconceptions as they move from grade to grade that are not addressed, and these misconceptions accumulate, making success at math seem impossible to the student. Students give up, decide they are not a "math person," and avoid math courses as they progress to the secondary level. This chapter discusses the power of frequent assessment in mathematics through a process called Math Review. Math Review is a daily, self-assessment, formative process coupled with feedback and reflection that provides benefits to students and teachers alike. Math Review puts the students into the assessment equation, where they belong, and provides the necessary support for them to deal with their misconceptions and to develop confidence in their ability to do math. More in-depth discussion of the Math Review process is provided later in this chapter.

Current challenges facing math classroom teachers are how to deal with all the different levels of math ability in one classroom and how to determine the student misconceptions that exist and the instructional source of those misconceptions. The power of frequent assessment for the teacher is discussed from the standpoint of the diagnostic information that can be collected from students within a Math Review–type process and how a high frequency of information gathering is vital. This level of frequency moves the formative process to the level of looking at how students actually think about the math; how they interpret the classroom instruction; and, most importantly, how they develop the misconceptions.

Lorna Earl (2003, p. 69) discusses the impact of an assessment system that uses student errors in assessment for learning:

> Motivation is enhanced when errors and mistakes are treated as a normal
> part of learning, with timely feedback and a chance to rethink and redo the

work, and when assessment is designed to provide students with access to their progress and allows them to stay engaged with the task. When assessment is designed to give students and teachers insight into what they are able to do independently as well as with guidance, students are empowered to seek help and the teacher is able to provide assistance at that point of learning, not at the end of instruction.

The following section provides a glimpse into a fourth-grade classroom that is using a Math Review process to support learning in mathematics.

A Few Days of Math Review in a Fourth-Grade Classroom

Teacher-Directed Days 1, 2, and 3

A fourth-grade class is starting its instructional time for math. Three problems are written on the white board below the title Math Review:

   1. Expanded notation 456 = _____

   2. Regrouping 454 − 129 = _____

   3. Fractions ¼ + ⅓ = _____

Students work on the problems independently for two minutes and then work with a student partner for six minutes to complete the problems. At the end of the eight minutes, students take out a marking pen and put away their pencils to begin the processing of the three problems. The teacher begins by having the students star their name, the date, and the title of the assignment on their paper to reinforce directions, then the processing moves on to the first problem. The teacher has the students star the term "expanded notation" on their paper. The class says "expanded notation" together. Students and the teacher write and chorally say, "The value of a digit is determined by its position," which is the concept statement for this problem. The teacher leads the students through error analysis by having them star the 400, then the 50, then the 6. Students are directed to circle any of the parts that are incorrect and make the corrections at that moment. Students then complete a reflective statement that is based on the error analysis and the extent to which the student feels he understands the concept involved in the problem. The same procedure is followed for the remaining problems. After the last problem is processed, students write a final reflection indicating skills or concepts they feel confident about and those they believe they still need to work on. The teacher collects the student papers and reviews the reflections. The same process will be followed for the next two days.

Student-Directed Days 4, 5, and 6

On the fourth day, the students start working on the same type of problems as on the first three days (the categories do not change, just the numbers used for the problems). Students work with an assigned partner for eight minutes. The teacher is circulating through the classroom, listening to student conversations about the problems and watching for students who could be invited to lead the class through the processing portion of Math Review. The teacher notices one fourth grader who has been showing good progress with expanded notation and extends an invitation to the student to explain that problem to the class. The teacher reminds the student to practice the key parts of the problem with his partner so that he will feel ready when he presents to the class. The teacher selects two other students to process the remaining problems on the Math Review. At the end of eight minutes, the students put away their pencils and take out their red marking pens. The student selected to process problem one comes to the white board and leads the feedback process for the class as if he were the teacher. The student completes the error analysis for the problem, asking the class if it agrees after each step; has the class write and chorally repeat the concept statement for this problem (the value of a digit is determined by its position); and directs the students to reflect on their performance for that problem. When the student completes his review, the class gives him a round of applause to celebrate his courage to present in front of his peers. The other two problems are processed in the same manner using the other two invited students. During the student presentations the teacher stands in the back of the room, prompting the student presenters if necessary with questions that will help them remember key components of the problems (concept statement, error analysis, key vocabulary).

Group Answer Days 7 and 8

On the seventh day, students continue to work on the same type of problems, but they work in groups of four using a collaborative group process called Group Answer. Before beginning work, the students number off in their group and write their number next to their name on their paper. The teacher checks to see which students are 1s, 2s, etc. The teacher explains that at the end of the work time (eight minutes) a number from 1 to 4 will be called and that number will indicate which student from each group will be presenting a problem to the class. The students begin working together on each problem. They solve problem one together, not going on to problem two until all group members agree with the answer and understand the problem. The groups continue working in this fashion until they have completed the three problems. At the end of the eight minutes, the teacher provides two minutes of rehearsal time for groups to make sure that each member is prepared to present each problem. During this on-task, collaborative student work, the teacher is circulating and listening intently to student conversation to gather diagnostic information about progress with the skills and concepts that have been part of Math Review during the last seven days. At the end of the rehearsal time period, the number 3 is called. All students with the number 3 from each group come to the front of the room. Six students come forward, so two are assigned to each problem for the purpose of processing the problems with the class. The students that are selected are told by the teacher that if they get stuck during their presentation they are welcome to ask the group they are representing for help during their presentation. The first two students lead the class through the feedback process for problem one, including the error analysis, the concept statement, key vocabulary, and student reflection. The other student pairs present the processing for the remaining two problems. Then all students complete an overall reflection that includes a sentence about how they performed personally and a sentence about how their group performed.

The Math Review Process—Daily Formative Assessment

The preceding scenario describes a class using Math Review. This process is part of an instructional model called Five Easy Steps to a Balanced Math Program, which is used by districts, individual schools, and individual classrooms across the United States from kindergarten to high school (Ainsworth & Christinson, 2006). The Math Review process involves students and teachers in a daily assessment and feedback process that has various benefits to both groups that result from its focus on student misconceptions. The Math Review process involves students in daily practice with concepts in mathematics that they should know at their current grade level but that they do not know. The process is based on the ideas of repeated reasoning and effective feedback—that if a student is trying to learn a concept he has been struggling with, he needs multiple opportunities to work on the concept (repeated reasoning). Furthermore, connected with those multiple opportunities must be feedback that is timely and specific (effective feedback). The math concepts are presented in categories that are determined by the grade-level teachers. Usually students work on three to five categories daily.

What sets the Math Review process apart from a typical warm-up activity is that students continue to work on the problems until an assessment shows that they are proficient with the concept and skill involved in that category. The assessment that is used to show proficiency is called the Math Review Quiz, which is described later in this chapter. The other distinguishing components of this process are a structured student feedback process that includes error analysis, student reflection, and development of student metacognitive skills and tactics that create a collaborative classroom environment conducive to the learning of mathematics.

When each Math Review problem is processed, students are provided with key vocabulary, a concept statement, and a distinct error analysis that will help students become aware of and correct their misconceptions pertaining to the problem. To enhance student engagement and promote student conversation around mathematics, several methods are used to provide the necessary feedback for each problem. When problems are new to students, the teacher-directed method is used, which involves the teacher giving all the feedback information for the problems. After two or three days, when students are more comfortable with the problems, the student-directed method is used, which involves students in providing the necessary feedback information. The two methods were exemplified in the scenario described earlier. As students gain confidence with the problems presented on Math Review, the collaborative technique Group Answer is used to process the Math Review problems, which will provide valuable formative information to the students and the teacher before students take the Math Review Quiz. Periodically, a Math Review Quiz is given to provide assessment information for the student and the teacher as to the effectiveness of the daily self-assessment feedback activity that has been practiced in the Math Review process.

Key Assessment Components of the Math Review Process

The Feedback Process

In *Visible Learning*, John Hattie (2009, p. 173) discusses the power of feedback:

> When teachers seek, or at least are open to, feedback from students as to what students know, what they understand, where they make errors, when they have misconceptions, when they are not engaged—then teaching and learning can be synchronized and powerful.

As mentioned earlier, the critical component that distinguishes the Math Review process from a traditional warm-up activity is the structured feedback process that students participate in daily. Feedback is essential to the learning process, especially when students are trying to correct misconceptions they have developed about a concept in math. The Math Review process provides students feedback that is specific to the problems being practiced on a daily basis. The feedback is given initially by the teacher, then by other students, and then by peers in a collaborative setting. The feedback elements (a specific error analysis, a concept statement, and key vocabulary) are designed to provide students with enough information to self-assess their understanding of a concept on a daily basis. This self-assessment process allows students to discover their misconception and then to move toward the correct understanding.

The engaging, interactive nature of this feedback process allows the teacher to gather formative information on a daily basis about student understanding related to the concepts on Math Review. The teacher becomes aware of how some students understand the concept and, more importantly, why other students struggle with a given concept. This daily diagnostic information leads to an interesting part of the feedback process called "concept statements." Concept statements are concise statements about the mathematics involved in a concept that the students are having a difficult time understanding. The statements are developed by the classroom teacher as he collects information about student misconceptions related to a concept. Here are two examples of concept statements:

> Place value—the value of a digit is determined by its position.

> Regrouping—a quantity can be rearranged and is still the same quantity.

A concept statement is attached to each category in the Math Review process so that students can write and say the statement daily. Many students find the statements helpful when studying for and taking the Math Review Quiz. The benefit of this process to the classroom teacher is that it focuses the feedback and instructional support on the essential component of the concept that is causing confusion for the majority of the students.

The daily nature of this type of feedback process allows the student to self-assess over several days so he can actually correct the misconception and begin to gain confidence in his ability to understand mathematical concepts. Other components of the daily feedback process—peer explanation, peer interaction, key vocabulary practice, and concept statements—support the student in his attempt to relearn a concept. Learning with understanding, especially trying to relearn a notion that you have developed misconceptions about, is a gradual process that is dependent on effective feedback and self-assessment over time.

Error Analysis

To allow students to discover their misconceptions about a concept or skill, they have to be able to look at the components that make up that concept or skill. The error analysis process in Math Review provides students with a daily opportunity to examine which components of a problem they understand and which components they still need to work on. This process begins with the teacher determining an acceptable sequence or procedure that could be used to solve the problem. During the first few days that students begin working on the Math Review problems (the teacher-directed method mentioned earlier), the teacher sets the expectations for the established sequence or procedure, which allows students to receive very specific feedback on a daily basis. Each day, students will indicate which part of the sequence they were successful with and which part they still need to work on. Many teachers have students use a red pen to draw stars next to components of the problem that are correct, circle the components that are incorrect, and correct those components immediately on their paper.

Error analysis used within the Math Review process has many benefits for students in terms of self-assessment. Many students who struggle with math become singularly focused on the answer. They decide that if the answer is incorrect, they do not know anything about math and they are not a math person. The error analysis process can help change this attitude by making students aware of the individual parts of a procedure or sequence. This awareness allows the students to focus on what they do know and what they do not know. By participating in a very specific self-assessment process, the students actually start thinking that it is possible to correct their misconceptions. Instead of feeling that the whole situation is hopeless, the students find that they actually do know more mathematics than they thought they did, which in turn brings about a positive attitude change regarding their ability to learn mathematics. The specific and repetitive nature of this error analysis process is naturally engaging to students, and it creates a classroom environment that enhances students' responsibility for their learning. The students start feeling hopeful that they will be successful.

For teachers, the process of developing the error analysis sequence that they will present to students within the Math Review process creates instructional clarity and helps teachers to gain awareness of the possible sources of student misconceptions. Because the daily error analysis process provides teachers with valuable formative information about student understanding, it helps teachers adjust instruction to help more students become proficient with a skill or concept that is being practiced on Math Review. As students become more involved in the explanation part of the Math Review process (the student-directed method and Group Answer), teachers are able to collect valuable diagnostic information about student understanding from actual student explanations of the error analysis sequences for each problem.

As teachers of various grade levels from the same school start involving students in a self-assessing error analysis process, the teachers begin to have conversations about how an error analysis based on a given concept should look as it gets more difficult at various grade levels. Teachers realize that a vertical conversation is needed about how the concept is taught, what student work should be shown for a problem related to the concept, and especially what an error analysis should look like at each grade level. This vertical conversation helps create consistency in the use of mathematical language and consistency of teacher explanation for a given concept. An interesting side benefit of this endeavor is that teachers find that their own understanding of the concept is enhanced. This type of discussion can also lead to secondary math teachers deciding as a group what work should be shown to solve an equation and all math teachers at that school or district expecting the same work on Math Review processes and on unit assessments. This type of consistency, matched with student awareness from the error analysis process, allows more students to be successful.

In fact, when students become aware of the components of a concept, learn how to assess their knowledge of the components, and know what the teacher expects in terms of how to show their knowledge of those components, they almost cannot help but be successful.

Reflection/Metacognition

Effective assessment practices offer students an opportunity to reflect on what they are learning. It is through this reflection that students experience assessment as a part of learning, rather than as a separate evaluative process.

In *Visible Learning*, John Hattie (2009, p. 174) discusses the next step that students must take with feedback provided:

> It is also worth noting that the key is feedback that is received and acted upon by students … many teachers claim they provide ample amounts of feedback but the issue is whether students receive and interpret the information in the feedback.

The final step in processing each problem in the Math Review process is to have students write a reflective statement that indicates their progress with the concept that the problem represents. Students use the results of the error analysis presented by the teacher or a classmate and their understanding of the concept statement to devise their reflective statement. The reflective statement indicates parts of the concept that they understand and parts that they still need to work on. After all the problems on Math Review have been processed, students write a general reflection that indicates how the students feel they are doing overall. This reflection tends to act as a plan for improvement for the next day. This vital final step of the process starts building student responsibility for their learning.

The reflection part of Math Review allows students to see how all the parts of this self-assessment review process fit together. As students pay more attention to their personal results from the error analysis for each problem, they find that their reflective statements become more and more specific to the concept they are striving to understand. Another benefit of students participating in reflective practices is that it enhances student metacognition (students thinking about their thinking), which is an important step in a student determining his misconception and then moving toward repairing that misconception.

Of course, the student reflections are not just valuable diagnostic information for the teacher about student progress with the problems on Math Review; they also provide indicators of students' attitudes toward math and their levels of efficacy with the presented concepts. The daily, formative nature of Math Review allows the teacher to use student reflections to see if students are making progress on the problems or if students are becoming frustrated. This information also helps teachers make informed instructional decisions. As teachers use this process over time, they find that student reflections help them more readily determine the source of the student misconception pertaining to a concept.

Not Moving On

The main criteria for category selection in the Math Review process is "what students should know when they enter a given grade level but they do not know," which means that the main purpose of Math Review is to provide a system that allows students to fill gaps of understanding and correct misconceptions. This purpose necessitates that the Math Review process afford students the necessary opportunities to meet this goal. As previously stated, the basis of the Math Review process is that students need multiple opportunities to work on a skill or concept that they have struggled with, and that those multiple opportunities need to be coupled with timely and specific feedback. When Marzano, Pickering, and Pollock (2001, p. 67) looked at the research surrounding the practice of a skill that is being learned, they found, "It's not until students have practiced upwards of 24 times that they reach 80-percent competency."

Their research studied students learning a new skill, so just imagine what is necessary for students who have seen a concept in math over several years and have developed several misconceptions about that concept. The unique feature of Math Review that students appreciate is that the teacher does not just "move on" to other concepts because of pressure to cover material; instead, the teacher stays with a concept on Math Review until the assessment data shows that students have reached a determined level of proficiency. Students get to experience the power of continual daily self-assessment combined with a supportive feedback process. They start to believe that they can understand the concept and that they can be successful with mathematics.

> The subject of mathematics in particular promotes expressions of anxiety that take such forms as tension and dislike (attitudinal features); worry, helplessness, and mental disorganization (cognitive features); and fear (emotional feature). The consequences of anxiety include avoidance of courses and an inability to achieve in the subject (Ma, 1999). (Hattie, 2009, pp. 49–50)

A common response from students and teachers across the United States involved in implementing Math Review is that the supportive, "not moving on" nature of the process immediately begins to lower math anxiety for students who have previously struggled with math. After a short time those students typically experience success and a change of attitude about their math ability.

Engaging Methods to Provide Feedback

Teacher-Directed Method—
Setting the Expectations, or Providing the Model

Making sure that students understand the goal is a critical first step in creating a useful feedback system. In "Less Teaching, More Assessing," John Wilcox (2006) quotes Grant Wiggins: "If you want me, as a student, to meet the standard, then you better make sure I know what the standard is," Wiggins advised. "We have to work very hard to eliminate mystery and secrecy about what excellence is."

Wiggins continued, "You can't achieve a goal as a learner without a clear model of what you are trying to accomplish. If you want people to achieve a result, they need a model of what you want them to achieve."

The teacher-directed method goes a long way toward setting these expectations, or providing the model for achievement. As mentioned earlier, it is used to process new problems for the first three days that students work on those problems. This method helps the teacher to clearly establish the main components for the processing of each problem (error analysis, concept statement, and key vocabulary). The teacher-directed method is geared to provide very direct feedback to the students to allow for their initial self-assessment. This method does not involve the teacher trying to draw the information out of the class through questioning. At the end of the three days the students have a clear idea of what is expected for each problem, and at that point it is time to engage more student involvement in the processing of the problems.

Student-Directed Method—
Adding Student Explanation to the Classroom Environment

The student-directed method, which takes place on days 4–6 of the Math Review process, involves students in the presentation of feedback using the model that the teacher had established during the three days employing the teacher-directed method. The method, in which student volunteers lead the class through the key components of each problem, introduces student explanation into the classroom environment, which is immediately diagnostic for the teacher and helpful to students. Many times a student's explanation can be as helpful as, if not more helpful to other students than, a teacher explanation. The teacher gets to hear firsthand to what degree students understand a concept, which will help him determine the source of students' misconceptions. If classroom teachers do not hear students' explanations, they really do not know what students are thinking about a given concept. This method also promotes practice of metacognitive skills: students become more and more aware of their thinking as they work to deal with their misconceptions. It also allows more balance in the classroom between teacher talk and student talk and keeps Math Review much more student centered. In short, the student-directed method facilitates daily assessment for the teacher about student understanding and feedback about the effectiveness of the error analysis and concept statements designed for the problem.

Group Answer Method—a Collaborative, Informal Assessment Activity

The scene on days 7–8 described at the beginning of the chapter is an example of students participating in Group Answer, a collaborative activity for Math Review introduced earlier. In the Group Answer method, students have been working on the Math Review problems for several days. This informal assessment activity allows students an opportunity to find out how they are progressing. The students complete the problems on Math Review together as a group without teacher assistance and make sure that all members of the group are prepared to present each problem to the class. In this method, the students complete the problems one at a time, making sure everyone in the group has achieved understanding of each problem before moving on to the next. The method is used a day or two before the Math Review Quiz, which serves as a final self-assessment for the students on the concepts being practiced on Math Review.

The Group Answer method provides students with a very engaging self-assessment activity that involves collaboration, on-task conversation, verification of solutions, and appropriate peer interaction. The student reflection completed at the end of the activity can also be used by students to devise a study plan for Math Review Quiz if the teacher offers such an option.

Group Answer is beneficial to teachers because of all the information that can be obtained about the students and effectiveness of instruction. As the student groups work on presenting information about the problems, the teacher can consider some of the following questions: Did the error analysis work? Was the concept statement effective? What adjustments need to made in instruction? Which students still seem to be struggling? What is my prediction for the quiz results? Are other misconceptions developing? How are the groups functioning? Is more training in collaboration necessary? Are there underlying skills that still need to be dealt with? Did I hear some great student explanations that would be models for other students?

Math Review Quiz, or How Are We Doing?

Within the Math Review process, students are formally assessed once every two weeks on the problems they have been working since the previous quiz. The students take a Math Review Quiz that is made up of two or three problems of each type covered in the review. The students complete the quiz independently. When all students are finished with the quiz, they take out a red pen and put away their pencil in preparation to correct the quiz. Students correct their own quiz so that they receive immediate and specific feedback about their progress. The same error analysis processing that had been used daily in Math Review is used to correct each problem. Students indicate which parts of a problem are correct and which parts are incorrect. On the back of the quiz they either congratulate themselves for a proficient performance or write a specific plan for improvement based on the problems that they did incorrectly. The emphasis of the Math Review Quiz is to provide students with formative information about how effective their practice has been over several days. The frequency of the Math Review Quiz and its alignment with the daily practice, feedback, and the Math Review self-assessment process allow students who have typically not been successful in math to begin to find success. The immediate result of this newfound success for these students is a new attitude of hope. They actually start believing that they can learn mathematics, or at least the concepts on the current Math Review. The complete student involvement in the assessment process allows students to view mistakes as events to learn from and begin to realize that struggling is part of the learning process. Instead of just following a procedure to get an answer, students strive to understand, to have the math make sense.

Furthermore, the frequent nature of the Math Review Quiz allows the classroom teacher to collect information about individual student performance and overall class performance on the concepts on Math Review. Teachers typically set a level of performance on the quiz that indicates proficiency. Students who do not reach that level of performance are provided support during Math Review such as being a member of a flex group or being provided a peer assistant. These students also become eligible for a reteaching, retesting opportunity, which provides a significant measure of hope and motivation for struggling students. Teachers also use Math Review Quiz data to find students who, on the basis of their continued outstanding performance, might be interested in peer tutoring training.

The quiz results are also used to determine when a category should change on the Math Review process. Typically, when 85 to 90 percent of the students in a classroom show proficiency with a given concept, that category changes and another category is placed on Math Review.

Vertical Alignment of Instruction: A District-Wide Benefit

An approach to assessment in mathematics that is applied more frequently and is more student centered helps the teacher become increasingly aware of student misconceptions. As teachers become aware of why kids do not understand, they tend to do a better job of instructing and start seeing that instruction in math needs to make sense and be consistent across the grades.

As the Math Review approach to assessment takes hold across a school or school district it becomes apparent that student gaps in understanding pertaining to a given concept often are due to instructional practice, highlighting a clear need to vertically align instruction in math. When the vertical discussion takes place along with implementation of a Math Review–type process, gaps from prior grades are identified and resolved much sooner and students move through the grades with fewer gaps, better understanding, and more confidence about their ability to learn mathematics. Students also start to trust that they will be supported if they do not understand a concept the first time it is "covered" in class. The greatest benefit of the vertical alignment of math instruction Math Review is that more students successfully reach the end goal of the math curriculum of a school district.

Common Core State Standards in Mathematics— a Brief Discussion

The Common Core State Standards Initiative (2010) states, "The K–5 standards provide students with a solid foundation in whole numbers, addition, subtraction, multiplication, division, fractions, and decimals—which help young students build the foundation to successfully apply more demanding concepts and procedures, and move into applications."

It further states, "The standards stress not only procedural skill but also conceptual understanding, to make sure students are learning and absorbing the critical information they need to succeed at higher levels—rather than the current practice by which many students learn enough to get by on the next test but forget it shortly thereafter, only to review again the following year."

It is obvious from these quotes that the Common Core State Standards for mathematics expect students to understand the mathematics that they are learning and to retain what they have learned. Procedural approaches to teaching mathematics in recent history in the United States have not served us well in terms of student success and especially in terms of student retention of mathematical concepts. The Common Core State Standards emphasize not only understanding but also moving students to application, which means involving students in problem solving using the concepts they are learning. It will become even more important that student misconceptions are dealt with on a timely and effective basis. As teachers begin to focus their instruction on the Common Core State Standards, their students will greatly benefit from a student-centered self-assessment process such as Math Review so that students do not continue to accumulate misconceptions. Frequent assessment will help the classroom teacher with the shift to more meaning-based standards. Classroom instruction for procedural standards was more answer driven and not as dependent on knowing what the student was thinking, but once you move toward the realm of standards based on understanding, it is imperative that teachers pay attention to how the student is interpreting instruction. Frequent, student-centered assessment allows the teacher to obtain the necessary diagnostic information to determine whether classroom instruction is effective. The Math Review process also puts into place classroom environmental components such as student interaction, metacognitive practices, verification, collaboration, and student engagement activities that support development of understanding mathematical concepts.

Summary: The Power of Frequent Assessment in Mathematics

The use of frequent assessment in mathematics coupled with a self-assessment feedback system like Math Review is beneficial to students and teachers and has a positive impact on the math classroom environment.

Such a program benefits students by:
- Facilitating student self-assessment
- Providing sufficient feedback to allow students to correct misconceptions
- Allowing small, immediate successes that provide hope and lead to confidence
- Becoming student centered, which creates a feeling of responsibility for learning
- Promoting reflection, which allows students to think about feedback

Following are some benefits to teachers of this type of program:
- Teachers are challenged to consider student interpretation of instruction.
- Teachers receive current student diagnostic information.
- Teachers gain information about student thinking and student misconceptions.
- The experience of thinking through error analysis is clarifying for teacher and student.
- As the assessment approach becomes more student centered, instruction becomes more effective.

The impact on the classroom can also be felt in the following ways:
- Mistakes are seen as valuable events by which to obtain information.
- Students learn from each other and are supportive of one another.
- Student explanations and student thinking become vital parts of the math classroom.
- Students realize that we learn math through conversation and interaction.
- A wrong answer does not mean a student does not know anything about math, just that he is struggling with one part of a process or concept.
- A greater balance of teacher talk and student talk is achieved.
- Students are involved in all aspects of the assessment process.

References

Ainsworth, L., & Christinson, J. (2006). *Five easy steps to a balanced math program for upper elementary grades.* Englewood, CO: Advanced Learning Press.

Common Core State Standards Initiative. (2010). Key points in mathematics. Retrieved from http://www.corestandards.org/about-the-standards/key-points-in-mathematics

Earl, L. M. (2003). *Assessment as learning: Using classroom assessment to maximize student learning.* Thousand Oaks, CA: Corwin.

Hattie, J. (2009). *Visible learning: A synthesis of over 800 meta-analyses relating to achievement.* New York, NY: Routledge.

Marzano, R. J., Pickering, D. J., & Pollock, J. E. (2001). *Classroom instruction that works: Research-based strategies for increasing student achievement.* Alexandria, VA: ASCD.

Wilcox, J. (2006). Less teaching, more assessing: Teacher feedback is key to student performance. *Education Update, 48*(2), 1–8.

CHAPTER FOUR

Connecting Science Standards
and Assessments

LYNN HOWARD

Ms. Bryd's kindergarten classroom is abuzz with excitement. The students have a variety of items, including a marble, marshmallow, cracker, metal screw, and raisin. They have completed the science standard on making observations and building an understanding of the properties of common objects. The "sink or float" assessment will allow them to demonstrate what they have learned. The teacher has prepared a lab response sheet so students can record their observations for each item. Ms. Bryd is an exceptional educator who designs her science instruction around conceptual understanding and performance assessments. She incorporates behavioral observations, written work, and performance tasks to assess what her students know and are able to do.

Assessing student achievement in science has recently gained national attention across the United States. This increased interest is due in part to the No Child Left Behind Act's requirement of statewide testing in science starting with the 2007/08 school year (NCLB, 2002). Under federal law, local education agencies require annual assessments in core academic subjects, such as science, as related to the state standards. These standards reflect, for example, science concepts from multiple disciplines, such as life, earth, environmental, and physical sciences, as well as the incorporation of the science process skills.

This chapter provides a framework for implementing state and local science standards. The conceptual unit format, along with appropriately designed assessment items, allows educators to truly understand the structure and processes embedded in their state science standards. This progression of recognizing how standards and assessments are correlated builds professional and collaborative learning communities in which science teaching and learning is making a difference for students.

So What's Standing in Our Way?

With the amount of work required of classroom teachers today, they have difficulty balancing the demands of curriculum and standards, instructional methods and assessments, and data collection. Many teachers are frustrated yet committed to providing students with a strong science program, but they are often overwhelmed with the daily requirements and routines. In particular, teachers face impediments imposed by the following factors.

Many teachers have not received sufficient and sustainable professional development in teaching science. In some cases, teachers who have no educational background or experience are hired to teach science. These educators need specific professional development, not only in science methods and pedagogy but also in relationship building, classroom management, and a number of other areas that seasoned teachers take for granted. When given the framework and the tools that build skills and knowledge for teaching science, educators feel more confident in implementing the essential components of a balanced science program.

Often, district-mandated science programs are not aligned with the state standards, or testing to district standards can be confusing and addresses too much content to be taught during the course of one year. The National Science Education Standards (NSES) state, "assessments provide an operational definition of standards, in that they define in measurable terms what teachers should teach and students should learn" (NRC, 1996, pp. 5–6). The NSES and the National Research Council (NRC) stress that if science teaching is to be reformed, then students must be engaged in "active and extended scientific inquiry" (NRC, 1996, p. 52). The science textbook that is adopted by the district often does not align with the state testing or the class being taught but still becomes the predominant model for which to follow the curriculum. Today's educational arena is full of standards, assessments, and system mandates that govern what and how educators should teach. There is not enough time in the school year to physically "cover" all of the material in the curriculum and/or textbook. In addition, many teachers perceive gaps in the adopted programs and supplement them with additional lessons and activities from other resources.

Teachers are under enormous pressure to teach science procedures, conceptual understanding, and problem solving *and* prepare students for state tests. Science tends to be a "compartmentalized" subject, with multiple units presented to students each year. Although many state curricula tend to spiral or repeat in greater depth at later years, teachers often emphasize what is on the state test and de-emphasize the skills and concepts needed for a deep understanding of science. By combining a balance of science understandings and skills, teachers can implement the methods that incorporate all of the components of effective science teaching and learning.

Science is often taught in isolation and is not integrated with other subject areas.

Teachers who integrate science with other subject areas such as art, music, drama, literature, and history allow their students to go deeper into a scientific understanding of concepts and content. As teachers grow more competent with the science content, the integration of the arts and other core subjects becomes a natural connection for the teacher and the student. The NSES support coordinating and connecting science with other subjects, including technology. This integration allows a more efficient use of instructional time and enhances student achievement and learning.

Time, materials, and costs must be considered when designing science curriculum and assessments. The design of assessments makes selected-response items more attractive than performance assessments, which can be costly to develop and implement. Science performance assessments may be up to 100 times more expensive than multiple-choice items (Stecher & Klein, 1997).

A Basic Understanding

There is agreement in the science community that our present methods for assessing student achievement do not align with the current national standards. A disconnect exists between what is assessed and what students are expected to know and demonstrate.

The National Assessment of Educational Progress (NAEP) science assessments provide a view of what U.S. students know and can "do" in science. The assessment was developed by a committee of science and measurement experts to focus on the goals of the NAEP Science Framework. This framework is organized around two major dimensions: the fields of science and the knowing and doing of science. Earth, physical, and life sciences were included in the assessment, which consisted of multiple-choice and constructed-response questions. In addition, hands-on tasks were included.

There is a basic recognition among scientists and science education experts that science instruction should promote meaningful understanding of science concepts, processes, and thoughts. Students should not just be memorizing scientific facts or vocabulary but also developing a global understanding of how science works. The state standards present teachers with a long litany of goals, objectives, and benchmarks that often do not support conceptual understanding. This is why science is so "departmentalized" and promotes unit-to-unit teaching. With a more concise, structured approach to science teaching, students would be more productive in their learning environments and with science opportunities.

In an article entitled "Conceptual Understanding of Science," by Dorothy Gabel (2003, p. 70), she states:

> If we want to improve the conceptual understanding of science, teachers
> must be selective in the concepts they include in instruction. Much depends
> on the background that students bring to the course. This means not that

more content should be moved to lower grade levels but that the National Science Education Standards (1996) should be used as a guide to provide reasonable levels of content. The Standards carefully delineate what leading experts in the field deem appropriate for most students at each grade level. Increasing the content may force students to memorize and turn out to be detrimental to conceptual understanding.

Collaboratively Planning Science Conceptual Units

Teams of teachers across the country are faced with an overwhelming amount of information about effective teaching and student learning. Many schools are classified as "schools in crisis" by national, state, and local criteria. Friday Middle School in Gastonia, North Carolina, spent several years transitioning from individual, compartmentalized instruction to the Data Teams format. Student achievement was dismal in all grades, and teacher morale was at an all-time low prior to implementing a strategic planning approach across the content and grade levels. Because teaching is an isolated profession, the idea of teaming was very new to this school, and obstacles to overcoming the "my room, my lesson" mind-set had to be addressed in the beginning. From the first day of implementation, the school was committed to making a difference for the students. The hard lesson was that the teachers had to "look inward" and address personal issues before moving forward. The school implemented a conceptual unit design process to move beyond the traditional textbook and more into identifying Priority Standards, best instructional practices, and common formative assessments.

Science Conceptual Units

The NSES are comprehensive in science content, inquiry, and problem solving and inclusive of the process skills. The standards lend themselves to designing assessments with multiple "right" answers and require a hands-on approach that illustrates student understanding of the content. Science educators must have an opportunity to thoroughly understand their grade-level content standards so a purposeful intent for teaching is achieved. The standards must become "real" and useful to the teacher so that meaningful assessments and feedback can be used to adjust teaching and learning.

Designing conceptual units in science is an effective process for educators to move beyond the conventional practice of using the science textbook as a guide on what to teach and how to access student learning.

To help educators meet the learning needs of *all* of their students, the conceptual unit must:

- Incorporate the components of a balanced science program, using the textbook or science series as a resource

- Align the standards with best practices in instruction and assessment
- Incorporate strategies that support the science process skills, vocabulary, and reading and writing integration

Conceptual Unit Design

Science has typically been a subject in which students memorize isolated scientific facts with little understanding of broad, interrelated concepts. The new standards movement is asking students to demonstrate a deep understanding of a few fundamental ideas (AAAS, 1993; NRC, 1996). The way that science information is organized, presented, and assessed forms the workings of effective science instruction. Many districts have designed curriculum maps that tell the teacher the what, how, when, and why of teaching science. If this map does not promote learning with understanding, framed with a series of lessons, then science is often taught in isolation.

A conceptual approach to learning science allows students to deepen scientific understanding by connecting science concepts to science meaning. To effectively design a conceptual unit for science, Lynn Howard (2010), in *Five Easy Steps to a Balanced Science Program*, suggests the following 12 steps to sequence through planned instruction and assessment.

Step 1. Identify the priority science standards and "unwrap" to identify the key concepts and skills. Priority Standards are those that are the most important for students to know and be able to do. These standards must meet three criteria: (1) they are derived from the state standards, (2) they are important for learning in the next grades, and (3) they have lifelong implications for student learning. "Unwrapping" the standards identifies the major concepts (nouns and noun phrases) and skills (verbs) found in the standard and objectives. There may be an integration of standards based on the unit.

Step 2. Determine the science process skills that will be addressed during the unit. The basic science process skills are what we do when we conduct scientific exploration and experimentation. As teachers select the Priority Standards, the science process skills should be included (observing, communicating, classifying, measuring, inferring, and predicting) if the "unwrapped" skills are not inclusive.

Step 3. Determine the priority vocabulary from the concepts. Science textbooks contain many new words that students are expected to learn and understand. Although these words represent important concepts that are essential to science understanding, they can be overwhelming for many students. Successful instruction in science targets the essential vocabulary that is necessary for conceptual understanding.

Step 4. Determine the Big Ideas and Essential Questions. Big Ideas, according to Grant Wiggins and Jay McTighe in *Understanding by Design* (2005), are enduring understandings of what we want the students to retain and remember after leaving a unit.

These are decided by a grade-level team that asks, "What are two or three essential big-picture understandings that we want the students to discover on their own after they complete the conceptual unit?"

Essential Questions are written by grade-level teams of teachers to share with students at the beginning of the unit. These guiding questions are matched with the Big Ideas and represent the learning outcomes for the unit. The purpose of the Essential Questions is to help students make connections with the skills and concepts from the standard. Big Ideas help clarify the main ideas that students need to know about the standard. Students should respond to the Essential Questions with their own Big Ideas after completing the unit.

Step 5. Determine the materials, resources, and time frame needed to complete the unit. These components will be determined by the standards. Some districts have pacing guides that drive the instructional time for the content. Materials and resources should be located prior to implementing the unit so that smooth transitions occur from day to day.

Step 6. Decide on a discrepant event to introduce the unit. A discrepant event is an outcome that surprises, startles, puzzles, or astonishes the observing student and, in some cases, adults. The "basic rules of science" do not appear to be consistent, and the outcomes are unexpected or conflict with what the student predicts before the event. Discrepant events motivate students to investigate the science concept. It is important for the teacher to present the discrepant event as a science problem that the class will be investigating or trying to solve. The true science concept is not immediately revealed to the students but is one that evolves over the teaching of the conceptual unit.

Step 7. Develop writing prompts. Select several writing prompts that are aligned with the standards. Depending on the grade level and the time frame for the unit, have students write one or two writing prompts each week.

Step 8. Develop a problem-solving task. The problem-solving task should align with the standard(s) for the unit. It is suggested that a problem-solving task be completed every two weeks.

Step 9. Plan pre- and post-assessments and scoring guides, then administer the pre-assessment. Once the skills, concepts, and Big Ideas have been identified, grade-level teams design a pre- and post-assessment. The end-of-unit assessment should be matched to your Big Ideas and Essential Questions.

Step 10. Select best instructional strategies. Robert Marzano, Debra Pickering, and Jane Pollock (2001), in *Classroom Instruction That Works*, identified nine categories of effective teaching practices. Teachers should consider which of the nine best fit the instructional techniques needed for student learning to occur during the conceptual unit.

Step 11. Deliver unit instruction. Determine the time frame, materials needed, and instructional methodologies. If the district or school has a pacing calendar, it may serve as a guide for the time frame for the unit.

Step 12. Administer the end-of-unit assessment. Students complete the end-of unit assessment guided by an accompanying scoring guide, with students completing peer and self-assessments of their work. The teacher completes the final evaluation of the student work and provides feedback.

A Success Story

Multnomah Education Service District, based in Portland, Oregon, under the direction of Judy Custy, curriculum coordinator for the Department of Instruction, developed conceptual units in biology and physical science that serve as models for other districts and schools. A group of biology and physical science teachers collaborated on conceptual units and are completing a comprehensive set of assessment items aligned with the Priority Standards. Each month, these educators met to design conceptual units based on the format described in this chapter. The assessments include selected- and constructed-response items and performance tasks that represent the best instructional practices for problem solving, communicating in science, and the science process skills.

Common Formative Assessments in Science

The conceptual unit forms the framework for the development of common formative assessments. The assessments are collaboratively designed by a grade-level team of teachers and administered to all of the students during the implementation of the science unit. The results of common formative assessments allow teachers to evaluate the level of student understanding of the Priority Standards. The results of the assessments are analyzed through a Data Teams process, with information being shared with all grade-level teachers. This review provides timely feedback so that teaching may be differentiated based on the learning needs of their students. The ultimate goal is for the common formative assessment to drive and inform instructional practices.

The data provided from summative assessments are often limited and not timely, and they frequently do not indicate how well students know or have learned the material being taught. The state assessment is an assessment *of* students' learning that is summative, whereas the common formative assessments for classrooms are assessments *for* learning. Both are useful and necessary. Teachers use pre- and post-assessment results to plan and adjust instruction, lessons, interventions, and informal classroom assessments. The pre-assessment results can be used to identify students who are excelling and those who need extra support. This assessment may guide the differentiation process within the classroom so that teachers can modify assignments within small-group work time. Teachers who use the pre-assessment as a "lens" by which to view and frame the post-assessment are providing their students with a format that prepares them for additional testing.

Rationale for Common Formative Assessments in Science

Black and Wiliam (1998) state in "Assessment and Classroom Learning," "In reviewing 250 studies from around the world between 1987 and 1988, we found that a focus by teachers on assessment *for* learning, as opposed to assessment *of* learning, produced a substantial increase in students' achievement." The formative assessments are collaboratively designed, administered, scored, and analyzed within each grade level throughout the school year. Common formative assessments provide teachers with valid feedback regarding the students' current understanding and knowledge of the content and science process skills.

The purpose of common formative science assessments is to determine what your students know and are able to do with regard to the standards you are teaching. They are designed to be multiple-measure assessments that allow students to demonstrate their scientific understanding in a variety of styles. Each grade level is able to establish consistent expectations for standard implementation, student achievement, instructional practices, and aligned assessments. When assessment results are analyzed in a Data Teams process, they carry a predictive value about how students will succeed on additional assessments.

Formats and Focus

Common formative assessments are similar in design and format to end-of unit assessments and district and state assessments. These assessments should only target the Priority Standards from the conceptual unit. Most common formative assessments contain two types of items: selected response (multiple choice, matching, true/false) and constructed response (short-answer and problem-solving tasks). The common assessment may include items from more than one science standard. Students are required to demonstrate both their procedural understanding (the science process skills) and their conceptual understanding (Big Ideas).

Important Considerations Regarding Common Formative Assessments

First, common formative assessments should be aligned with the district benchmarks and end-of-course assessments no matter when they are given. Second, results from the common formative assessments must be analyzed in a Data Teams format so that mid-course corrections in teaching and learning can be made before a summative assessment. Third, common formative assessments must mirror the format of the state and local benchmarks and tests. Released test items are available in most states and serve as a guide to assessment item design.

Types of Response Items for Science Assessments

Selected-Response Items

Selected-response items require students to select one response from a list of answers. Most state tests are designed in the multiple-choice format, so it is suggested that grade-level teams use this configuration when creating selected-response items for their common formative assessments.

One of the benefits of selected-response items is that they can be answered quickly by the students and can be objectively scored as correct or incorrect. This effectively assesses students' knowledge of factual information, priority vocabulary, and basic skills. However, this type of question tends to promote recall or memorization of facts rather than demonstrate evidence of higher-level thinking and understanding. Selected-response items do not support writing and creative thinking unless they are specifically designed to do so.

The following is a sample question from the biology assessment at Multnomah Education Service District:

1. Which of the following best describes the structure of DNA?
   a. a double strand of nucleotides twisted into a helix
   b. a double helix of amino acids
   c. a single strand of nucleotides twisted into a helix
   d. a single helix of amino acids

Constructed-Response Items

This is the portion of the common formative assessment where students demonstrate through writing, speaking, or performance their integrated understanding of the "unwrapped" concepts and skills—at the level of rigor specified in the standard. For example, if the standards say "describe," then the constructed-response item would reflect this cognitive skill. Constructed-response items include short responses (word, phrase, and sentence; problem-solving steps; or multiple sentences or paragraphs). This type of question requires students to organize their thinking and use concept knowledge and skills to answer a question or complete a task. Teachers are able to determine whether students have gained an understanding of the Priority Standard. The benefit of constructed-response questions is that they provide the teacher with a valid inference about student knowledge. However, they take longer to score and require a scoring guide or statement of proficiency to determine the level of mastery.

Constructed-response items may be written so that students *physically* demonstrate their understanding of the targeted concepts and skills. Their performance and corresponding degree of proficiency can then be evaluated by using a scoring guide, or rubric.

Here is a sample question from a grade 6 assessment administered at Multnomah Education Service District:

> 3. Using scientific instruments, describe ways to measure mass and volume of an object.
>
>   *Proficiency*: In order to be proficient, the student includes using a scale or balance to find the mass, using length, height, width to find volume using a standard or metric measurement, or using displacement to find volume using a graduated cylinder.

Performance Tasks

Performance tasks give students the opportunity to demonstrate the level to which they have mastered the Priority Standard. These open-ended products and performances are designed to show what the student should know and be able to do after completing a conceptual unit.

The Office of Technology Assessment of the U.S. Congress (1992) defines performance assessment as "any form of testing that requires a student to create an answer or a product that demonstrates his or her knowledge or skills."

Effective performance assessments contain tasks that are engaging and worthwhile to the student. Performance assessments contribute to student learning by giving them challenging, high-level tasks that require them to apply skills and knowledge learned prior to the assessment. Many teachers find that performance tasks developed individually or by grade-level teams provide better data about student learning than traditional assessment methods.

Performance tasks should consist of complex challenges that reflect current science trends.

Science performance tasks should:
- Allow students to demonstrate and communicate their knowledge of standards, goals, objectives, and science content
- Allow students to demonstrate their understanding of science by requiring them to demonstrate more than one plausible solution
- Integrate science with other core content disciplines
- Provide meaning, interest, challenge, and real-world relevance to the content
- Allow for a deep investigation into the task

Designing a Performance Task

Good performance tasks require that students use higher-level thinking and the science process skills in solving the question or task. Consider the following when designing a performance task:
- Ask the questions "What are we going to do in this task? What do we want our students to accomplish?"
- Develop an overview of the performance assessment including:
  - An engaging scenario
  - Three to four tasks to be completed
  - Student understanding of the Big Ideas
  - Differentiation for varying abilities
  - Nonfiction and fiction connections to the task
  - Multiple levels of thinking skills
  - The time frame for completion
  - A scoring guide for evaluation
- Scaffold (increase the complexity of) the task to build understanding of concepts and skills.
- Determine the materials needed.
- Establish a time frame for completion.

Sample Grade-Level Performance Tasks

Kindergarten students are asked to complete a performance assessment after studying a unit on animals. The task involves designing a zoo for a panda bear including the habitat, food, safety issues, and other factors necessary for panda bear survival. Students are able to use the Internet to research the task and design an acceptable zoo habitat for their panda bear.

Fourth-grade students are asked to complete a performance assessment after studying a unit on the properties of matter. The task involves having students make simple observations, conduct experiments, collect data, use tools and measurement techniques, and communicate results.

A sixth-grade unit on the transfer of energy has students determine the best materials for use as insulators. Students are presented with a survival scenario in which they were stranded in a snowstorm on the side of a road. They are to use the materials to simulate the situation, determine the variables, conduct the experiment, and communicate the results.

A physics unit on force and motion has students designing and conducting experiments to demonstrate the effect of speed on collisions. Using toy cars and student-selected materials, the science process skills are integrated into the research and investigation to draw conclusions related to force, mass, and acceleration.

Biology students are applying their knowledge of genetics to the occurrence of traits on their family tree. The task assesses students' ability to apply their understanding to Mendel's Laws of Heredity by collecting, analyzing, and interpreting data.

Conclusion

This chapter is designed as a framework for implementing science standards and assessments. As you read through the chapter, take time to reflect on your current practices with science teaching and learning. Use this information as it is presented or adapt it to meet individual state, district, teacher, and student needs.

References

American Association for the Advancement of Sciences (AAAS). (1993). *Benchmarks for science literacy.* New York, NY: Oxford University Press.

Black, P., & Wiliam, D. (1998). Assessment and classroom learning. *Assessment in Education: Principles, Policy, and Practice, 5*(1), 7–73.

Gabel, D. (2003). Conceptual understanding of science. *Educational Horizons, 81*(2), 70–76.

Howard, L. (2010). *Five easy steps to a balanced science program.* Englewood, CO: Lead + Learn Press.

Marzano, R., Pickering, D., & Pollock, J. (2001). *Classroom instruction that works.* Alexandria, VA: ASCD.

National Academy of Sciences. (1996). *National Science Education Standards* (pp. 11, 13–15, 104–106). Washington, DC: National Academies Press.

National Academy of Sciences. (2000). *National Science Education Standards: A guide for teaching and learning.* Washington, DC: National Academies Press.

National Research Council (NRC). (1996). *National Science Education Standards.* Washington, DC: National Academies Press.

No Child Left Behind Act of 2001 (NCLB). (2002). Public Law 107-110. Retrieved from http://www2.ed.gov/policy/elsec/leg/esea02/107-110.pdf

Olson, S., Loucks-Horsley, S., & the Committee on the Development of an Addendum to the National Science Education Standards on Scientific Inquiry. (2000). *Inquiry and the National Science Education Standards: A guide for teaching and learning.* Washington, DC: National Academies Press.

Stecher, B. M., & Klein, S. P. (1997). The cost of science performance assessments in large-scale testing programs. *Educational Evaluation and Policy Analysis, 19*(1), 1–14.

U.S. Congress, Office of Technology Assessment. (1992). *Testing in American schools: Asking the right questions* (OTA-SET-519). Washington, DC: Government Printing Office.

Wiggins, G., & McTighe, J. (2005). *Understanding by design* (2nd ed.). Alexandria, VA: ASCD.

CHAPTER FIVE

Common Formative Assessments for English Language Learners

LOAN MASCORRO

Believe in something big. Your life is worth a noble motive.
WALTER ANDERSON

About 34 years ago, a little girl came to the United States from Vietnam. Her family had fled Vietnam in the middle of the night on a fishing boat with hopes of survival and one day attaining freedom in the country of opportunities. Her father and mother were well aware of the tremendous danger but knew that if they stayed in Vietnam the family would eventually be broken up by the Viet Cong. They had two options: stay, and the family would be enslaved, or risk everything for a chance for freedom. Their dreams came true in November 1977, when they arrived in the United States after living in a refugee camp in Malaysia for six months.

Suddenly a new gift of freedom and the opportunity to continue schooling in America meant that an invaluable prospect for a promising future could be obtained through education. But the girl faced a multitude of challenges in assimilating to a new culture, school, and community. Learning became a daunting task, and going to school every day was an act of courage. These questions crossed her mind daily: *Will I be able to make friends? Will I be able to understand and do the work? Will my teacher like me? How will I communicate?* She tells herself, *Don't cry. Smile.* Every day she came to school, she asked herself, *How will I speak to other people? I speak Vietnamese and Cantonese.* She wondered if, when attempting to repeat a word, she would sound funny. She already felt a lot of fear and anxiety but wanted everything to be all right. She hoped it would be.

The Impact of Common Formative Assessments for English Language Learners

Authentic assessment, rooted in the simplicity of knowing a student's name and acknowledging his background, language level, and cultural history, allows the educator to develop common formative assessments for learning at all levels inclusive of the district level, department or grade level, state level, school level, and individual level. Balanced learning can be achieved through formative approaches when using intentionally created assessments for all students to determine their current level of understanding of an academic area while crafting access to social and instructional understanding. "Schools with the greatest improvements in students' achievement consistently used common assessments" (Reeves, 2004).

Common formative assessments are ongoing, collaboratively developed assessments that gauge and give insight into the students' learning at measured, scheduled times (Ainsworth & Viegut, 2006). These assessments are not summative but rather are based on the necessary appropriate instruction targeted to proficiency to guide student success toward literacy and fluency. For example, if an educator gives a student a piece of sheet music for a song without knowing the level of the student's skill, it might inspire the student to write a song or discourage him from ever studying music at all. Conversely, if an educator knows the level of proficiency and interest—obtained by administering a common formative assessment—and plays a song for the student, with the stated goal being that eventually he could write the music or play the piece independently, the student is inspired and guided toward composition fluency and appreciation of music across a broad spectrum of knowledge, instrument selection, genre, career choices, and appreciation.

Making inferences about student learning involves knowing the strengths and weaknesses of the learner, which allows the educator to shape, modify, guide, and design a curriculum that determines the outcomes, growth, and success of the student. Different types of common formative assessment for English language learners (ELLs) may include the following:

1. Checklists
2. Rubrics
3. Observations
4. Oral responses
5. Group responses
6. Individual responses
7. Performance-based responses
8. Criterion-referenced state or district tests
9. Text-driven guides

The role of the educator when developing assessments for the ELL is to be aware of the student's language acquisition level (Exhibits 5.1 through 5.5). The result is appropriate assessments that guide interests, introduce academic concepts, and disseminate essential information as part of the curriculum. Multiple opportunities for success throughout the assessment process allow fluency, achievement of proficiency, leverage for basic skills to develop and grow, and building steps to advance knowledge and comprehension. Therefore, setting explicit language and content objectives for ELLs is critical for effective teaching and learning. Implementing common formative assessments in an integral process with a view toward providing the data needed to inform educators on student learning needs impacts instructional effectiveness. This process should inspire teachers to learn about their students and encompass responsive teaching as a result of personalized, differentiated support for individual students' learning needs (Tomlinson, 2010).

EXHIBIT 5.1	Language Acquisition Level 1	
General Descriptor	**Students Can**	**Teachers Should**
Student moves from silent stage with no comprehension to physical responses with minimal comprehension. Student continues to one- or two-word responses with limited comprehension to speaking in simple sentences with comprehension of highly contextualized information.	• Respond nonverbally to respond in simple sentences • Respond in L1 • Respond physically • Sing and draw • Make connections with prior knowledge • Categorize objects and pictures • Use context to make meaning • Identify people, places and things • Repeat and recite • Reproduce what they hear • Label drawings and diagrams • Describe concrete things, events, places, and people • Explain simple academic concepts • Learn "big ideas" in content areas • Recognize and read basic vocabulary and write words and simple sentences • Associate sound and meaning • Role play • Listen and respond with greater comprehension • Compare and contrast	• Provide listening and speaking opportunities • Create a language-rich classroom • Create high context for shared reading • Use art, mime, and music • Use predictable, patterned books • Ask Yes/No, and Who? What? Where? Questions • Have students label, manipulate and evaluate pictures and objects • Ask questions requiring responses of lists of words • Ask open-ended questions • Have students describe personal experiences • Use self-created books • Use props and realia during instruction • Assess prior knowledge and build background knowledge • Encourage active participation of listening, speaking, reading, and writing at the students' levels

Note: English learners are capable of higher-level thinking but are often unable to communicate their thoughts and ideas in spoken or written English.

Source: Reprinted from The Leadership and Learning Center's Accelerating Academic Achievement for English Language Learners Seminar by Bonnie Bishop. Copyright 2010.

EXHIBIT 5.2	Language Acquisition Level 2	

General Descriptor	Students Can	Teachers Should
Student moves from minimal comprehension and some proficiency in communicating simple ideas to comprehension of highly contextualized information. Student continues to speak in simple sentences with approximations. Reading and writing progress with scaffolding and support.	• Reproduce familiar phrases • Originate and speak in simple phrases • Speak with frequent errors in the patterns and structure of English • Make increased connections with prior knowledge • Use context to make meaning and increased connections • Simply describe people, places and things along with more abstract concepts and ideas • Simply retell main events and the sequence of a story with some detail • Explain and describe simple academic concepts • Learn "big ideas" and details in content areas • Recognize and read basic vocabulary and write words and simple sentence • Listen and respond with greater comprehension	• Give more comprehensible input • Give students increased opportunities to produce academic and social language • Create a language-rich classroom • Create high context for shared reading • Use art, mime, and music • Ask Yes/No, and Who? What? Where? Questions • Develop story frames • Provide increased practice of key grammatical structures in context • Have students describe personal experiences • Use self-created books • Use props and realia during instruction • Assess prior knowledge and build background knowledge • Encourage active participation of listening, speaking, reading and writing at the students' levels • Do informal assessments on an ongoing basis • Continue to monitor progress • Be patient

Note: English learners are capable of higher-level thinking but are often unable to communicate their thoughts and ideas in spoken or written English.

Source: Reprinted from The Leadership and Learning Center's Accelerating Academic Achievement for English Language Learners Seminar by Bonnie Bishop. Copyright 2010.

EXHIBIT 5.3	Language Acquisition Level 3	

General Descriptor	Students Can	Teachers Should
Student moves from comprehension of contextualized information and proficiency in [communicating] simple ideas to increased comprehension and communication skills. Student begins to speak in complex sentences with approximations. Reading and writing progress with scaffolding and support.	• Use context to make meaning and increased connections to academic understanding • Engage in conversation and produce connected narrative • Interact with native speakers • Make errors with irregular patterns and structures in English • Read from a variety of genres with scaffolding from the teacher • Identify and describe main ideas and details • Simply summarize story or informational text • Make descriptions with increased details • Draw comparisons • Define new vocabulary	• Encourage students to describe personal and secondhand experiences • Provide explicit instruction in irregular patterns and structures in English and idiomatic expressions • Develop student study skills, such as making predictions and inferences • Explain text features [such] as headings, charts, maps, and graphics • Provide opportunities to access technology • Engage students in directed reading-thinking activities • Use reciprocal teaching and learning to teach clarifying, questioning, summarizing, and predicting • Continue to develop vocabulary skills by providing comprehensible input • Develop cognitive skills through reading and writing • Ask how and why questions as well as open-ended, higher level thinking questions • Introduce explicit grammatical instruction • Do informal assessments on an ongoing basis • Continue to monitor progress • Be patient

Note: English learners are capable of higher-level thinking but are often unable to communicate their thoughts and ideas in spoken or written English.

Source: Reprinted from The Leadership and Learning Center's Accelerating Academic Achievement for English Language Learners Seminar by Bonnie Bishop. Copyright 2010.

EXHIBIT 5.4   **Language Acquisition Level 4**

General Descriptor	Students Can	Teachers Should
Student has good comprehension of information and is proficient at communicating well using both social and academic language. Student has an adequate vocabulary to achieve academically. Student is approaching grade-level standards in reading and writing.	• Make fewer errors with irregular patterns and structures in English • Read from a variety of genres with little scaffolding from teachers • Identify and describe complex main ideas with details • Summarize story or informational text • Give opinions and reasons for opinions • Summarize, draw comparisons and contrasts, and justify views and behaviors • Demonstrate both social and academic understanding of English • Demonstrate ability to use higher-order language, synthesize, analyze, and evaluate • Persuade and debate with preparation • Engage in extended conversations and produce complex sequential narratives • Develop listening, speaking, reading, and writing skills with increased comprehension	• Structure group discussions • Provide opportunities for readers, such as theater and literature circles • Provide for a variety of realistic writing opportunities • Guide use of reference materials and technology • Provide reading opportunities in a variety of genres • Publish student writing • Focus on academic language and vocabulary • Ask questions to provide students with opportunities to synthesize, analyze, and evaluate in oral and written communication • Expand explicit grammatical instruction • Do informal assessments on an ongoing basis • Continue to monitor progress • Be patient

Note: English learners are capable of higher-level thinking but are often unable to communicate their thoughts and ideas in spoken or written English.

Source: Reprinted from The Leadership and Learning Center's Accelerating Academic Achievement for English Language Learners Seminar by Bonnie Bishop. Copyright 2010.

EXHIBIT 5.5	Language Acquisition Level 5

General Descriptor	Students Can	Teachers Should
Student has very good comprehension of information and near-native proficiency at communicating both social and academic language. Student has an expanded vocabulary to achieve academically. Student is at or above grade-level standards in reading and writing.	• Make fewer errors with irregular patterns and structures in English • Read from a variety of genres with little to no scaffolding from teachers • Comprehend and generate discussions and presentations in social and academic settings • Have developed fluency with a wide range of topics • Read and comprehend grade-level texts • Organize and generate written compositions based on purpose, audience and subject matter • Have a sense of his or her own voice • Respond to and use figurative language and idiomatic expressions appropriately • Prepare and deliver presentations and reports across grade-level content areas that use a variety of sources, and that include purpose, point of view, transitions, and conclusions	• Continue explicit grammar instruction • Encourage students to lead group discussions and teach • Provide opportunities for student-generated pres-entations • Provide for a variety of realistic writing opportunities in a variety of genres • Encourage independent use of reference materials and technology • Continue to publish student works • Provide increased opportunities for students to develop higher-order thinking skills • Do informal assessments on an ongoing basis • Continue to monitor progress • Be patient

Note: English learners are capable of higher-level thinking but are often unable to communicate their thoughts and ideas in spoken or written English.

Source: Reprinted from The Leadership and Learning Center's Accelerating Academic Achievement for English Language Learners Seminar by Bonnie Bishop. Copyright 2010.

Unless educators target specific language acquisition skills, the learner is left to try to comprehend in an environment where words are merely sounds rather than a bridge to academic areas supported by literacy and grade-level content knowledge and standards. The bridge between a student staying in survival mode to being a part of a curriculum that involves application, creativity, active participation, involvement, ongoing hope, enthusiasm for progress, aspirations to achieve, and confidence to try in all academic areas is central to the importance of assessment for learning. The process of guiding learning through periodic, systematic testing of knowledge and skills serves as a platform of the intricacies needed to build social, instructional, and academic language acquisition.

Benefits of Common Formative Assessments for English Language Learners

For the individual student, the benefits of language acquisition are, simply, the ability to be a powerful communicator. Communication allows students to develop proficiency through multiple measures of assessment and formats and draws them into academic and social areas of participation on a daily basis.

For ELL students to achieve language acquisition, educators must be purposeful in defining their goals and objectives in instruction and planning, in collaborating among colleagues to provide for a similarity of assessments across district and state requirements, and in giving regular feedback to students attaining critical standards and success as participants in a learning environment.

A school culture that features collaborative assessments promotes powerful support for students whose language acquisition is directly related to their success as learners, community participants, and members of a social environment where language fluency is the bridge to opportunities at every level.

In this effort, it is imperative that all teachers of ELLs know and understand the English language development (ELD) standards in order to employ effective instructional strategies and practices to increase student performance levels. In many school settings, the responsibility of teaching ELLs lies with the English language development teacher because of the notion that ELLs are unable to learn much in a mainstream classroom and thus these students are better served by specialists to meet their needs. The reality is that teaching English language skills is not the sole responsibility of the English as a second language teacher, but the responsibility of all teachers.

Realistic expectations based on differentiated English language performance assessments guide instruction for students and form a bridge to meeting English language arts standards. Skills related to listening and speaking, reading, and writing (Exhibit 5.6) can be taught in all content areas, not in isolation but as part of differentiated instruction. Skills assessments should be crafted in alignment to what students can "do" at each language acquisition level. Additionally, assessments can be adapted for preproduction, early production, speech emergence, and advanced fluency students by asking tiered questions that increase in the level of complexity associated with their level of language acquisition to check their comprehension and to help them acquire basic summarization skills. Starting with the levels of language acquisition, teachers can provide multiple experiences within the context of developing literacy and communication through common formative assessments that include a variety of item types, performance tasks, response types, scoring guides, and rubrics while accounting for specific levels of competency resulting in long-range expectancies for advanced fluency.

When all teachers are familiar with the ELD standards, they will become more skillful in their teaching because they will choose the appropriate questions, prompts, strategies, and practices to engage ELLs (Flynn & Hill, 2006). Furthermore, knowing and understanding the characteristics of each stage of language acquisition is critical to planning effective assessment formats that will more accurately measure ELLs. This directly impacts students' level of confidence as they successfully engage in learning that meets their needs.

When large-scale assessments are used as the only source of data, educators must keep in mind that an individual child's academic growth has minimal impact on the cognitive demand desired during the course of study (Popham, 2001). Traditional assessments such as these will not measure ELLs' knowledge and skills adequately. Although the data from these large-scale assessments can be useful, the need for more specific and timely data behooves us to change our assessment methodology to one that yields information for teachers to design and refine their instructional discourse for their students on a daily basis. Furthermore, assessment tools need to be distinguished between tests and assessment. While tests guide instruction toward mastery of skills, discernment between an overall picture of student knowledge and abilities provides direction for instruction, enabling a curriculum to go beyond a declarative, fact-based focus to one that allows a student to demonstrate through varied opportunities differentiated performance of his abilities in all academic areas.

Student assessments that require advanced language skills are obstacles for ELLs to demonstrate mastery of a skill or concept. Therefore, a variety of interim, formative, and summative assessments that acknowledge the language proficiency level of a student provide for differentiated instruction while making it possible for the ELL students to advance as communicators in listening and speaking, reading and writing.

Common Core State Standards

Given the widespread adoption of the Common Core State Standards, all students will be expected to demonstrate higher levels of proficiency in English and mathematics. What will be some of the challenges for educators providing support for ELLs? Which strategies and support structures will remain the same, and in what areas will a broader

EXHIBIT 5.6 **Differentiated English Language Performance Assessment: K–2 Beginning Level**

	Listening and Speaking	Reading	Writing
English Language Development Standards	Respond to simple directions and questions using physical actions and other means of nonverbal communication. LS-3 Begin to speak with a few words or sentences using some English phonemes and rudimentary English grammatical forms. LS-1 Answer simple questions with one- or two-word responses. LS-2 • Independently use common social greetings and simple repetitive phrases (e.g., "Thank you," "You're welcome"). LS-4	Respond orally to stories read aloud, using physical actions and other means of nonverbal communication. RC-1 Identify using key words or pictures the basic sequence of events in stories read aloud. RC-5 Recognize English phonemes that correspond to phonemes students already hear and produce in their primary language. RW-1 Read aloud simple words in stories or games. RF-1	Copy words posted and commonly used in the classroom. WS-2 Copy the English alphabet legibly. WS-1 Write a few words or phrases about an event or a character from a story read aloud by the teacher. WS-3 Use capitalization when writing one's own name. WC-1

Performance Tasks	After multiple experiences with the reading of *The Rainbow Fish*, ask the following questions:
	
	1. What is your name?
	2. Can you point to the book?
	3. Point to a fish.
	4. What is the name of the fish in the story? Point to the name of the fish. Thank you.
	5. Show me what the fish did.
	6. Tell me what the fish did.
	7. Point to the word that tells what Rainbow Fish did.
		• Picture walk
		• Key Vocabulary Prediction with a picture card deck to predict what the story might be about.
		• Multiple experiences with the reading of *The Rainbow Fish*. Teacher reads story and uses realia and total physical response (TPR) to act out story.
		• Using picture cards with scenes from the story, ask student to properly sequence the major events.
		• Student will respond to the story using physical actions or other means of nonverbal communication. (Point to the rainbow fish, etc.)
		
		After sharing the word bank, use word cards and ask student to point to the following words:
		  coral (cognate)
		  in
		  and
		  ocean
		  fish
			After multiple experiences with *The Rainbow Fish*, direct student to do the following task (use TPR to ensure that students understand the task):
			
			Write your name on the paper. Draw a picture of Rainbow Fish sharing his pretty scales. Show me where Rainbow Fish lives and include some of the characters in your drawing. Using the word bank, write some words that describe what you drew. Tell me who is in your picture. Label your picture.
			
			Scoring Guide:
			Mastery
			–Student writes name legibly using appropriate capitalization.
			–Student uses words from the word bank or from the classroom word wall to describe the drawing.
			–Student labels the picture correctly.
			Approaching
			–Meets two of the proficient criteria
			Beginning
			–Meets fewer than two of the proficient criteria

range of interventions be required? The answers to these questions are currently unknown, but educators should endeavor to explore and embrace the expectation of the higher standards through the lens of evaluation. The process of planning, implementing, and monitoring the Common Core State Standards must include reflection on the current state of each district's existing ELD program, which will allow opportunities to conduct curriculum audits and identify any gaps. Furthermore, developing and communicating a clear, systematic Common Core implementation plan regarding expectations and outcomes will be pivotal to the success of all students.

All teachers will need to be prepared to deliver not only a rigorous but also a relevant curriculum for all students that encompasses complex content and application of knowledge through higher-order thinking skills with strong language skills through reading, writing, speaking, and listening. In addition, teachers must have an understanding of the principles of Specially Designed Academic Instruction in English to provide a supportive, nurturing learning environment for ELLs. While maintaining a focus on common standards, it would necessitate the content-area instruction be modified to include ELD (Diaz-Rico & Weed, 2002). Specially Designed Academic Instruction in English strategies, implemented effectively in a mainstream classroom to provide access to learning, feature the following characteristics: the context for instruction must be full of hands-on learning and cooperative learning opportunities, and presentation of new content should be tailored to make it more comprehensible, and hence accessible.

With that being said, let's take a look at an example of a writing standard from the Common Core State Standards and pay particular attention to how the content and skills within that standard develop in terms of rigor and complexity, and the implications for instruction this progression has for ELLs. Exhibit 5.7 illustrates how concepts and skills develop with increasing complexity through the grades for Writing Anchor Standard 3. The learning progression expectations spiral around the same concept every year, with new skills added to increase complexity. This cycle is a gradual process in which students have multiple exposures to the same concepts, working toward learning expectations that are attainable for both the teaching and learning goal. For example, consider the criteria set by the standards when assessing a student in fifth grade who is demonstrating that he is proficient in *establishing a situation and introducing characters* but lacks the skill *orienting the reader, along with organizing events logically and sequentially.* The grade level the student is currently performing at with those particular writing skills can be easily deciphered by looking back and forward on the learning progression. This is the beauty of the learning progression structure in the Common Core State Standards. One can look back and look forward to see where students are performing along the specific learning trajectory for each standard. Through careful alignment of the student's English language acquisition level, ongoing common formative assessments, and sheltered instructional strategies, a teacher can provide ELLs the support needed to accelerate toward academic achievement.

EXHIBIT 5.7

Grade-Specific Standards for Writing: Standard 3

The example below illustrates how skills and concepts for end-of-year, grade-specific expectations for a given standard are both reinforced and expanded as students advance through the grades. The result is a **"spiral effect"** where students repeatedly practice mastered competencies from the year prior in the context of new competencies being "added" each year as the standard increases in complexity and sophistication. New skills and concepts "added" to each grade level from the year prior are noted in **bold**.

W.CCR.3	**CCR Writing Anchor Standard 3** **Write narratives to develop real or imagined experiences or events using effective technique, well-chosen details, and well-structured event sequences.** =
W.11-12.3a **Grade 11–12 students:**	Write narratives to develop real or imagined experiences or events using effective technique, well-chosen details, and well-structured event sequences. a. Engage and orient the reader by setting out a problem, situations, or observations, and **its significance**, establishing one or multiple point(s) of view, and introducing a narrator and/or characters; create a smooth progression of experiences or events. +
W.9-10.3a **Grades 9–10 students:**	Write narratives to develop real or imagined experiences or events using effective technique, **well-chosen details**, and well-structured event sequences. a. Engage and orient the reader **by setting out a problem, situation, or observation**, establishing one **or multiple point(s) of view**, and introducing a narrator and/or characters; **create a smooth progression of experiences or events**. +
W.8.3a **Grade 8 students:**	Write narratives to develop real or imagined experiences or events using effective technique, relevant descriptive details, and well-structured event sequences. a. Engage and orient the reader by establishing a context and point of view and introducing a narrator and/or characters; organize an event sequence that unfolds naturally and logically.
W.7.3a **Grade 7 students:**	Write narratives to develop real or imagined experiences or events using effective technique, relevant descriptive details, and well-structured event sequences. a. Engage and orient the reader by establishing a context and **point of view** and introducing a narrator and/or characters; organize an event sequence that unfolds naturally and logically. +
W6.3a **Grade 6 students:**	Write narratives to develop real or imagined experiences or events using effective technique, **relevant descriptive details**, and well-structured event sequences. a. **Engage** and orient the reader by **establishing a context** and introducing a narrator and/or characters; organize an event sequence that unfolds naturally **and logically**. +
W.5.3a **Grade 5 students:**	Write narratives to develop real or imagined experiences or events using effective technique, well-chosen details, and well-structured event sequences. a. Orient the reader by establishing a situation and introducing a narrator and/or characters; organize an event sequence that unfolds naturally. +
W.4.3a **Grade 4 students:**	Write narratives to develop real or imagined experiences or events using effective techninque, **well-chosen details, and well-structured** event sequences. a. **Orient the reader** by establishing a situation and introducing a narrator and/or characters; organize an event sequence that unfolds naturally. +
W.3.3a **Grade 3 students:**	Write narratives **to develop real or imagined experiences or events using effective technique, descriptive details, and clear event sequences.** a. **Establish a situation** and **introduce a narrator and/or characters; organize an event sequence that unfolds naturally**. +
W.2.3 **Grade 2 students:**	Write narratives in which they recount a **well-elaborated event or short** sequence of events, include **details to describe actions, thoughts, and feelings**, use temporal words to signal event order, and provide a sense of closure. +
W.1.3 **Grade 1 students:**	**Write narratives** in which they recount **two or more appropriately sequenced events**, include **some details regarding what happened**, use temporal **words to signal event order**, and **provide some sense of closure**. +
W.K.3 **Kindergarten students:**	**Use a combination of drawing, dictating, and writing to narrate a single event or several loosely linked events, tell about the events in the order in which they occurred, and provide a reaction to what happened.**

Source: Adapted from CCSSI, 2010, pp. 19, 20, 43, 46.

Not only will it be essential for teams of teachers or departments to collaborate on common formative assessments to ensure their content is relevant and the data to be extrapolated provides specific information to guide the next steps of instruction and learning, but in addition clear and specific feedback must be provided to the student to advance. It goes without saying that feedback must be specific and timely. Traditionally, providing feedback focuses on the past, a student's mistakes, and a grade and/or mark. What needs to become a habit of mind is the engagement of providing feedback for the future; whether it is a conference between student and teacher or teacher and parent, it is a conversation that focuses on goals for the future, which is referred to as "feedback forward." For example, in Exhibit 5.8, an assessment sample of a narrative is provided. How would you gauge this student's performance? What is the student's language acquisition level? Has the student met all of the criteria for writing standard 4a in grade 4? What specific feedback would you provide to the student to advance his writing going forward? Keep in mind that this is a formative assessment.

EXHIBIT 5.8	Student Writing Sample: Narrative
Assessment Sample: Writing Standard 4a	
Student Sample Grade 4—Narrative "Small Moments"	I sat there. Just me. I sat there looking at my long beautiful hair. "Could I see my hair shorter?" I asked myself. I felt my long glossy hair tickle my neck. My reflection looked back at me. Was my reflection about to change? Or was I about to change? "Click! Click!" I looked behind me. There stood my mom. "Ready for your haircut Sophie?" she asked. I gulped. "I guess." I said softly. The shiny metal of the scissors gleamed in the afternoon sun. The click that the scissors made gave me a chill down my spine … *the story continues*

Who's the Little Girl?

That little girl, being me at the tender age of six, spent a lot of time listening, and watching. I was given a stack of cards with a picture of a word. The cards had a magnetic strip that ran through a machine, after which the device would repeat the word. That is how I learned vocabulary. I was pulled out of the classroom and sent to another room to learn in isolation. Fortunately, my teachers were pleasantly surprised that I displayed confidence in math and was able to demonstrate understanding of some math skills without linguistic skills, so they allowed me to have a little more interaction with my classmates than I might have had otherwise. But most of the time I was lost because I could not understand anything or engage in the learning. When it came time for me to complete an assessment, needless to say, I was overwhelmed and did not want to attend school on those days. The sheer anxiety of taking a test made me want to escape. What excuses could I conjure up to miss school? At one time, I thought perhaps weekly appointments to the dentist or orthodontist for preventive dental care would be a rational reason to not be at school. Who would question that? Nonverbal communication skills were the key to my survival at school, each and every day. I wanted so badly to understand, to learn, to be successful, and to feel like I belonged.

So how can educators focus assessment to gauge language acquisition in order to help recent immigrants and students with varying degrees of native language proficiency? How do educators facilitate learning for students who know a few vocabulary words and help them make sense and develop the different language levels of acquisition?

Common formative assessments play a critical and fundamental role in developing fluency for students to progress as academic learners and formative speakers while avoiding linguistic obstacles that prevent language acquisition. Systematic and thoughtful instruction and assessment can diffuse the level of anxiety that prevents a student from being too afraid to ask simple questions about the location of the restroom, obtaining help, or understanding the rules. Educators need to engage in assessment discourse that evaluates the students' performance, and levels of acquisition and language skills, on an ongoing basis. Such discourse promotes the provision of accommodations and development of processes that optimize a venue for success for ELLs to become powerful communicators, who are then able to attain high levels of academic achievement and are prepared to demonstrate the skills needed for college and twenty-first-century careers. In other words, they are set up for success.

References

Ainsworth, L., & Viegut, D. (2006). *Common formative assessments: How to connect standards-based instruction and assessment.* Thousand Oaks, CA: Corwin Press.

Common Core State Standards Initiative (CCSSI). (2010). *Common Core State Standards for English language arts & literacy in history/social studies, science, and technical subjects* [PDF document]. Retrieved from http://www.corestandards.org

Diaz-Rico, L. T., & Weed, K. Z. (2002). *The crosscultural, language, and academic development handbook.* Boston, MA: Allyn and Bacon.

Flynn, K., & Hill, J. (2006). *Classroom instruction that works with English language learners.* Alexandria, VA: ASCD.

Popham, W. J. (2001). *The truth about testing: An educator's call to action.* Alexandra, VA: ASCD.

Reeves, D. B. (2004). *Accountability in action* (2nd ed.). Englewood, CO: Lead + Learn Press.

Tomlinson, C. A. (2010). *Leading and managing a differentiated classroom.* Alexandria, VA: ASCD.

Transforming Teaching Through Standards and Assessment

As you read the chapters in this section you will see the following themes: rigor, synergy of practices, and the focus on learning for the twenty-first century. The authors address the teaching and learning process and show us the impact of standards and assessment in the classroom. Each chapter will increase your understanding of how teachers use standards and assessment as an instructional tool. These authors shine a bright light on the need to change our instructional pedagogy to better meet the needs of the students of today and the students of tomorrow.

Brandon Doubek challenges a traditional approach to teaching and learning by helping us to view standards and assessment through different contexts and, therefore, applications. In his words, standards and assessment are the "centerpiece for teaching and learning." In order to further emphasize their importance, Brandon helps to frame our practice through the use of contexts, as understanding the contexts is critical to leadership, to teaching, and to student learning. He takes us on a journey and engages us in the condition of *leadership* through a case study. He then places our learning in the contexts of *curriculum, planning for instruction, instruction,* and then *assessment.* This chapter will help you frame or even reframe your practice and thought processes of using standards and assessment to improve teaching, learning, and leadership. Brandon offers a compelling conversation for change.

Laura Benson also takes us on a journey with standards and assessment—one with compasses, maps, and guiding principles. She teaches us about the "important" priorities in formative assessment: *knowing every student as an individual, focus, assessment systems, feedback, collaboration, questioning, and listening.* Based on her interactions with teachers about standards and assessment, she shares many practical classroom strategies. Laura reminds us that formative assessment does make our jobs as teachers much easier, and it places the focus of instruction on our students. She passionately speaks to the importance of helping students see they are supported and valued by teachers. Laura accomplishes all this by showing us how to use formative assessment as a tool for learning and as a valuable experience for students.

Thomasina Piercy exposes the current state of reading comprehension in our schools and shows us the gaps between school experience, exposure, and standards with the demands of postsecondary education and career readiness. She provides a wealth of research and history on literacy standards, school experiences, instruction, and assessment. Thommie guides us toward deeper understanding with text complexity and shows us a framework that will increase rigor and, in turn, deepen student understanding. She does a stellar job of showing the connections between the Common Core State Standards, twenty-first-century learning standards, and disciplinary literacy standards. While disciplinary literacy provides teachers with instructional procedures to guide informational learning, it also shows us the need to increase our standards, rigor, and expectations of our students. This chapter will inspire you to create a rigorous, literacy-rich environment in which to adequately prepare our students for a postsecondary career or college experience.

CHAPTER SIX

Contexts and Applications for Standards and Assessment

BRANDON DOUBEK

It seems funny that most of the writing and planning I am able to accomplish most efficiently happens at around 38,000 feet in the air each week. Of course, this notion presupposes that there are no crying babies, and no one is inadvertently invading my chair space, but it is one of the easiest places for me to focus and isolate myself. Each of us has our own context for most things we do in life, and this is part of *my* context for planning and communication.

When thinking of the word "context," it conjures a sense of surroundings, situations, and history. *Merriam-Webster's online dictionary* defines "context" as "the interrelated conditions in which something exists or occurs." So it would seem that almost any definition, characterization, or explanation of something deemed important would require an understanding of its context to gain necessary background for the purpose of interpretation. Take, for instance, the level of preparation required to perform a piece of Classical instrumental music. One can learn the notes, rhythms, and musical markings on the page and still perform the piece like a robot. But playing any instrument with the intention to emote feeling requires a deeper understanding of who the composer was, the era in which the piece was written, and the reason and/or for whom it was written; these are crucial, contextual starting points. One might also learn all the rules of football and never help a team score a touchdown due to a lack of understanding about team dynamics.

The case for understanding contexts of standards and assessments is not only critical to teaching and learning but is also at the heart of the levels at which instruction, curriculum, and assessment are interpreted. So often the planning stage of instruction begins with teachers looking at a textbook and choosing chapters from a book or some other materials to deliver instruction, rather than starting with the target curriculum standard to determine what is delivered to students. The first approach usually leads to a process of prioritizing content over process, of teaching too much content without allowing the time for students to process and reflect on the most critical information. And sometimes, even when we do begin by examining the standards first, the prerequisites cannot be accounted for because each class of students may vary in their levels of previous mastery from year to year. Moreover, the Bloom levels at which teachers evaluate curriculum standards can make the difference between targets being taught and assessed at the appropriate levels or not. Therefore, this may potentially impact state test scores in a negative way. For example, while some standards might be interpreted at level 2 (understanding) of Bloom's cognitive taxonomy, they might be measured on a state test at level 4. Therefore, this interpretation can determine student success or failure in an entire system of assessment and instruction.

Marzano (2003) relates the five ranked school-level factors impacting achievement the most, with number one being a "guaranteed and viable curriculum." These attributes, guaranteed and viable, were based on two original factors: "opportunity to learn" and "time." *Guaranteed* in this case seems to suggest that all students have access, and they will receive the same basic information from one teacher to the next. This concept lends itself well toward teacher collaboration in that teachers need to discuss the "what" that is being taught for optimum consistency from classroom to classroom. *Viable* seems to imply that standards are practical and relevant to current world developments, like twenty-first-century technology, and that curricula have the potential to transform organically as the world around us changes. To ensure that curricula are not stagnant, they must be evaluated from time to time in order to remain current. Hence, the context for instruction begins with an examination of curriculum as the first stage in the process.

In order to provide a guaranteed and viable curriculum for students, school districts may create time for teachers to discuss the most important parts of the curriculum to prioritize which standards are most critical for students to know and be able to "do." Because there is simply not enough time for teachers to deliver all that is provided in most state curriculum documents (Reeves, 1996), teachers must prioritize skills, processes, and concepts over content. By delineating these Power Standards (Ainsworth, 2003), students have more time to internalize information at the required level of cognition, rather than trying to learn a plethora of fact-based information they may forget later in time.

So often students are not connected to the information they are asked to learn. When teachers collaborate to prioritize standards by using endurance, leverage, and readiness (Ainsworth, 2003; Doubek, 2010), taking into consideration the high-stakes state tests—not teaching *to* the test—they begin to make important connections to real-world situations, which they convey to students. Teachers need time to create value for this material so that students find new information relevant and meaningful. The "hooks" for learning that contain text-to-world connections are critical in order for students to understand why they must learn new information. Without this "priming," it is difficult for students to internalize and retain new material (Jensen, 2005). This process of collaboration is even more effective when it is completed while calibrating a vertical alignment (Jacobs, 1997).

Creating Change One Step at a Time: A Context for Leadership

Washington Court House, Ohio, is a small school district 45 miles southwest of Columbus with approximately 2,200 students and a population of 13,631. Superintendent Keith Brown initiated a district partnership with The Leadership and Learning Center in January 2009 by focusing on district leadership, identifying district goals that included the proposed improvement of reading, math, and graduation rates. The district had experienced state test score challenges, with its lowest scores in the middle school. The district leadership team participated in the seminar Daily Disciplines of Leadership (Reeves, 2002) in January, and teachers and all administrators experienced two seminars, Data Teams and Writing to Learn, by May 2009. Washington Middle School teachers received an additional seminar, Powerful Strategies for Effective Teaching, in March 2009. They also experienced numerous site-visit follow-up days to ensure deep implementation at all grade levels.

In June and August 2009, over a period of four days each month and with the guidance of Susie Bailey, director of Data and Curriculum, teachers met in grade-level teams by math- and reading-related content areas to begin a second pass at prioritizing and aligning the curriculum using the 2002 Ohio state standards. In each grade-level content team, teachers began without curriculum documents first to decide which skills, processes, and content would form the "safety net" curriculum (Reeves, 2003). Organizing by categories that were derived from the state curriculum document, teachers then calibrated the vertical alignment Power Standards choices and matched the state language from the Ohio state standards. Teachers who were present at these meetings deliberated over the Power Standards to be included by using sticky notes on poster paper and by talking through their choices and either keeping or changing Power Standards based on other grade-level decisions. At the beginning of the 2009/10 school year, teachers created pacing guides to "map" the curriculum to begin planning for instruction.

In July 2009, district leadership, including Superintendent Brown, Assistant Superintendent Beth Justice, Director Bailey, and Title 1 Director Peggy Zimmerman, along with four building principals, met for two days to discuss monitoring and implementing Data Teams within Professional Learning Communities. Mr. Brown announced at this meeting that the district would begin a "late start" on the first Wednesday of each month for dedicated time on Data Teams within Professional Learning Communities for all teachers in the district. This retreat also included significant planning around leadership communications to all stakeholders and training on walk-throughs to monitor the instructional process. In September 2009, all teachers and administrators were trained using the text and seminar Common Formative Assessments (Ainsworth and Viegut, 2006), work that would be developed and collaboratively scored in Data Teams.

By October 2009, all Data Teams were implementing with high fidelity in three of four schools, and all building administrators were conducting walk-throughs each week. Principal Eric Wayne and Assistant Principal Tracy Rose at Washington Middle School developed and implemented a rather simple walk-through protocol with the intention of providing both written and oral feedback to teachers. The form only included binary result information (yes/no) with an emphasis on Power Standard learning targets, engagement, and feedback. In a school that had previously experienced little teacher collaboration and mostly summative teacher evaluations, the most significant change reported by Assistant Principal Rose was that teachers began inviting administrators into classrooms so they could receive and discuss more feedback. In most cases, the feedback was from the teacher to the administrator about what had occurred.

By May 2009, the middle school improved its state ratings from "effective" to "excellent" for the first time while the district maintained an "effective" rating. By May 2010, the district also moved from "effective" to "excellent." During a building site visit to the middle school in December 2009, Mr. Rose stated that he knew something had changed in his building when conversations with teachers were more focused on instruction than on logistics and complaints. In a recent conversation with the author via e-mail, Mr. Rose commented on the process of collaboration at this school:

> I believe our monthly department meetings help us maintain focus and accountability with curriculum mapping, assessments, and strategies (best practices). This preparation each month is to ensure not only the guaranteed and viable curriculum, but to foster support and create/maintain an environment in which teachers have shared ownership and common goals. All stakeholders need to be active participants for us to make shared decisions in the best interest of our students. One of our social studies teachers, Troy Montgomery, begins and ends each lesson discussing the learning target, making connections for the students so they understand why they are learning the information, and he discusses how they will be assessed, so students feel that he is setting them up for success. An interesting fact: He assigns a lengthy research paper each year. Two years ago the completion rate for all his classes was 80%. Since the utilization of learning targets and a shift in his teaching style that emphasizes connections and an understanding of "why do I need to know this," his completion rate for the research paper this year was 98%.

Implementation site visits from The Leadership and Learning Center continued to focus on leadership, Data Teams, common formative assessments, and powerful strategies for effective teaching during the 2009/10 school year. In an effort to emphasize the importance of leadership, it should be noted that at least one central office administrator was present at all site visits and all trainings, engaging in extensive communication before each seminar, training, or site visit. Communications with the district were consistent through e-mail and phone conversations, and they provided context for the strengths and obstacles that were encountered in current situations.

In May 2010, the district achieved an "excellent" rating, with the most significant gains seen in student achievement as measured by the Ohio Achievement Assessments (OAA) listed in Exhibit 6.1 (Ohio Department of Education, 2010). It also moved into the 94th percentile in the state in terms of gains indicated in state ranking documents for 2009/10. Although the data listed in this exhibit measure apples to oranges (different students each year), they are the current metric presented in most state statistics.

In July 2010, a second leadership retreat focused on monitoring instruction not just by building administrators but also by central office administrators several times each week. Although formative walk-throughs were originally grieved by the teachers' union,

EXHIBIT 6.1	Ohio Achievement Assessments Student Achievement Measures: 2007/08 versus 2009/10	
Grade Level/Content Area	**2007/08 % Proficient**	**2009/10 % Proficient**
Grade 3 Reading	71.5	75.5
Grade 4 Math	68.5	75.8
Grade 5 Math	60.6	65.1
Grade 6 Reading	76.3	79.9
Grade 6 Math	67.5	76.1
Grade 7 Reading	71.3	81.1
Grade 7 Math	68.3	83.9

they were ultimately accepted as instruments of formative feedback rather than summa-tive judgment. In December 2010, Director Bailey stated that teachers welcome central office administrators into their classes and welcome the opportunity for feedback. In a most recent e-mail conversation she stated: "We've seen a gradual shift in the attitude of our staff members toward collaboration and the acceptance of data and research as bases for decision making. We're definitely headed in the right direction."

While the district evidenced significant gains in math scores, the gains were still not enough to make adequate yearly progress (Ohio Department of Education, 2010). In October 2010, math teachers in grades 3 through 12 participated in the seminar Five Easy Steps to a Balanced Math Program from The Leadership and Learning Center, which emphasized Step 1 (computational skills), Step 2 (problem solving), and Step 4 (math facts).

Teachers in grades 3 through 5 received additional site visits in October and Decem-ber 2010 to reevaluate their prioritized curriculum standards in order to reconfigure their curriculum pacing maps in math and reading. This work began with an analysis of several data sources, including state test data (OAA); Measures of Academic Progress, developed by Northwest Evaluation Association; and common formative assessments. By analyzing several data sources, or triangulating data, and reflecting on the realities of what they experienced using the common assessment process, teachers worked collab-oratively to restructure what and how they taught.

Several realizations came to light as teachers examined their previous curriculum maps: (1) there were too many Power Standards in several of the months, (2) some of the skills on which students were most proficient repeated on occasion, (3) some of the skills with which students struggled were placed all in one month, and (4) some of the teachers who made original decisions about what to place in which month were no longer teaching that grade level. Additionally, by reflecting on the common formative assessments that accompanied their current pacing guide, teachers conveyed that (1) most assessments were too long to be collaboratively graded in a timely manner, and (2) in several cases, the assessment seemed artificial because the teachers had not had time to adequately teach everything on the pacing guide for a given time period.

The result of these four days of data analysis and curriculum reevaluation (two days for grade 3 math and one day each for grades 4 and 5 reading) included (1) reducing the redundancy of specific Power Standards on which students performed well; (2) more evenly distributing Power Standards for those skills with which students struggled; (3) incorporating specific instructional strategies tied to each Power Standard, emphasizing Step 4 of the Data Teams process; (4) reducing the number of Power Standards to two to four maximum per two months; and (5) reducing and rebalancing (quantitative and qualitative questions) common formative assessments. Moreover, on the last day of this meeting with reading teachers, Principal Bob Runnels of Belle Aire Intermediate, grades 3 through 5, met with these teachers at their request to discuss redistributing students during certain blocks of time to differentiate instruction so a response to intervention (RTI) could become more equitable for all students. Exhibit 6.2 shows the result of a revised curriculum map for the month of October for grade 3 mathematics. It is important to note that teachers not only indicated the power indicator and cluster but also worked to codify a generative list of instructional strategies matched to the curriculum.

Setting the Pro Verbial Stage: A Context for Planning

To plan most effectively for instruction, several pieces of background information must be taken into consideration that provide context for the process. These include, but are not limited to:

1. the level of Bloom's taxonomy (Anderson & Krathwohl, 2001; Bloom & Krathwohl, 1956) required by the curriculum standard,

2. a knowledge of where students are in relation to that standard (pretest assessment),

3. how students will achieve that level of cognition (instruction),

4. how we will know they have achieved that level (posttest assessment), and

5. a reasonable time for the journey.

Although planning is a critical component of teaching and learning, it is often done "on the fly" or in compliance with administrators' mandates. Unless a context is provided for this task—the "Why do I need to do this?" factor—many teachers feel it is an unnecessary evil that yields little reward, a veritable "check-off" to complete by a due date. The fact is that planning for instruction ultimately determines the flexibility of human performance in teaching, and because Bloom levels command laser-like accuracy to ensure that they are measured and instructed to the required level, the inferences for this context should be addressed well before this planning stage of instruction takes place. Moreover, while it may be said that the "best laid plans [schemes] of Mice and Men oft go awry" (Burns, 1786), we can never truly anticipate how a group of students, even those we teach daily, will receive, react to, and value new information (Clark, 1999). Planning for the unexpected is not common practice in teaching, so unpacking context in advance of the instructional practice is one of our safest routes to achieve the most effective instruction.

EXHIBIT 6.2   Revised Curriculum Map for Grade 3 Mathematics

*Cat	Power Indicator	Cluster Indicators	Instructional Strategy	Assessments
*NS	*Use place value concepts to represent whole numbers and decimals using numerals, words, expanded notation, and physical models.* **For example: model the size of 1,000 in multiple ways, e.g., packaging 1,000 objects into 10 boxes of 100, modeling a meter with centimeter and decimeter strips, or gathering 1,000 pop-can tabs.**	1. Identify and generate equivalent forms of whole numbers, e.g., 36, 30 + 6, 9 × 4, 46 − 10, number of inches in a yard.	• Flash cards • Rainbow number cards • Expanding objects • Base 10 blocks • Number neighborhood	October CFA and CSA (some will do differentiated formative assessments, including pre-tests)
NS	Add and subtract whole numbers with and without regrouping.	1. Model and use the commutative and associative properties for addition (and multi-plication). 2. Explain and use relationships between operations such as: a. Relate addition and subtraction as inverse operations. 3. Write, solve, and explain simple mathematical statements such as 7 + ! > 8 or D + 8 = 10. 4. Express mathematical relationships as equations and inequalities. 5. Make estimates for **perimeter**, area, and volume using links, tiles, cubes, and other models.	• Build furniture within house with newspaper, given dimensions (perimeter) • Math playground video • Cubes and dice • Human perimeter • Addition with dice • Subtraction with dice • Computational strategies (vs. traditional regrouping) • Counting up strategy • Basic subtraction— "think addition"	

*Cat stands for category. NS in this case stands for number sense as a category from the Ohio state standards.

What the Cat Dragged In:
A Context for Curriculum

The "Unwrapping" Conundrum

When we think about the level at which we teach and measure information in class-rooms, that level should be determined by the level at which the curriculum standard falls into Bloom's cognitive taxonomy (Anderson & Krathwohl, 2001; Bloom & Krath-wohl, 1956). In many cases, it is difficult to ascertain what writers were thinking as they assembled certain documentation, as is the case with any form of text. Hence, the title of this section represents the attempt to figure out what was intended by the writers of the standards—what the cat brought into the house—as it poses a visual challenge.

Recently, one of my close friends and I wrote a series of e-mails to each other that we misinterpreted. The result was some initial words that were more serious than usual, then we both ended up laughing about the fact that one cannot discern tone in e-mail. Such is often the case with interpreting standards. It is hoped that these levels are neither random nor arbitrarily conceived at the state or national level but that they form indicators of mastery that have been carefully scaffolded by grade level and content area to mirror the appropriate grade/age/developmental stage of what students need to know and be able to do.

The mistake that is made most often, however, is trying to rely entirely upon the verbs found in the standard as the sole metric for the Bloom level most closely associated with the direction of instruction and assessment. In order to fully comprehend and evaluate the context of the standard, one must look beyond the verb to the nouns and sometimes even the prepositional phrases (in which nouns hide) to discern the intended Bloom level. Moreover, identifying the level at which standards are written treads upon a gray area of understanding that is neither outlined by curriculum writers nor communicated by school districts. Herein lies the problem of context within curriculum standards that becomes the basis for instruction and assessment in the teaching and learning process.

Even with the standardization of the Common Core State Standards for 2014, there is nothing written in the document that concerns the specifics of teaching the standards. This omission does not imply that standards should dictate the particular instructional strategies or methodologies for instruction that teachers should use. However, some direction about the taxonomical interpretations of standards could increase levels of teaching and learning. For example, during a training on "unwrapping" the standards as part of the common formative assessment process, Barbara Bonnes, curriculum director for Mentor (Ohio) Public Schools, noticed that although teachers in her district were delivering instruction at high levels of complexity, they struggled to interpret the Bloom levels in the current state curriculum. This incident is not isolated by any means. Many teachers in school districts find major challenges in evaluating the rigor of standards because curriculum writers provide little direction about the intended level that should be taught. Whether districts are using Bloom or some other metric of classification (e.g., Depths of Knowledge, Marzano's reinterpretation of Bloom), this contextual level of meaning for the standard is crucial for translating curriculum into instruction and then checking understanding with assessments.

The most difficult interpretations involved trying to determine the correct level of Bloom's cognitive taxonomy (see Exhibit 6.3) using the 2001 version for several of the Ohio state standards. As educators, we all want to "get it right." In order to practice with this information, several standards from the national core curriculum were used to serve as a model and guided oral practice during the seminar (see Exhibit 6.4).

In 2010, more than 500 teachers in six states (California, Hawaii, Missouri, Ohio, Washington, and West Virginia) reacted to the standard displayed in Exhibit 6.4 with the same basic responses. They evaluated the first strand, "gather relevant information...," as either level 3 or 4 (apply, analyze), and they rated the second one, "assess the credi-

EXHIBIT 6.3   Bloom's Cognitive Taxonomy

The Knowledge Dimension	The Cognitive Process Dimension					
	(1) Remember	(2) Understand	(3) Apply	(4) Analyze	(5) Evaluate	(6) Create
Factual Knowledge	List	Summarize	Use	Order, classify	Rank	Combine
Conceptual Knowledge	Describe	Interpret	Experiment	Compare	Assess	Plan
Procedural Knowledge	Tabulate	Predict	Calculate	Differentiate	Conclude	Compose
Meta-cognitive Knowledge	Appropriate use	Execute	Construct	Achieve	Action	Actualize

Source: Wikipedia (n.d.).

EXHIBIT 6.4   Common Core State Standards for English Language Arts, Grade 6

Research to Build and Present Knowledge
- Gather relevant information from multiple print and digital sources
- Assess the credibility of each source
- Quote or paraphrase the data and conclusions of others while avoiding plagiarism

bility...," as level 5 (evaluate). But when they estimated the last strand, "quote or paraphrase the data and conclusions of others while avoiding plagiarism," their responses were widely divergent. Teachers literally appraised this strand at all six levels of Bloom's taxonomy. When asked about their thinking around this strand, teachers who assessed the strand at levels 1 and 2 stopped on the words "quote" (level 1) or "paraphrase" (level 2). Teachers at the other end of the spectrum rated the strand at level 5 because the words "avoiding plagiarism" seemed to suggest that students must be able to judge what constitutes plagiarism, and teachers who responded with level 6 stated that because the strand suggests students must incorporate this information into some form of a research paper, they would have to create something new from what they already had.

The repercussions of such variance among teachers' interpretations may have a direct impact not only on the interpretation of curriculum but also on instruction, in terms of the levels at which students are scaffolded, and on assessment, in terms of the way teachers assess student learning. An even more profound outcome of this variance may show itself as districts are rated on high-stakes test scores. Therefore, it seems that the safest route in this regard would be to err on the side of the higher Bloom level so that students are not "caught" on high-stakes tests without the necessary practice to demonstrate mastery of an objective.

Give a Man a Fish:
A Context for Instruction

While teachers undoubtedly work very hard to prepare lessons for their students, it is questionable whether they all begin with the end in mind (Wiggins & McTighe, 2005) or establish what students should be able to do as a result of the process of teaching and learning. Teaching is both an art and a science (Marzano, 2007). They must go beyond teaching with the assessment results as an end result. Many factors must be considered in the delivery of instruction that ultimately make a difference in whether a child succeeds or fails in life, can successfully support themselves financially, and can make significant contributions to society, or they give up on life altogether—and of course, the outcomes that fall somewhere in between. The one thing we know for sure is that teachers make the difference (Fullan, 2010; Reeves, 2010, 2011; Sternberg & Grigorenko, 2000).

Often when children respond to the question, "What is your favorite subject in school?" the response is about the teacher and how he or she "does" things—this is one cultural context for learning. Students occasionally mention that they are "good at" one subject or another, but a deeper unpacking of those layers usually points again to the teacher. The irony of this situation is that teachers use curriculum to make choices about what to teach (the constant), but how they challenge, communicate with, encourage, engage, facilitate learning of, mediate for, and stimulate students (the variables) is very much up to their own choices, which seem to center around attitude, instructional methodology, and personality. Marzano (2007, p. 4) states that "It is certainly true that research provides us with guidance as to the nature of effective teaching, and yet I strongly believe that there is not (nor will there ever be) a formula for effective teaching."

Many experts in the field of education agree that there is some "x factor" in great pedagogues, but those factors that are controllable and that educators can have some influence over (Covey, 1989) include structures and routines based on the curriculum from which educators base instruction. Linda Darling-Hammond (2010) states: "Clearly, if students are expected to achieve 21st-century learning standards, we can expect no less from their teachers and from other educators." She continues to explain that the variance in teacher preparation programs accounts for a large portion of achievement gaps. Although extensive research on instructional strategies that are most effective exists (Danielson, 2007; Hattie, 2009; Hunter & Russell, 1981; Hyerle, 2000; Jackson, 2011; Joyce, Weil, & Calhoun, 2000; Marzano, 2007; Nessel & Graham, 2006; Perry, 2009; Richardson, Morgan, & Fleener, 2004; Rothstein, 2000; Slocumb, 2004; Stronge, 2007; Tatum, 2005; Tomlinson, 2001; Van de Walle & Lovin, 2006), few models of teaching make connections between curriculum standards and the process of teaching and learning by connecting them to specific instructional strategies as categorized by strands within the curriculum.

A Before-During-After Framework: Connecting Bloom's Taxonomies

Once teachers have evaluated curriculum standards and decided which strands receive the highest priorities, the next step is to estimate how long it will take to teach these strands; the third step is to plan for the instructional process. Pacing guides should take into consideration the time it takes to teach a prioritized standard in its entirety, rather than skimming through the "facts of the information." Indeed, some mathematical consideration using estimated Bloom levels within the standard should be one factor in determining how long a standard is to be taught. The most effective and researched

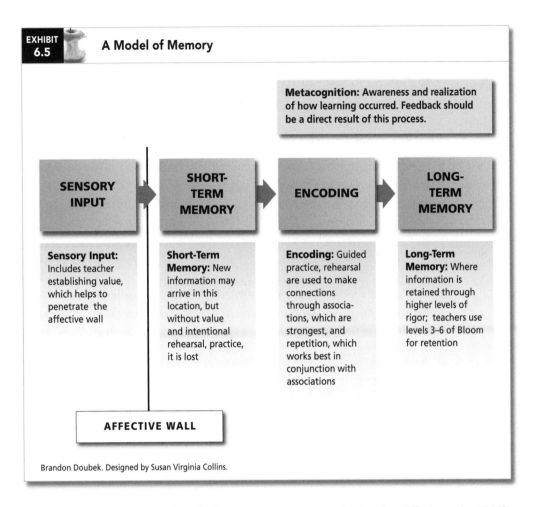

EXHIBIT 6.5   **A Model of Memory**

Metacognition: Awareness and realization of how learning occurred. Feedback should be a direct result of this process.

SENSORY INPUT → **SHORT-TERM MEMORY** → **ENCODING** → **LONG-TERM MEMORY**

Sensory Input: Includes teacher establishing value, which helps to penetrate the affective wall

Short-Term Memory: New information may arrive in this location, but without value and intentional rehearsal, practice, it is lost

Encoding: Guided practice, rehearsal are used to make connections through associations, which are strongest, and repetition, which works best in conjunction with associations

Long-Term Memory: Where information is retained through higher levels of rigor; teachers use levels 3–6 of Bloom for retention

AFFECTIVE WALL

Brandon Doubek. Designed by Susan Virginia Collins.

model of instruction includes a before-during-after model (Van de Walle & Lovin, 2006). This model is called many different names by various instructional researchers, including priming, processing, and retaining for mastery (Jensen, 2005); preparation, assistance, and reflection (Richardson, et al., 2004); and anticipatory set, guided practice, and closure (Hunter & Russell, 1981). However, when this framework is superimposed with Bloom's affective and cognitive taxonomies, it very closely resembles what Eggen and Kauchak (2007) refer to as the cognitive information processing model (see Exhibit 6.5).

Because educators are most concerned with the new information that students must retain to master specific curriculum standards, a before-during-after framework for instruction allows teachers to scaffold instruction to ascend the levels of Bloom's cognitive taxonomy. Furthermore, by addressing Bloom's affective taxonomy (See Exhibit 6.6) as part of the stimuli from the environment, teachers are helping students to move toward valuing information (Krathwohl, Bloom, & Masia, 1973) that is new by establishing relevance to the content standard. This presentation of new material for students is a critical characteristic of learning that occurs during the first—before—stage of the framework. When students are connected to novel information with which they are familiar, they are more likely to persist in the learning process (Driscoll, 1994; Gill, 1993; Robinson, 1993; Sullo, 2007).

This process of creating value for students requires the connection of the curriculum standard to real-world applications in order to find the most appropriate "hooks" for instruction. This "before" stage of instruction (see Exhibit 6.7) contains no new information for students but builds on their prior knowledge. Many instructional strategies are well suited to this first stage of instruction, including anticipation guides, list-group-label, and alphabet taxonomies. Creating a "before" hook for instruction may become as simple as finding the theme of a story (e.g., conflict) and then asking students how many of them have experienced the phenomenon (in this case, had conflicts with their parents). For math instruction, the more mathematical concepts are applied to real-world situations, the more mathematics is not a disconnected set of symbols and procedures (e.g., we can find slope in handicapped ramps, airplane takeoffs, and escalators).

EXHIBIT 6.6   Bloom's Affective Taxonomy

Category
Receiving Phenomena: Awareness, willingness to hear, selected attention. Using the five senses to access information.
Responding to Phenomena: Active participation on the part of the learners. Attends and reacts to a particular phenomenon. Learning outcomes may emphasize compliance in responding, willingness to respond, or satisfaction in responding (motivation).
Valuing: The worth or value a person attaches to a particular object, phenomenon, or behavior. This ranges from simple acceptance to the more complex state of commitment. Valuing is based on the internalization of a set of specified values, while clues to these values are expressed in the learner's overt behavior and are often identifiable. Teachers must help students to create value for new information by making explicit connections to real-world contexts.
Organization: Organizes values into priorities by contrasting different values, resolving conflicts between them, and creating a unique value system. The emphasis is on comparing, relating, and synthesizing values. Because the brain creates hierarchical systems, values are sorted and organized by priorities.
Internalizing, or Living by, Values (characterization): Has a value system that controls their behavior. The behavior is pervasive, consistent, predictable, and most importantly, characteristic of the learner. Instructional objectives are concerned with the student's general patterns of adjustment (personal, social, emotional).

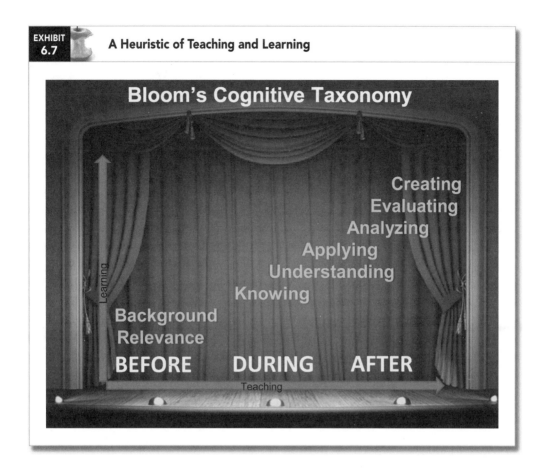

EXHIBIT 6.7   A Heuristic of Teaching and Learning

The "during" phase of instruction is the first phase in which new information is introduced; it is the place in which students are guided through the beginnings of Bloom's cognitive taxonomy. This scaffolding is not instantaneous, and it requires time for students to process, rehearse, and encode new information. Students require guided practice and feedback during this stage so they are able to clarify any misunderstandings or problems with understanding how a concept works. Hattie (2009) clarifies the idea of feedback as that from the student to the teacher, rather than from the teacher to the student. Several instructional strategies, including concept attainment, known as the Frayer model, and reciprocal teaching are helpful during this middle phase of instruction. In 25 years of observations of classrooms around the world, visiting many rooms on a minimum monthly basis, I have watched many teachers beginning and ending in the "during" phase of instruction. When I discussed this observation with the teachers, their responses included three main reasons: (1) they were trying to cover too much content, (2) there are too many standards to teach, or (3) the pacing guide does not allow for the "before" or "after" phases. The fact is that all three phases are required for students to truly internalize and retain new curriculum that is foreign to them. The last phase of instruction consists of students using what they know, and it is the time that new material reaches a higher level of flexibility and complexity.

The "after" stage of instruction takes students to the final level of Bloom's cognitive taxonomy that a curriculum standard requires. The last phase of instruction should allow students to perform an activity by practicing in different ways, comparing and contrasting, sequencing, judging, or creating something new from what is known. In this end phase of instruction, students should reflect on the information in some way before a summative assessment takes place. In some cases, I have observed teachers substituting assessment for this phase of instruction, which mistakenly assumes that, because students have been guided up to this point, they are able to move to full independence/autonomy. However, feedback is required for all stages of the instructional process, and if it is to occur with guidance by an instructor, then students must receive formative feedback in this stage, as in the previous two phases. Hattie (2009) states that "the more challenging the task, the more critically feedback is needed." Because the "after" phase of instruction includes the most abstract and complex activities in learning, formative feedback is a crucial component of this stage. Several strategies that have been used in the "before" phase of instruction can be used again in a new context or by adding an element at a new level of complexity with the same strategy. Other strategies that may be useful during this stage include nonlinguistic visual representations, final word protocol, and Socratic seminars.

In essence, Exhibit 6.7 relates on the horizontal axis how teachers use time to deliver before-during-after instruction (teaching). The level of cognition connected to the curriculum standard is represented by the vertical axis (learning). While each level of Bloom's taxonomy subsumes, or takes in and becomes part of, the previous levels, these highest levels, also known as higher-order thinking skills, require that students have mastered all of the steps leading up to this point. Because students begin at different places based on their previous learning, it is often necessary to differentiate instruction in a meaningful, intentional, and organized manner (e.g., having all students learn the same prioritized standard but using different content based on their interest, then coming back together to evaluate theme or tone). Differentiation that requires the unreasonable expectation of teachers to create 15 different lesson plans is unwarranted; however, useful activities, particularly at the upper levels of Bloom's taxonomy, emphasize students' strengths and capitalize on talent development (Sherer, 2006). Because some students can become lost when they are unable to understand a new concept or when a feedback mechanism to the teacher is not in place, an RTI may become most appropriate in order for students to master prioritized standards.

Look Before You Leap: An Inclusive Methodology for Response to Intervention

"RTI is a framework that guides instruction for all students" (Gregg, 2010). It is not a process that leads to special education but a general education model that allows teachers to take a different track when students do not respond to instructional strategies provided in daily lessons. Hence, all students are part of this process whether they are in general education, gifted education, or self-contained special education. In essence, RTI is another form of differentiating instruction combined with data-driven decision making. Because the components of RTI suggested by the language of the federal government include multiple forms of assessment (universal screenings of academics and behavior, student assessment with a classroom focus, and continuous progress monitoring during interventions), this approach seems to mirror pretest methodology and formative assessment. In addition to these assessment components, the instructional components suggested by federal language include using high-quality, research-based classroom instruction, implementing appropriate research-based intervention, and teaching behavior-fidelity measures, all of which should be included in regular instruction and a before-during-after framework.

Because this is a multitiered intervention system (see Exhibit 6.8), in which 80 to 90 percent of students should be part of tier 1, with students receiving more intensive

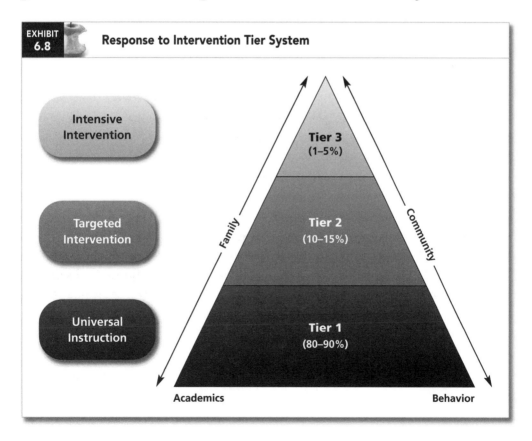

EXHIBIT 6.8 **Response to Intervention Tier System**

Intensive Intervention

Targeted Intervention

Universal Instruction

Tier 3 (1–5%)

Tier 2 (10–15%)

Tier 1 (80–90%)

Family

Community

Academics

Behavior

instruction in tier 2 (10 to 15 percent) and more individualized attention in tier 3 (1 to 5 percent), it is often mistakenly understood that when students do not "seem" to respond to regular instruction they should move up into the next tier. The problem is that tier 1 instruction is not always stable, so many schools across the nation show what is usually thought of as an inverted pyramid.

Tier 1 does not negate the process of reteaching new information just because students don't "get it" the first time around; it suggests that when universal instruction has included various forms of instructional strategies (graphic organizers, Math Review, etc.) and students continue to struggle, then they need more attention in a smaller group environment (tier 2) where they can give and receive appropriate feedback so they can clarify misunderstandings or resolve a lack of engagement with the material (Hattie, 2009). The goal of RTI is that, if students need more intensive instruction in tier 2 or 3, eventually they are able to work back toward tier 1. In essence RTI is a "red flag" system that prevents the overidentification of special education students while helping all students, regardless of their labeled status, to achieve to their fullest potential.

While many districts throughout the nation, particularly in their elementary schools, have created a special time in the day for interventions, this is not always a viable option for secondary schools, nor is it suggested in any of the federal language that this should be mandated. The point of RTI is that it is an all-day, everyday occurrence in K–12 classrooms for all students in terms of affective and cognitive growth. And because RTI is not just about academics but also concerns behavior, active classroom routines, structures, and teacher responses are critical components of the tier 1 process. Response to intervention relies heavily on the formative assessment process, which is equally critical for student success.

In St. Paul (Minn.) Public Schools, many elementary schools have adopted a model in which RTI occurs during a 30- to 45-minute separate block of instruction and in which intensive interventions are possible when human resources (e.g., community volunteers, college students) are available to assist in this process. This situation seems to be helpful, particularly when an inverse pyramid exists, or more plainly, when more students require tier 3 interventions. At Humboldt Senior High School in St. Paul, the principal, Mike Sodomoka, put together a committee to create a secondary context for RTI, in which an extra period of the school day, financed by a special grant, allowed teachers to create an intervention structure for students who are struggling, an enrichment for those in tier 1, and a progress-monitoring mechanism (formative assessments) to keep these groups flexible. In essence, some assessment procedure must be in place for this process to occur in any building.

Are We Almost There Yet?
A Context for Assessment

While I was a supervising university professor, I asked one of my student teachers how he knew when his students truly understood what he had taught in a lesson that day. He responded that he knew they had processed the lesson "because he could see it in their eyes." Yet I have been in conversations on more than one occasion when I realized my mind had drifted, I was uninterested, or I was distracted—it is human nature. After all, becoming inattentive at times is a natural part of brain function. However, even though my engagement level or cognition was not 100 percent, I could still respond with "Uh huh." Students know the "school game," and they are capable of responding in any number of ways that they have learned to pacify teachers.

The process of assessment is possibly one of the most complex tasks that teachers must perform because it requires making an inference from the response to some form of question, and there is little if any guarantee that any one question will directly measure the intended level, or rigor, of a curriculum standard or the instruction that has accompanied the teaching of that standard. However, rarely do college or university curricula include a course for undergraduate preservice teachers on testing and measurement or instructional evaluation. For this reason, many forms of assessment are used for grading purposes rather than the most important function of assessment: generating reciprocal feedback for teachers and students.

Assessing Prerequisite Skills

Because curriculum standards are written at various levels of Bloom's cognitive taxonomy, and because students arrive in classes with various "levels of knowing" in regard to specific standards, pretesting various taxonomy levels may be the only way to fully understand where students are in relation to that standard. Often students are rewarded with high achievement grades for coming into a class having already mastered a learning objective. Because they learned the material at a previous time, they are sometimes labeled as "smart," while other students who come into contact with the information for the first time are often labeled as "struggling." The teacher and levels of instruction determine whether these labels are assigned or growth is the intended outcome. In order to safeguard against this occurrence, pretests can be administered to measure the starting point of what students need to know and be able to do. The use of pretest data in the Data Teams process is one way to set goals to ensure growth for all students. Growth can then be measured most accurately by measuring the difference between pretest and posttest gains in achievement. However, when a majority of students show significant mastery of a standard before it is taught, it is then appropriate to compact curriculum (Renzulli & Reis, 1997) and prioritize other standards or to differentiate instruction and

EXHIBIT 6.9	Example of Increasing Assessment Complexity
Simple Formative	No paper and pencil, no grade, mostly observational, allows for feedback without writing over a fewer number of curriculum standards, should provide predictive validity for complex formative assessments
Complex Formative (pre-tests and post-test)	Includes paper and pencil, no grade, data-collection device to allow feedback with writing over two or more curriculum standards at a time, should provide predictive validity for simple summative assessments
Simple Summative	May or may not include paper or pencil depending on task or performance; for a grade; allows for feedback over two or more curriculum standards to demonstrate proficiency; should provide predictive validity for complex summative assessments; may include chapter, vocabulary, or weekly tests
Complex Summative	May or may not include paper or pencil depending on task or performance, but is most often written in some form; for a grade; has a tendency to provide less feedback (but should in some way); measures the largest number of curriculum standards in a cumulative manner; may or may not immediately inform instruction depending on the author and time given; may include unit tests and high-stakes assessments

provide enrichment for students who immediately demonstrate mastery on pretests (VanTassel Baska, 1997).

Another function of pretests is to evaluate the viability of a curriculum. When several groups of students, over a period of several years, in the same grade level or course, reveal proficiency on the same standard year after year, it would seem that this standard or strand is no longer a priority and should be changed or replaced to reflect a more current necessity in a particular course of study.

It is important that posttests measure the ultimate level of a curriculum standard and that assessment measures are balanced and include both quantitative and qualitative items so that students have multiple opportunities to demonstrate proficiency (Doubek, 2010). Posttest formative assessment measures allow students to demonstrate a level of proficiency and still accommodate a reciprocal feedback mechanism before a summative assessment is administered. Achieving a desirable balance between formative and summative assessments is often an enigmatic process and requires a system of authentically prioritized standards.

A Tiered System of Assessments

The most important quality of a tiered assessment system is that one level of the process informs, or provides predictive validity for, the next higher level in some way (see Exhibit 6.9). Because the goal of assessment is to provide reciprocal feedback between students and teachers and to help teachers make instructional decisions based on that feedback, assessment systems should fit "hand to glove" so that with each individual task, or level of rigor in Bloom's taxonomy, the student has the opportunity to achieve clarity. Hattie (2009) indicates that feedback "fills the gap between what is understood and what is aimed to be understood." In this way, each level of an assessment system should provide information to students that allows them to increase in task complexity.

Each level of assessment should have some predictive validity for the next level of measurement, so that each tier supports the next (see Figure 6.10). Over the years, I have listened to many administrators who challenge testing and measurements as they currently exist because current grading policies have little if any predictive validity for high-stakes tests, which are the current metric of school and district performance. When

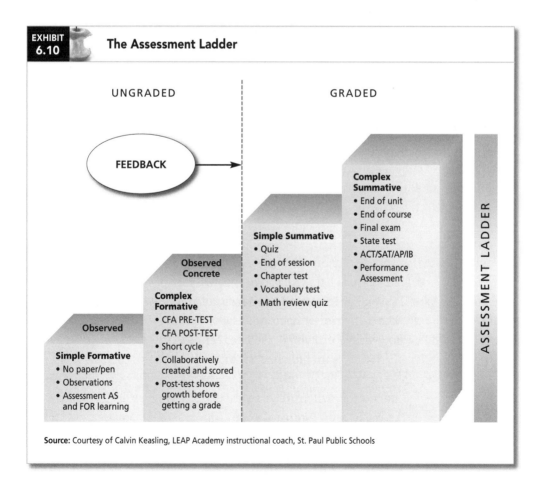

EXHIBIT 6.10 **The Assessment Ladder**

UNGRADED   GRADED

FEEDBACK

Simple Formative
• No paper/pen
• Observations
• Assessment AS and FOR learning

Observed

Complex Formative
• CFA PRE-TEST
• CFA POST-TEST
• Short cycle
• Collaboratively created and scored
• Post-test shows growth before getting a grade

Observed Concrete

Simple Summative
• Quiz
• End of session
• Chapter test
• Vocabulary test
• Math review quiz

Complex Summative
• End of unit
• End of course
• Final exam
• State test
• ACT/SAT/AP/IB
• Performance Assessment

ASSESSMENT LADDER

Source: Courtesy of Calvin Keasling, LEAP Academy instructional coach, St. Paul Public Schools

assessment systems are constructed so that they are balanced, provide reliable data that inform instruction for making midcourse corrections, evaluate curriculum for viability, and lead to changes in instructional methodology, they become a centerpiece for teaching and learning. When assessments allow students to share specific information about why they attained a correct answer or failed to achieve a desired response, then assessments generate reciprocal feedback between students and teachers. Finally, teachers and administrators need to make careful decisions about which data are most helpful in the teaching and learning process; otherwise, they can become overwhelmed with data.

Triangulating Data

Because educators use data from assessments to make decisions about curriculum (prioritizing, viability, and compacting) and instruction (reteaching, tiered interventions, grouping), these decisions should not be made in isolation or based on only one data point, one assessment, or one observation. On the other hand, we must be careful that students are not overtested (Reeves, 1996). The more critical the decision is in regard to student success, the more adults should make conscientious decisions about the data points that are chosen. For this reason, it is important to balance data points in terms of quantitative and qualitative information so that data are balanced to include multiple opportunities for students to demonstrate what they know and can do.

While negotiating quantitative and qualitative data points is challenging, the use of rubrics or checklists can help to objectify observed qualitative information. Often decisions about students, policies, and procedures are made using only numbers, with little regard to context. This approach to decision making can lead to an erroneous sorting of students that is neither accurate nor complete. Data must be winnowed so that the most helpful data, rather than all possible data, are used to inform decision-making processes and to most effectively impact positive student achievement.

References

Ainsworth, L. (2003). *Power standards: Identifying the standards that matter most.* Englewood, CO: Lead + Learn Press.

Ainsworth, L., & Viegut, D. (2006). *Common formative assessments: How to connect standards-based instruction and assessment.* Thousand Oaks, CA: Corwin Press.

Anderson, L. W., & Krathwohl, D. R. (eds.). (2001). *A taxonomy for learning, teaching and assessing: A revision of Bloom's taxonomy of educational objectives* (complete ed.). New York, NY: Longman.

Bloom, B. S., & Krathwohl, D. R. (1956). *Taxonomy of educational objectives: The classification of educational goals, by a committee of college and university examiners. Handbook 1: Cognitive domain.* New York, NY: Longman.

Bloom's taxonomy. (n.d.). In *Wikipedia*. Retrieved from http://en.wikipedia.org/wiki/Bloom's_Taxonomy

Burns, R. (1786). To a mouse. In *The Norton anthology of English literature* (vol. 2, 4th ed., 1979). New York, NY: W.W. Norton & Company.

Clark, D. (1999). Bloom's taxonomy of learning domains: The three types of learning. Retrieved from http://www.nwlink.com/~donclark/hrd/bloom.html

Context. (n.d.). In *Merriam-Webster online dictionary*. Retrieved from http://www.merriam-webster.com/dictionary/context

Covey, S. (1989). *The seven habits of highly effective people.* New York, NY: Simon & Schuster.

Danielson, C. (2007). *Enhancing professional practice: A framework for teaching.* Alexandria, VA: ASCD.

Darling-Hammond, L. (2010). *The flat world and education: How America's commitment to equity will determine our future.* New York, NY: Teachers College Press.

Doubek, M. B. (2010). Standards and assessment in the data team process: A practical lens. In *Data teams: The big picture.* Englewood, CO: Lead + Learn Press.

Driscoll, M. P. (1994). *Psychology of learning for instruction.* Boston, MA: Allyn and Bacon.

Eggen, P., & Kauchak, D. (2007). *Educational psychology, windows on classrooms* (7th ed.). Upper Saddle River, NJ: Pearson.

Fullan, M. (2010). *All systems go: The change imperative for whole school reform.* Thousand Oaks, CA: Corwin Press.

Gill, J. H. (1993). *Toward a philosophy of education.* Atlantic Highlands, NJ: Humanities Press International.

Gregg, L. A. (2010). Response to intervention joins data teams. In *Data teams: The big picture.* Englewood, CO: Lead + Learn Press.

Hattie, J. A. C. (2009). *Visible learning: A synthesis of over 800 meta-analyses relating to achievement.* New York, NY: Routledge.

Hunter, M., & Russell, D. (1981). *Increasing your teaching effectiveness.* Palo Alto, CA: Learning Institute.

Hyerle, D. (2000). *A field guide to using visual tools.* Alexandria, VA: ASCD.

Jackson, Y. (2011). *The pedagogy of confidence: Inspiring high intellectual performance in urban schools.* New York, NY: Teachers College Press.

Jacobs, H. H. (1997). *Mapping the big picture: Integrating curriculum and assessment K–12.* Alexandria, VA: ASCD.

Jensen, E. (2005). *Teaching with the brain in mind.* Alexandria, VA: ASCD.

Joyce, B., Weil, M., & Calhoun, E. (2000). *Models of teaching* (6th ed.). Boston, MA: Allyn and Bacon.

Krathwohl, D. R., Bloom, B. S., & Masia, B. B. (1973). *Taxonomy of educational objectives, the classification of educational goals. Handbook II: Affective domain.* New York, NY: David McKay Co.

Marzano, R. J. (2003). *What works in schools: Translating research into action.* Alexandria, VA: ASCD.

Marzano, R. J. (2007). *The art and science of teaching: A comprehensive framework for effective instruction.* Alexandria, VA: ASCD.

Nessel, D., & Graham, J. (2006). *Thinking strategies for student achievement: Improving learning across the curriculum, K–12* (2nd ed.). Arlington Heights, IL: Skylight.

Ohio Department of Education. (2010). Retrieved from http://ilrc.ode.state.oh.us/

Perry, A. (2009). *Writing matters in every classroom.* Englewood, CO: Lead + Learn Press.

Reeves, D. B. (1996). *Making standards work.* Englewood, CO: Lead + Learn Press.

Reeves, D. B. (2002). *The daily disciplines of leadership: How to improve student achievement, staff motivation, and personal organization.* San Francisco, CA: Jossey-Bass.

Reeves, D. B. (2003). The "safety net" curriculum. In L. Ainsworth, *Power standards: Identifying the standards that matter most.* Englewood, CO: Lead + Learn Press.

Reeves, D. B. (2010). *Transforming professional development into student results.* Alexandria, VA: ASCD.

Reeves, D. B. (2011). *Finding your leadership focus: What matters most for student results.* New York, NY: Teachers College Press.

Renzulli, J. S., & Reis, S. M. (1997). The schoolwide enrichment model: New directions for developing high end learning. In N. Colangelo & G. A. Davis, *Handbook of gifted education* (2nd ed.). Boston, MA: Allyn and Bacon.

Richardson, J., Morgan, R., & Fleener, C. (2004). *Reading to learn in the content areas* (6th ed.). Belmont, CA: Thomson.

Robinson, A. (1993). *What smart students know.* New York, NY: Three Rivers Press.

Rothstein, E. (2000). *Writing as learning.* Glenview, IL: Skylight.

Sherer, M. (2006). Celebrate strengths, nurture affinities: A conversation with Mel Levine. *Educational Leadership, 64*(1). Alexandria, VA: ASCD.

Slocumb, P. (2004). *Hear our cry: Boys in crisis.* Highlands, TX: Aha! Process.

Sternberg, R. J., & Grigorenko, E. L. (2000). *Teaching for successful intelligence to increase student learning and achievement.* Arlington Heights, IL: Skylight.

Stronge, J. H. (2007). *Qualities of effective teachers.* Alexandria, VA: ASCD.

Sullo, B. (2007). *Activating the desire to learn.* Alexandria, VA: ASCD.

Tatum, A. (2005). *Teaching reading to black adolescent males: Closing the achievement gap.* Portland, ME: Stenhouse.

Tomlinson, C. A. (2001). *How to differentiate instruction in mixed-ability classrooms.* Alexandria, VA: ASCD.

Van de Walle, J. A., & Lovin, L. H. (2006). *Teaching student centered mathematics.* Boston, MA: Pearson.

VanTassel Baska, J. (1997). What matters in curriculum for gifted learners: Reflections on theory, research, and practice. In N. Colangelo & G. A. Davis, *Handbook of gifted education* (2nd ed.). Boston, MA: Allyn and Bacon.

Wiggins, G., & McTighe, J. (2005). *Understanding by design* (2nd ed.). Alexandria, VA: ASCD.

CHAPTER SEVEN

Assessment for Literacy Learning and Assessment as Literacy Learning in the Twenty-First-Century Classroom

LAURA BENSON

As a girl, I constantly had maps spilling over the sides of my nightstand table and peaking out of the top of my book bags. With my family moving more than 17 times, we were constantly navigating new territories. It was easy to feel lost, always being new. Maps were comforting. And maps were necessary. Absolutely necessary.

One summer, my dad gained a small assignment that took us to the small Greek island of Corfu. As this trip was unexpected, we had no time to search for maps in London, where we were currently living. "No problem," my dad explained. "We'll pick up a great map at the airport."

What my dad had not expected was how small and how fledging the Corfu airport was. No gift shop. No bookstore. No maps.

Setting out past the airport to the house we had rented on the other side of the island, we had the good fortune to find a gas station of sorts with a "Rumpelstiltskin" collection of maps. Most looked like they were left over from World War II. Finding one in full color with a couple of photographs, we grabbed it, feeling victorious—for a minute, anyway, until we realized that the entire map was in Greek.

"Your dad's an engineer. He can figure anything out," my mom assured us.

Studying the map together, my dad, brother, and I determined a few key landmarks to look for so that we would know we were going in the right direction.

"Okay, here's where we need to go," my dad said, pointing to a small beach on the west side of the island. "Let's backtrack from there to here to figure out the best way to get to Pelekas."

We problem solved how we would navigate this new map in this unknown language. "We should see a huge olive grove just before we need to make our first right turn"—I drew in a tree and wrote "olive" next to a word in mostly unrecognizable letters to remember this spot—"and look for a sign with this word next," Dad continued.

Following the map with the markers we had determined before we set out for our house, we knew whether we were on the right path, and we also knew if something was amiss.

After a half hour or so, my brother said, "I think we should have seen the ocean by now, Dad."

"You're right. I think we turned a bit too early at that café back there," Dad countered.

Understanding where we should end up, paying attention to what we expected to see, and making adjustments when we did not find what we expected, we found our way to our new summer home. Once again, maps saved us.

Knowing where to go, knowing what to look for, knowing what to do to self-correct one's journey—my early and continuing map experiences reflect our work as educators. To know what we need to teach and to craft responsive ways to engage students in learning, we have to know them well, and we must have a clear idea of where we need to go together.

Standards name the destinations of our teaching-learning work with students. Identifying, detailing, and working toward these end goals collaboratively as colleagues and with students, we gain a sharper vision of what literacy proficiency is. Assessment tools and rituals, especially formative assessments, insightfully guide our work, just as the maps of my childhood steered and corrected so many of my journeys. Formative assessments help us determine where our students are individually in their journey toward a specific literacy standard. By knowing every student as an individual reader, writer, learner, and thinker with our use of formative methodology, we are better able to craft standards-focused instruction so that it fulfills genuine student needs in response to their strengths, curiosity, and current stages of development.

A Few "Whats" and "Whys" in Defining Formative Assessments

Authentic. Practical. Focused. Revealing. Edifying. Classroom based, student centered, and teacher led. These are some descriptors I offer when asked to define formative assessment. Formative assessments are ongoing assessments, observations, summaries, and reviews that inform teacher instruction (Fisher & Frey, 2007) and provide and provoke students' feedback. Whether through oral, written, and/or artistic responses, formative assessments help to harvest students' understanding of a key skill, strategy, or concept. Open-ended questions, one-on-one conferences, self-evaluations, exit slips, projects involving teaching a younger student, blogs entries, wiki book reviews, photo essays of a scientific process, summaries told through drama and music, student-generated and teacher-created rubrics, video conferences comparing two historic events, and personal learning goals are just a few examples of formative assessments. These are *for learning* assessments because the priority in their design and practice is to promote students' learning (Black, Harrison, Lee, Marshall, & Wiliam, 2004; Darling-Hammond, 2001); provide information to learners about what to do to improve (Clarke, 2008); and guide teachers' instructional decisions in considering, for example, cause-and-effect adaptations to responsively meet students' learning needs. In fact, formative assessments are only *formative* when teachers use them to *inform* their instruction (Reeves, 2010; Popham, 2008; Marzano, 2009). As detailed in numerous studies (Reeves, 2003, 2004a, 2007; Stiggins & Guskey, 2007; Ainsworth & Viegut, 2006; Schmoker, 2006; Clarke, 2005; Johnston, 1997; Darling-Hammond, Ancess, & Falk, 1995), frequent assessment of student progress is a common characteristic of high-achievement schools. The best teachers frequently check for student understanding (Schmoker, 2011).

Formative assessments keep teachers in the driver's seat of their evaluative efforts because it is teachers who design and decide when and which formative assessments they will engage their students in to deepen their evaluative knowledge about each child. Formative assessments involve teachers as action researchers (Clarke, 2005). Teachers use formative assessments before and during students' learning practice with the focused intention of determining student proficiency of a specific literacy skill, strategy, or concept and to elicit students' metacognition. Formative assessment is not random or informal; rather, it is a planned process in which teachers and students use assessment-based evidence to adjust what they are currently doing (Popham, 2003; Overmeyer, 2009). Formative assessment sharpens our lens in knowing our students, reflecting on the effectiveness of our instructional efforts, and determining the next steps of our teaching.

Feedback is the central theme of formative assessment (Clarke, 2005). Formative assessments are all about *informing*—informing the learner about himself; informing us as teachers about where a student is, and where all our students are, in their learning journeys; and informing us about the effectiveness of our efforts to help our students grow and progress. The feedback we give to and gain from students fuels our collective work. Formative assessment consists of providing feedback that leads pupils in recognizing their next steps and how to take them (Black & Wiliam, 1998). In this way, feedback becomes instruction. As John Hattie (1992, 2009) details in his groundbreaking meta-analyses, the most powerful single moderator that enhances achievement is feedback. O'Connor (2009) seconds Hattie's research and the foundational message of this book: "Clear, concise feedback matched to standards will promote student achievement." By using formative assessments to know and monitor students' understanding over a long period of time in a variety of contexts and contents, teachers gain a *focused lens* and thus can better know students and provide them with and draw from them more descriptive feedback.

Descriptive feedback is specific and relates directly to learning. Its purpose is to enable and empower growing readers and writers to take on the thinking strategies of proficient readers and writers. It is related to performance and makes comparisons to exemplars (Davies, 2000). Descriptive feedback is most effective when it points out both the strengths in the work and the areas needing improvement. Students need to understand what they can do well as readers and writers. When teachers substituted comments for grades, students engaged more productively in improving their work (Black, et al., 2004). Students must be given the opportunity to apply the feedback by trying again (Black & Wiliam, 1998). Using descriptive feedback, students revise, practice, and retry.

Precise feedback is at the core of data-driven, focused instruction (Fullan, Hill, & Crevola, 2006). Assessments that provide such fine-grained feedback help learners to "avoid damaging generalizations" about overall ability in a subject area based on limited understandings of mastery (Stiggins, Arter, Chappuis, & Chappuis, 2004). The virtue of descriptive feedback, drawn from our formative assessment rituals, is especially important when it comes to offering students' feedback about the invisible literacy skills of reading and thinking. When we apprentice students in using thinking strategies, our feedback is vital in illustrating these "in the head" processes used to integrate new information with what is already known and detail the operations that allow the learner to use, apply, transform, relate, interpret, reproduce, and re-form information for communication (Clay, 1991). Whether the class is social studies, readers' workshop, science, art, or English, naming and describing the thinking work needed as that performed by social anthropologists, readers, scientists, artists, or writers helps students know what to replicate when they engage in their own independent work (Benson, 2000, 2002; Quate & McDermott, 2010; Piercy & Piercy, 2011).

Developing and maintaining a culture of feedback provides a great benefit not only to students but also to ourselves as adult learners and colleagues. Cassandra Erkens echos this point in *The Principal as Assessment Leader* (Guskey, 2009a):

> If we employed the practice of descriptive feedback, we could inform our understanding of the science of teaching, helping everyone, including master teachers, see and hence solidify their own craft knowledge. With such specific, informational feedback, we can better support all teachers trying to master their craft.

Frequent monitoring of the feedback we give and get from students and the goals we establish from our formative assessments are the foundation of accountability that is student centered (Marzano, 2009) and should be frequent focal points of our Professional Learning Communities/Data Teams. Clarifying essential outcomes also allows teams to redesign systems of reporting student performance. No longer are parents and students limited to general grading for entire content areas or units of study. Instead, feedback can be shared at the individual skill level, highlighting student strengths and weaknesses within discrete performance categories (Marzano, 2009).

Guiding Principles in Developing
Edifying Formative Assessment Practice and Partnerships

As a professional and a scholar, I want my work to stand on the shoulders of research. But I have always been drawn to assessment rituals because, first and foremost, they help me get to know my students and develop trust and connection with them. Through my formative assessment rituals over the last 32 years, I have come to know my students not only as readers and writers but as human beings. I have learned about who has a sick dog and whose grandma is coming to visit. Students have shared jokes, dreams, questions, and fears, too. And I vividly remember the time when I was sitting with a chid who, for the very first time in four years, talked about witnessing the murder of his mother and seeing his uncle dragged away into a police car. Formative assessments are in many ways a sacred *conversation* between students and teachers and between students and themselves.

Edifying feedback grows from trusting and respectful relationships. When a student shares his thinking, especially when he writes it down or speaks it in a one-on-one conference, the child is going public with a bit of his soul. Realizing this many years ago, I began to reflect on how to best give and gain student feedback by journaling and, sometimes, videotaping my interactions with students. From my jottings over the last 32 years, the following guiding principles blossomed. These tenets explicate the thinking behind my assessment and evaluation work. To illustrate what each principle looks like "live and in action" with students, I have included a few of my formative assessment tools and rituals.

In the spirit of Margaret Wise Brown's *The Important Book* (Harper Collins, 1949), my formative assessment efforts are shaped by determining what is most important and staying true to these priorities.

- The importance of knowing every student as an individual
- The importance of focus
- The importance of an efficient, practical, and richly informative assessment system
- The importance of continuously offering and soliciting student feedback
- The importance of establishing student proficiency with corroboration and collaboration
- The importance of questioning
- The importance of listening, listening, listening

The Importance of Knowing Every Student as an Individual

Growing connected relationships with my students is at the heart of my formative assessment practices. I want to—and I have to—know every student as an individual reader, writer, learner, and thinker. Formative assessments enable me to know and respond to my students as individuals and as a community of learners. In conferences and in "quick writes," I ask open-ended questions—questions I do not know the answer to so that students know I really want to hear their unique thoughts (and so that they know there is not a "gotcha!" factor to my efforts). I work hard to be chiefly a listener (not an interrogator) when I engage students in formative assessments. I will not gain deep and rich data if students do not trust me. Helping students know how important it is to me to get to know each of them is foundational to establishing an effective and informative assessment system.

Even with the clarity of standards, even with a well-articulated curriculum, how will I know how to make these goals relevant to my students if I do not know them well? Getting to know each child and the class as a whole helps me make responsive and differentiated teaching decisions. As I look back at our standards-based curriculum and units of study with the focused lens of my formative assessment data, I ask myself, "Is this lesson for all of my students, for some of my students, or for one of my students?" and "How can I make this content relevant and compelling for this group of students? What instructional strategies and contexts would help students not only progress but thrive?" My formative assessment rituals also help me consider what else I need to know about my students. If I am puzzled about a student's growth, having a well of formative assessment tools to draw on enables me to problem solve many of the challenges of my teaching work.

Nothing enables me to get to know students as individuals more than conferring. Years ago, one of my beloved mentors, Don Graves, shared the original meaning of the word "assessment." "Laura," Don explained, "in Latin the word assessment means to sit beside." As passionate practitioners of conferring, Don and I found that definition delicious. There is just no better way of getting to know students than sitting with them one on one. Engaging in authentic and probing conversations to understand a student's thinking is always at the heart of my formative assessment practices. And conferences represent an essential form of feedback all readers and writers need and long for (Benson, 2001, 2004).

Rituals and routines structure and guide my conferring and give my individual instruction predictability and focus. My conferences are not haphazard or random because I know what each student and I need to gain from our one-on-one collaborations. My decisions about why and how to engage a student in a conference are shaped by my (1) relationship with the student and (2) instructional intentions or purpose for the conference.

In new relationships, building trust with the reader/writer is paramount. Over time, I can nudge students in conferences to take more risks because they know that my suggestions are coming from unconditional caring and sincere inquiry. Maintaining connected and strong relationships with students is always at the heart of effective teaching and, thus, absolutely paramount in developing edifying conferences. In his brilliant book *Conferring*, my friend Patrick Allen (2009) shares one of our favorite quotes on this subject from one of our beloved mentors, Donald Murray (1989):"Once you have established a basic pattern for conferring, then you can develop variations on a conference style. But only when you know and trust each other. And trusting yourself is absolutely essential!"

Here is a window into one of my trust-building, assessment-for-learning conference rituals:

Listen, Name, Nudge

Listen for evidence of the reader's/writer's use of focus strategy/skill/concept. I might begin a conference with an invitation such as:

- *Tell me about your thinking/reading/writing.*

- *How can I be of help to you today?*

- *We've been studying why and how to make connections in our reading/writing. How can I be of help to you today in making connections as you read/write?*

As I get to know students, and they get to know me, I often do not have to say anything because they know I am most interested in listening to them first. So, as I sit next to a student, he just begins to tell me about his literacy work.

As the student shares his reading/writing, I listen and look for direct connections to our current learning focus and record the student's strengths and/or needs in implementing this focus effectively. If I am not sure about the reader's/writer's use of the focus lesson or if the child is very quiet, I might need to nudge my evidence gathering with a prompt such as:

- *We've been studying how questions focus a writer's work. Tell me about how you are using questions to guide your writing.*

- *We've been studying how questions guide and energize a reader's thinking. Show me where/tell me how questioning is helping you understand what you read/this text.*

Name how the reader/writer is using the focus strategy(ies) effectively. The naming may need to come from the teacher first, but students should be encouraged to name their strengths/effective practices as soon as possible and as often as possible. Encouraging metacognition is key. In this part of my conference, I might say one of the following statements to the student to affirm successful literacy habits and trigger students' self-evaluations:

- *Your "I bet..." inferring really seems to be helping you understand the character's feelings.* I might add, *What are you noticing about your inferential thinking?*

- *Your thinking is much deeper because you are focusing on identifying the most important ideas as you read these nonfiction texts.* I might add, *What helps you know what is important in nonfiction text/this text?*

- *I noticed that you problem solved this part/this word so that you really understand the section.* I might add, *How did you know to do this?*

- *Name something you are doing well here in your writing.*

- *What are you doing to help yourself think/understand as you read? What is helping you understand what you are reading?*

Leave the reader/writer with an assignment. I might do so with a simple and straightforward comment such as:

- *Before I came to confer with you, you were working really hard. I know that you will continue to work hard in your writing/reading as I leave. Good job, Bud!*

- *You seem to really be in the habit of inferring in this book. Remember to stop and infer as you get to the other texts in your book box* (collection of diverse genres developed for students' independent reading). *Sound good?*

Or I might provide more instructional support by saying:

- *We talked about how to figure out a new word (as you write) by using your visual memory—by having a go at it on this piece of scratch paper so that you can see if it looks right. You are already in the habit of using your phonics to figure out new words. Hooray! So, when you want to use a new word in your writing, stay courageous and know that you now have a few ways of problem solving or cross-checking a new word—using your phonics to sound it out and writing it out to see if it looks right to you. Keep using those two strategies as you continue to write today and when you are writing at home tonight, too. And let's check back in with each other tomorrow to see how this is working for you, OK?*

Or I might offer the reader/writer some intriguing challenge or rigor:

- *From what you shared about why and how you are summarizing as you read, you understand so much about this way of thinking. Would you be our focus lesson/mini-lesson teacher tomorrow and teach the rest of our class about how they can summarize?*

- *You have grown so much—I see that you are monitoring your understanding by stopping and talking to yourself. I wonder if you might stop a bit more often to understand more of the author's ideas here. I think you might be stopping to self-talk after many pages, and that might be making it hard for you to remember all the great things that are happening and being said here. I think stopping after every paragraph or even after a few sentences might help you understand more deeply. What do you think? . . . Let's tip in some sticky flags in your book to figure out a good stop-and-think pacing for your reading. . . . Later today/tomorrow, let me know how this feels and if it is helping you understand more and enjoy your reading more—always cool, right?*

Conference Record Notes

Following my demonstration lessons, I am often asked, "What did you write down when you were conferring with the kids? Can we see your notes?" What to record can be a bit bewildering. After all, how can we meet with all 22 to 36 students, and when are we going to have time to read our conference notes, anyway?

Focus is the key to creating informative conference record notes. My rule of thumb is focus. Rather than writing down the 5,789 things I could write down about any given student's strengths or needs, my conference record notes are about and aligned to the focus of our focus lesson/modeled lesson (most often with the whole group) and collaborative learning (sometimes with the whole group; often, however, learning students practice and gain from small-group fellowships).

Record it. Maintain records of your conferences in a method that feels most comfortable and informative to you. There is no way that you and I can remember each pearl or puzzle students share in one-on-one conversations. So, recording what you observe, hear, see, read, and so forth in conferences is crucial. Developing and using a straightforward and practical way of recording your observations of students and your suggestions to students will help you know how to pace your conferences. ("Hmm, just looking at my conference record notes, I see that I haven't met with Darius yet." Or "Right! From the notes I took yesterday, I remember that I promised to get back to Veronica about her revisions today.") Having accurate and easily accessible "notes to yourself" keeps you at the cutting edge of what your students most need right now to grow as writers/readers/thinkers. Your conference records may look like the samples of my own notes that follow, or they may look very different. You may choose to use checklists, sticky notes, or a flip book with index cards as your note-taking tool. It does not matter whether we use the same template. It only matters that you develop and maintain a system of taking notes about individual students that works best for you. (I also have my conference note clipboard close by as I meet with students in whole-group or small-group gatherings so that I can add insights about a child.)

Note it. One of the best tactics you can use to record your thoughts from your one-on-one conferences with students is to develop your own shorthand. Keep your notes focused and simple. These notes are for you. As the only audience (at least in most cases), the notes only have to make sense to you. Rather than writing every word down, I use codes such as:

- "R" for reading
- "W" for writing

- "M" when I ask a student to mentor the rest of the class by teaching an upcoming focus lesson; I put a circle around the "M" when the child has served as our writing/reading teacher

- "PE" when students are writing from a personal experience; "BK" when students are using their background knowledge as writers/readers/learners

- "SC" for self-corrects (in reading or in writing)

- "p" when I prompted a student; when a behavior is not yet independently initiated by the student (such as voicing why and how to use our focus strategy in his own writing/reading, using correct punctuation, remembering to stop and self-talk to aid understanding)

- "Adv" for "What advice would you give to your kindergarten buddy about fiction writing?" to remember what I asked a student and to make sense of the response I gain from each child

- Color coding: blue for the student's strengths and red for his goals (I use a two-headed pencil, or I review my notes using a blue highlighter for strengths and a pink highlighter for needs)

Share it. As soon as students are able, invite them to take notes during your conferences. Kids can take their own conference records in small notebooks or on sticky notes or index cards (Taberski, 2000). If having a copy of the student's notes would be helpful to you, carry carbon paper on your clipboard to give to students (between two pieces of paper, of course) so that you both gain a record of the child's thoughts. The notes a student writer/reader makes can serve as a compass to guide his efforts when the conference is over.

On Thursdays, to lesson plan for the next week, and several times each semester, to evaluate my students' growth and progress, I pour over my conference notes to identify my students' strengths, needs, and passions. Conferring well with students requires that I have a vision of what I hope for them as readers and writers. Just as listening up close has everything to do with how to confer, stepping back to see the big picture is equally important (Hindley, 2000). Understanding students as readers and writers helps us know how to thoughtfully build groups of "kindred spirits"—students with the same or similar literacy strengths and needs. If our instruction is effective, the needs of the group should shift and invite the creation of new groups. Keeping groups fluid is of utmost importance so that students continue to work on the cutting edge of their capabilities and have the opportunity to interact with a variety of their classmates (Felknor, Winterscheidt, & Benson, 1999). Students need to see themselves as strategic, capable readers who are ready to move on to new learning.

The conference record notes included at the end of this chapter (Exhibit 7.2) are from my demonstration lessons in a fourth-grade class at United World College South

East Asia/Singapore; with kindergarten through seventh-grade students at Canadian Academy in Kobe, Japan; and with first- and third-grade students at the American School of the Hague. As I recorded my notes, I used the shorthand style I profiled here. So that you can understand my notes, I have written them out in more complete detail (for the first six examples) and included two (from my work at the American School of the Hague) which reflect my shorthand style of note taking (with a key embedded into these notes to help you understand my shorthand codes).

Writing is problem solving.

SHELLEY HARWAYNE
Lifetime Guarantees & Writing Through Childhood

The Importance of Focus

My formative assesments are tightly aligned to the current learning goal—the standard—my students and I are studying. They give me multiple opportunties to look for students' growth and progress of our focus goal. While I could be looking for and assessing 547 literacy skills, I focus my assessment efforts on the current goal of student learning and document students' use of this literacy skill/strategy/concept. It is more important and accurate to moderate or measure a few components frequently and consistently than to moderate or measure many of them once (Reeves, 2004b).

I model feedback and work to help students identify or clarify the purpose of feedback exchanges with focus. The following questions reflect a nudge I may offer a student to consider needed feedback: "What kind of feedback would help you right now?" "We've been focusing our writing studies on topic generation. What will you teach your kindergarten buddy about this?" "Tell me about why and how you are using inferring as you read." Articulating the kind of feedback they need helps students feel a strong sense of ownership of their learning process and gives me keen insights about what my students know and can do.

For example, when studying nonfiction writing with students, the goal of achieving success at nonfiction writing becomes the focus of my whole-group, small-group, and individual instruction in writers' workshop, and it becomes a process focus to strenghten my students' content-area learning. Students' writing samples are rich with the ore of their thinking as writers, and I find their nonfiction writing especially informative in evaluating their learning of many subjects. Writing to learn differs from learning to write because the writing produced in the former is not a process piece that will undergo multiple changes resulting in a published document. Instead, the purpose of writing to learn is to be a catalyst for further learning and meaning making (Knipper & Duggan, 2006).

Engaging students in frequent nonfiction writing is a hallmark of The Leadership and Learning Center's research. In The Center's 90/90/90 studies, for example, Douglas Reeves (2007) highlights the power of engaging students in writing: "Students process information in a much clearer way when they are required to write an answer. Teachers have the opportunity to gain rich and complex diagnostic information about why students respond to an academic challenge the way that they do."

Additionally, my colleague Angela Peery's many books thoughtfully detail how to cultivate students' writing skills and diagnose student understanding through their writing. As a teacher, you can gather valuable formative information from student writing and adjust your teaching immediately. Writing can also be part of a balanced assessment system that includes authentic performance tasks (Peery, 2009). You can't avoid thinking when you write (Alber, 2010). I love using students' writing as not only a primary learning tool but a primary assessment tool, too. Assessments, when used correctly in a formative way, can empower students and teacher not only to improve but, better yet, to believe in themselves as writers and teachers of writing (Overmeyer, 2009).

With the focus on nonfiction writing (or any genre of writing), an invaluable tool is working from a common rubric. Rubrics give students descriptors to detail what excellent writing looks like and sounds like. Rubrics and checklists can take the mystery out of writing for students and improve the quality of writing to learn. They also encourage writers to be more self-directed in their mastery of content learning (Hill & Ekey, 2010; Bromley, 2009; Hodgson & Bohning, 1997). The learner has to possess a concept of the standard (or goal or reference level) being aimed for, compare the actual level of performance to the standard, and engage in appropriate action that leads to a closing of the gap (Sadler, 1989; Dodge, 2009). As implied in the preceding text, in order for students to do excellent work, they have to know what excellent work looks like and sounds like (Wiggins, 2003). Rubrics and scoring guides not only help illustrate the external work of a writer's efforts but also articulate some of the internal work of readers, writers, or learners.

Scoring guides are most effective in promoting student success when they are used in conjunction with models or exemplars of student work. Models should be developmentally appropriate yet vary in meeting the criteria. With older students, a professional model can also be included. Students learn to use the scoring guide to analyze the model and, therefore, become even clearer about the requirements of the task before they begin work (Oliver, 2008).

To energize student writing and secure greater ownership of their writing learning, I prefer using student-generated rubrics. I ask students to study and reflect on mentor texts as a way to identify the qualities of good writing we should expect in specific genres. For example, when studying nonfiction picture books with intermediate-grade students recently, I asked the kids to bring their favorite nonfiction picture book to our talking circle/focus lesson.

As the kids reassembled with their favorite books in hand, we discussed what made these texts so beloved (and it should be noted that some of the mentor-exemplar texts were actually authored by students). I asked, "What is it you love about this book? What do you admire in this book?"

I recorded the students' responses on a chart, and periodically we stepped back to study what we were articulating about great nonfiction picture book writing with, "We said that we love the authors' use of photography in our favorite nonfiction books. So, I wonder if this is a craft we should consider using more often in our own nonfiction writing." The kids generated numerous possibilities for how and why they planned to strengthen their own nonfiction texts with photographs and graphics.

Continuing our discussion, I nudged the students' thinking: "We also named the authors' use of language and of words that 'are not boring' as a quality of great nonfiction writing. Because this skill/craft reflects what so many of us as writers are working on right now in our own writing, what about taking this idea and detailing it more?"

And, moving our discussion along, I then asked the group, "If we were to create a scoring guide for our own self-evaluation about nonfiction language (or word choice), what would the scoring guide profile or say? Having a tool like this could help each of us grow as writers, and it could really help me help you when we conference and when I work to plan lessons, too." By generating ideas about what to look for in their writing, the kids gained a deeper understanding about "good writing" and, fueled by their own insights, their writing was immediately more vivid and energized.

In developing scoring guides, it can be helpful to share exemplars with students. Writers need to read the genre they are learning to write, and reading scoring guides or self-evaluations tools can support growing writers in developing a tool that will be personally meaningful and offer specific feedback.

The Importance of an Efficient, Practical, and Richly Informative Assessment System

The only way we can become comfortable and confident with formative assessments is to make them plausible in our teaching lives. Early on, I learned that I needed to develop and maintain a sensible and fruitful system of assessment. Shirley Clarke (2005) wisely advocates an integrative and practical approach to formative assessment: Rather than thinking "How can I fit it all in?" consider "How can I restructure a whole lesson to include formative assessment, where the learning most powerfully takes place?" Likewise, rather than viewing assessment as an event or an add-on to my already too busy teaching life, I seize everyday experiences as formative assessment. I view and craft my formative assessments *for* learning and *as* learning, which Clarke (2008) defines as any practice that transforms the "what to improve" into "how to improve." Students' regular classroom work provides me with numerous formative assessment wells and countless ways for the kids and I to reflect on how they can improve and move forward as readers and writers. Because formative assessments are considered part of learning, they need not be graded as summative assessments are (Dodge, 2009). Instead, they serve as practice for students (Chappuis & Chappuis, 2007).

Every time I am with students, observing them at work, hearing their thinking, or reading their words, I note and record evidence of their progress toward our current learning goal or standard. When your students are practicing the processes and implementing the content of your course, opportunities for formative assessment are ripe. For example, as students are writing independently, engage in one-on-one conferences to talk with students about not just what they are writing but also how they are crafting their writing: "How did you know that this part needed to be revised?" At the end of class, reflect on literacy practice with your students in talking circles with self-evaluative questions such as "What are you learning about yourself as a reader?" or "What do you notice you do well as a writer?" The kids' responses in both of these contexts help us know what they understand about their own reading or writing processes and, equally as important or more, the students better understand something about their own reading or writing thinking.

When you feel yourself getting overwhelmed, listen and adapt your assessment practices. For example, rather than trying to assess every student's reading in a very guided reading group, designate one child per meeting as your focus student. With your focus student, you can take a running record; ask an open-ended, metacognitive question(s); or even administer a subtest of the Developmental Reading Assessment. You can do this during your group time or by having your focus student stay a few extra minutes to gain more information about him.

Or you might develop a rotation of your teaching and assessing practices, as Sharon Taberski (2000) profiles in *On Solid Ground*. At the beginning of the school year, Taberski designates Mondays, Wednesdays, and Fridays to meet with her students in one-on-one conferences during readers' workshop and devotes Tuesdays and Thursdays to guided reading groups. After the first six weeks or first few months of the school year, Taberski switches the rotations so that she meets with students in guided reading groups on Mondays, Wednesday, and Fridays. As I would prepare for report cards and parent conferences, I found it helpful to engage in more one-on-one conferences to confirm my evaluations and to engage my students in goal setting, including planning the student-led conference portion of my conferences with their parents.

Do not save all your "pouring over student data" evaluation work for 8:30–11:30 p.m. Instead, consider carving out a few minutes each day or at least every week to reflect on where your students are as a group of learners and/or to problem solve a puzzling student. These types of reflection opportunities can and will be possible when your students are engaged in their own authentic and independent literacy practice (i.e., reading and/or writing on their own or productively with a peer).

A perfect example of engaging in practical assessments is the "show me what you learned" assessment, an assessment ritual I learned from Bonnie Campbell Hill (Hill, Ruptic, & Norwick, 1998; Hill, 2001; Benson, 2001). Returning a piece of their earlier writing to students, ask them to "show me what you learned." This assessment engages students in self-evaluating a previous writing piece by revising it with the knowledge and skills they now have as writers. I generally have students record their revisions in a different-colored ink directly onto their original piece. This approach provides the student with a concrete way to talk about and see his "then and now" efforts. And each student's then-and-now writing provides me with excellent data to document what the writer understands about good writing and what he has yet to learn or may be confused about in producing excellent writing work. Additionally, you can ask students to attach the rubric descriptor(s) that they feel their piece successfully reflects as they show you what they now know and do as writers.

The Importance of Continuously Offering and Soliciting Student Feedback

The most powerful form of learning, the most sophisticated form of staff development, comes not from listening to the good words of others, but from sharing what we know with others. Learning comes more from giving than from receiving. By reflecting on what we do, by giving it coherence, and by sharing and articulating our craft knowledge, we make meaning, we learn.

ROLAND BARTH

Toni Morrison (2009) says that what every child wants to know is: *Do your eyes light up when I enter the room? Did you hear me and did what I say mean anything to you?* While our feedback is offered to help our students reach academic goals, first and foremost, I am always mindful of and energized by how our feedback helps students know that they are heard and that we care about them unconditionally.

The key to successful communication is to take the imaginative leap of stuffing yourself right into your listener's shoes to know what he is thinking and feeling in the deepest recesses of his mind and heart (Luntz, 2007). To ensure that my formative assessment conversations inform and edify students' hearts as well as their heads, I use feedback filters developed by Connie Moss and Susan Brookhart (2009): focus, comparison, function, valence, clarity, specificty, and tone. I want my feedback to students to bridge how they can and should use their literacy knowledge and skills not just in school but as life tools. To help students become college and career ready, we need to teach them how to apply what they are learning in school to the practical and intellectual tasks in their everyday life (Wolpert-Gawron, 2010).

Both external feedback (such as teacher feedback) and internal feedback (such as student self-evaluation) affect student knowledge and beliefs. Together they help students with self-regulation: deciding on their next learning goals, devising tactics and strategies to reach them, and producing work (Butler & Winne, 1995). *The Teacher as Assessment Leader* (Kramer & DuBose, 2009) and "Assessment and Classroom Learning" (Black & Wiliam, 1998) both cite benefits to replacing evaluative (judgmental) feedback with specific, descriptive, and immediate feedback. Useful feedback, says Thomas Guskey (2005), is both diagnostic and prescriptive. It reinforces precisely what students were expected to learn, identifies what was learned well, and describes what needs to be learned better.

A rich way I frequently engage students in self-evaluations is what my friend and colleague Bonnie Campbell Hill (Hill, et al., 1998) and I call the "Post-It note strategy." Periodically, we give students a sticky note with the following prompt: "Put this sticky note on a page in a book that you can read and understand (an important point of clarity, especially for young readers)." If students are old enough, we also ask each child to record his name; the date; the title of the text; and, if developmentally appropriate, a comment or two about the text on the sticky note. Then, we take the kids' books to the copy machine to duplicate the pages of text with their sticky note "data." Over the course of a school year, these text pages become a rich portrait of each student's reading and growth as a reader. (If you cannot duplicate all your students' book pages at one time, engage just a handful of students in this formative assessment every few days so that, by the end of a week or two, every student has had the opportunity to engage in this self-evaluative feedback.)

For younger students or students of concern, it is important to follow up and confer with each child about their Post-It note evaluations. Sometimes students overestimate their comprehension while others sometimes underestimate their capacity as readers. Either way, this data is important because it helps to paint a picture of how well the reader knows himself and may contribute to good book matching or may illuminate the need to support a child in selecting texts to read.

If you have to talk, you have to think.
I get to learn things
from other people I don't know.

FIVE-YEAR-OLD STUDENT
quoted in Clarke (2008)

Talk is a primary form of formative assessment for me. It's an efficient form of monitoring student progress and has the added benefit of helping students process and construct their understanding, as Carol Cooper and Julie Boyd (1996) advocate: "We often don't know that we know something until we hear ourselves say it in an interaction with another human being." The dominance of constructive, pupil "dialogic" talk in a classroom is a key identifier of a formative assessment culture, in which pupils are actively involved in thinking (Clarke, 2008).

A major focus of my literacy instruction and thus my literacy assessment, is self-talk. Self-talk is the internal dialogue one uses to support construction and maintenance of understanding (Benson, 1993, 2004). Self-talk nurtures and reflects one's metacognition or regulation—knowledge about one's own cognitive processes (knowledge) and the monitoring of these processes (skillfulness) (Hattie, 2009). Whatever the content area, teachers need to model why and how to construct understanding for and with students. As thinkers/learners/readers/ writers/viewers work to understand, they need to use self-talk to guide, sustain, and fuel their thinking.

Three frequent—and practical—oral formative assessments are "connect two," "strikes and wonders," and "talking circles" (of course, students can write their responses to these invitations in addition to or instead of providing them verbally).

Connect Two

Connect two is an oral formative assessment that engages students in compare-and-contrast thinking. (It can easily be used as a written formative assessment, as well.) This strategy is especially helpful in social studies and science classes and supports students in comparing genres, characters, and authors' styles in literacy classes. Ask students to engage in this type of thinking and response with the following stem: "*I would connect _____ and _____ because...*"

Strikes and Wonders

Strikes and wonders is a way to support students' identification of important ideas and to assess their judgment of important ideas. It is also a positive way of nudging or helping students generate their own questions. Invite students to engage in strikes and wonders with the following prompt: "A strike is something that stands out to you or makes you say *aha*! A wonder is something you have a question about. What strikes you as important about this (book/topic/process/issue/person)? What are you wondering?" With your teammates, think about what you would expect to hear (or read) in students' responses to determine whether they are making healthy progress and growth in learning your focus goal/standard.

Talking Circles

At the end of class or at the end of the day, I want to support students' reflections and metacognition. And I want to hear their thinking to inform my own work. I often do this by gathering them in a talking circle and ask them a question such as, "What did you learn about yourself as a reader today?" "What are you noticing about yourself as a writer?" or "How is learning about inferring helping you as a learner, reader, or thinker?" To further you own use of talk as formative assessment, I highly recommend Douglas Fisher and Nancy Frey's (2007) *Checking for Understanding.*

The Importance of Establishing Student Proficiency with Corroboration and Collaboration

My assessment practices were forever chiseled by baseball cards. As I studied the back of baseball cards with my son, I was stuck by the statistics listed for each player—a data profile developed over the course of a season from the player's performance in numerous games. Just as a baseball player's aptitude is measured from multiple sources of data, students' patterns of performance—patterns of strengths and patterns of need—are more accurately determined from a body of evidence. Thoughtful teachers make decisions based on multiple sources of information and by analyzing a collection of student data (Felknor, et al., 1999). Determing a student's proficiency is never achieved from just one day's performance or from one test score. By varying the type of assessment you use over the course of the week, you can get a more accurate picture of what students know and understand (Dodge, 2009), obtaining a multiple-measure assessment *window* into student understanding (Ainsworth & Viegut, 2006). We gain a more accurate evaluation of our students' learning and understanding by gathering a *photo album*, as opposed to a *snapshot* (Tomlinson & McTighe, 2006). Let's honor our students as we do our baseball players by gathering corroborating evidence about what they know and can do over a long period of time.

Informative assessment is not an end in itself, but the beginning of better instruction (Tomlinson, 2007/2008). Successful teachers fuel their teaching work with their knowledge about their students—again, insights established from multiple sources of evidence collected over a long period of time. Their every step is taken in an effort to craft relevant and empowering learning for and with their students. Through rituals such as one-on-one conferences, metacognitive self-evaluations and self-talk, Essential Questions, small-group learning discussions, personalized learning goals, and descriptive feedback, we gain knowledge of students as individuals, respond to them with effective instructional strategies, and promote their self-evaluation.

Crucial to developing responsive formative methodology and to building a feedback culture as a school is articulating student proficiency. I have learned what to look for and what to listen for in students' literacy work. And I give enormous credit for this capacity to my teammates and colleagues. By engaging in collaborative assessment conferences during much of the last 32 years, I have gained more diverse and detailed perspectives about what proficient readers and writers demonstrate at each developmental stage. As we poured over student writing samples, for example, my teammates and I were able to develop anchor papers that illustrated where our students were reflective of Hill's (2001) developmental continuums, one of our most valued formative assessment tools and an instrument thoughtfully aligned to our state standards. These collaborative assessment rituals are continuously advocated in the research of The Leadership and Learning Center (Reeves, 2004a, 2004b; Allison, et al., 2010; Anderson, 2010), Harvard University's Project Zero (Ritchhart, 2004, 2011), and numerous studies around the world.

Working collaboratively with your colleagues, ask one another, "What does student proficiency look like and sound like reflective of this standard?" Work together to develop anchor evidence or exemplars of proficiency to vividly illustrate what student proficiency of each of your prioritized standards looks like. Few charges of our work are as important as understanding student proficiency. We have to know what to look for in our students' literacy work to truly determine their levels of understanding and to craft the most effective teaching responses.

In their detailed work, the authors of the Common Core State Standards have striven to articulate what proficiency looks like:

- In reading
- In writing
- When students are using their literacy skills in science
- When students are using their literacy skills in social studies

While standards identify key learning goals for students, it is the development of common formative assessment that helps teams and schools detail what proficiency looks like in student work. As you study the Common Core State Standards with your colleagues and engage your students in learning these standards, develop formative assessments to help you determine your students' proficiency of each prioritized standard. As your team develops the Big Ideas and Essential Questions for a unit of literacy study and builds a corresponding assessment and scoring guide, flesh out exactly what students need to know and do to achieve the goal and reach proficiency.

You may find it helpful or necessary to recalibrate your formative assessments as you gain deeper insights about what student proficiency of each prioritized standard looks like and sounds like. Collaboration should be continuous. After all, we are learners first.

To learn more about developing common formative assessments, turn to Ainsworth and Viegut's (2006) *Common Formative Assessments: How to Connect Standards-Based Instruction and Assessment*, Fisher and Frey's (2007) *Checking for Understanding: Formative Assessment Techniques for Your Classroom*, Dodge's (2009) *25 Quick Formative Assessments for a Differentiated Classroom: Easy, Low-Prep Assessments That Help You Pinpoint Students' Needs and Reach All Learners*, and Clarke's (2003, 2005, 2008) formative assessments texts listed in the references for this chapter. And to embed more collaborative assessment partnerships into your work, check out titles by Seidel (1991, 1996); Allen (1995, 2007); Allen (2009); Allen, Blythe, & Powell (1996, 2007); Allen, Blythe, & Thompson-Gove (2004); Blythe, Allen, & Powell (1999); Overmeyer (2009); Buchovecky (1996); and Benson (2002).

The Importance of Questioning

Questions are a compass. Questions guide, nudge, and chisel our thinking. The first part of the word "question" is the word "quest," which seems so right to me because my questions send me on journeys —journeys on which I seek and innovate answers.

Questions, then, serve as a compass for my teaching work. They ignite and fuel my assessment efforts. *How can I help my students want to live a literate life? How can I best reach my students as growing readers and writers? What do my students like to read and write, and what do they avoid? What do my students know and understand as twenty-first-century thinkers? What do they need to know and do as twenty-first-century thinkers? What have they yet to learn? What are my students' ways of engaging in literacy outside of school? Are their literacy skills supporting their content-area studies, or is there more we need to do together to strengthen their capacity to "read the world"?* With questions as my compass, I determine what I most need to know about my students "right now" (Davies, 2000) and then either create or embrace a formative assessment tool to help me know and monitor my students' proficiency of a particular literacy goal.

I am sure that questions are a vital compass of your own teaching and leadership work. As you meet with your Professional Learning Community/Data Team, consider the following compass questions as you develop and deepen your formative assessment practices:

- What do our students need to know and be able to do as readers? What do our students need to know and be able to do as writers? What do our students need to know and be able to do as content-area thinkers?

- How will we help our students achieve these goals?

- How will we know our students have achieved these goals?

- How will we give our students feedback about what they know and can do? How will we give students feedback about what they have yet to learn?

- How will we elicit feedback from our students about what they understand?

- How will we respond to our students' data, especially when the data indicates that students are struggling to achieve these goals? How will we respond to our students' data when the data indicates that students are more mature than the maturity level required for meeting these goals?

- Reflective of this prioritized standard, what does student proficiency look like and sound like?

As you meet with students, use questions as formative assessment. Depending on your instructional focus—the specific goal of teaching—a probing question or two can help you gain insights about students' understanding of their literacy process (Hagerty, 2009) and/or content knowledge. Exhibit 7.1 is a sampler of questions I ask students as I meet with them in small groups or conferences to gain evidence of their learning of literacy or content standards.

A critical and proactive step in using questions deeply and informatively, especially in alignment with your standards, is to talk with your teammates about what you would expect proficient students to say in answering any one of these inquiries. For more ideas about how to use questions as a compass of your own formative assessment efforts, refer to Clarke's (2008) *Active Learning Through Formative Assessment*, which offers brilliant and easy-to-implement examples of questioning strategies as formative assessment.

The Importance of Listening, Listening, Listening

In my interactions with students, I am teaching them how to be a healthy, curious, and caring adult. And I am teaching them how to achieve and maintain connected and trusting relationships. One of the best gifts we can give our students is listening to them. We will not always know *the right thing* to say or ask in our formative assessments, but do not worry about that. Just listen and be ready to listen, and, over time, your students' responses will be the data you most need and most value.

If a nudge is needed to launch your listening assessments, consider prompts such as, "Tell me what you are thinking" "How's it going?" or "How can I be of help to you today?" These statements and questions are often enough of a nudge to get a student talking. At other times, you may want to frame assessment conversations with a prompt such as, "We've been studying why and how writers write with voice. Show me a part of your writing that reflects what you now know and do to infuse voice in your writing." Or "Let's switch roles. You be me/the teacher and I will be you/the student. What advice would be helpful for this reader/writer to hear?" Formative assessment rituals like conferences become part of our everyday life. Often, all we have to do is sit near a student or group of students and they will begin to share their thinking and insights with us.

To listen, really listen, I engage students in *self-evaluation*. Assessment for learning helps students to feel in control of their journey to success and to focus on improvement (Stiggins, et al., 2004; Overlie, as quoted in Guskey, 2009b). Assessment for learning can be boiled down to a student working through three questions, which were developed based on the work of Sadler (Stiggins, et al., 2004):

- Where am I going?

EXHIBIT 7.1   Sample Literacy and Content Standards Questions for Students

Reading	Writing	Science	Social Studies
Tell me what you are thinking here/as you read this text. Or, I see you're reading _____. What is this book/text about?	*Tell me what you are thinking as you write this piece. Or, What is your piece about?*	*Tell me what you are thinking about this concept/process.*	*Tell me what you are thinking about this issue/concept/event/ person.*
We've been studying inferring. Where have you used inferential thinking? How has it helped you as a reader?	*We've been studying inferring. Where have you used inferential thinking as a writer? How has it helped you as a reader?*	*We've been studying hypothesizing—what we also call inferring. Where have you used inferential thinking in your science learning? How do hypothesizing and inferring help you as a scientist?*	*We've been studying ____ and talking about how we sometimes have to infer when studying a culture/historic event. Where have you used inferential thinking in your social studies learning? How has it helped you as a social scientist?*
In fiction, we know that characters change and grow as they work to solve their problems. Describe what this character is like at the end of the story/how he changed from the beginning of the story to the end of the story.	*We're studying why and how authors revise their work. Show me a place where you revised your writing, and share your "why" thinking with me.*	*What new understand- ings have you gained from studying _____? Have you changed any of your thinking about _____?*	*What new under- standings have you gained from studying _____? Have you changed any of your thinking about _____?*
If you were going to teach your kindergarten buddy about this strategy (i.e., how to make connections before, during, and after reading; identifying important ideas), what would you teach him?	*As we plan to share our writing learning with our first-grade pals, what will you teach them about writing from memories (using and triggering connections as writers)?*	*Let's share what we are learning about _____ with our community. What should we include in our class newsletter about _____?*	*Learning about this culture/event, what is important for us to remember and share with peers/our kindergarten buddies?*
What connections are you making as you read this text/these texts? How is using your schema helping as a reader?	*How are you using your background knowledge/memories/ expertise as you write this piece? How does using what you already know help you as a writer?*	*Comparing and contrasting (this) with (that), what are you noticing? Or, What connections are you making as we study _____?*	*How is this like and not like other cultures/events we have studied in history? Or, What connections are you making as we study _____?*

      ◦ Students understand the learning targets they are working to master.

  • Where am I now?
      ◦ Students understand where their understanding is in relation to mastering the learning target.

  • How can I close my learning gap?
      ◦ Students understand what they need to do to improve on learning targets they have not yet mastered

Conclusion

Whether the context of student learning is readers' workshop, writers' workshop, a middle school English class, a fifth-grade social studies class, or a partner teacher's advanced placement science class, these formative rituals help evaluate students' literacy learning and provide the kids and the teacher with vital opportunities to reflect on their understanding of the literacy processes and content implementations. As we consider twenty-first-century demands, such as problem solving and innovative thinking, and Common Core State Standards, such as negotiating text complexity, persuasive presentations, and argumentative writing, formative assessments offer all teachers practical and rich ways to continuously monitor their students' growth and progress. Pivotal to making formative methodology a reality is for educators to no longer see assessment as seperate from learning but *as* learning and part of our everyday classroom lives. The fact is that most educationally significant assessment takes place in classrooms, mememt to moment, among teachers and students (Johnston, 1997). Teacher Franki Sibberson and Principal Karen Szymusiak (2008, p. 21) detail their standards-focused, formative assessment efforts:

> We have found that knowing the standards well is our best tool. We keep copies of our state standards handy and refer to them often. But instead of writing lessons so we can check off what standard we taught, we want to make sure to include much of that content into real conversations about books. We know that conversations are often the best and most authentic way to begin thinking about many of the standards. By knowing the standards *well*, we can introduce words such as theme and plot in read aloud discussions.... When we know the standards well, we can embed our standards teaching into authentic work of students who are reading books and talking about their reading every day.

Formative assessment rituals map my work with students. They continuously guide me to building stronger connections of learning for students and with students. Because they are aligned to standards, I have a more accurate and vivid vision of where my students and I are meeting the goals articulated by my school community. Most of all, I have seen how they empower students because, together, we create a supportive and edifying feedback culture. Living with standards and assessment in the ways I have shared with you in this chapter, students feel a strong sense of ownership and investment in their own learning. Thinking of assessment through the lens of partnership has the potential for building a sense of control and competency, which are needed for student engagement (Czikszentmihalyi, 1997).

Of course, formative assessments are one piece of the quilt of my work. "Formative assessment is a powerful vehicle for focusing on effective learning. However it is not a quick fix: it takes time, thought and discussion to become embedded. It also involves, in many cases, a gradual power shift, through modeling and training, engaging children to gradually take more and more control over their learning and the decisions they make to enhance learning" (Clarke, 2003). As Guskey (2005) and Reeves (2010) advocate, to embrace and informatively use assessments as part of our everyday teaching work, we must (1) use assessments as sources of feedback for both students and ourselves; (2) follow assessments with responsive, relevant, and, as necessary, corrective instruction; and (3) give students multiple oppportunites to demonstrate their understanding.

In our think tanks as a Leadership and Learning Center training team, Reeves starts our conversations with, "This is about what students need." Students need to know we know them and want to know them. They need to know themselves in vibrant Technicolor detail, gaining insights that are more plausibly tangible to students when they live in a culture of continuous and supportive feedback. Formative assessments are vital in helping us get to know and support each students' literacy learning. Effective assessment should make our job easier (Hill, et al., 1998). This is the radiant promise of formative assessments.

EXHIBIT 7.2   **Sample Conference Record Notes**

CONFERENCE RECORD NOTES from Laura Benson
United World College South East Asia, Singapore

Unit of Study/Focus: Fiction Writing   Date: November 17–20

Helen's 4th Grader Writers

Amanda	Michael	Ally	Andres
The Outback—she begins by writing, does not need planning tool or supports right now; "Ideas are spill out"—excellent flow and energy to her writing	Harry Potter inspiration in developing this scary story—boy lands on Mars; has a well-developed story in his head full of details and is able to transfer his thinking to paper with maturity and focus.	Very passionate and focused on objects and place of story; she said *"Since I was young, I have been interested in fairies and castles…"*	Draws inspiration and ideas from the books he reads—"You can get a lot of ideas from books"; developing a series—Adventures of Handee Patoo (sp.?)
"I use a notebook for ideas that flow in my head … sometimes I (also) include doodles…"	*"I did better than I thought I would (at writing fiction/as a fiction writer)!"* self-evaluation	*"This is a twin story … about best friends…"*	What advice would you give a kindergarten buddy (or a peer)? *"It's your imagination which is very important … daydreaming is important…"* (He offered many sophisticated insights about the value and power of daydreaming to inform and chisel a writer's thinking.) … *Think about the end … Watching the scene* (as he writes it or thinks about it—he's visualizing which is evidence of a deep understanding of how to craft and how to ponder possibilities!). *MENTOR: He could/should teach upcoming writing lessons—modeling his thinking would be very helpful to his classmates.
Adding her voice to our large group talking circles	Encourage him to name his growth, effectiveness as writer, and set his own goal(s).		Able to be metacognitive as he reflects on his writing (both his process and his products), seems very confident and comfortable adding his voice to our talking circles and in conferences.
	Seems very confident and able to be absorbed/engaged as independent writer.		Partnering with Darrin and Shan

| EXHIBIT 7.2 | **Sample Conference Record Notes** (continued) |

Ryan	Nicole	Jun Ho	Amelia
Super Dog! Retelling story when I asked him what he is saying inside his head—can summarize on the piece/product. Model and practice self-reflections and evaluations with him to grow his metacognition. Appropriately (to his development and age) focused on the action of the story. Seems to be drawn to developing not only action but humor, too. Growing understanding about character; support him in helping him develop his character(s) with a bit more detail and (over time) more awareness and articulation of internal attributes of his characters	Thinking about her process and product effectively— self-talk/ internal dialogue seems to help her think through her writing and explore thoughtful choices, too. Focused on "how everything changes"— boy taking quiz/quizzes; character = girl; dogs	The Ominous Mind (Not sure I have it spelled correctly—it sounds like such a cool title!). Character = Jim Get ideas by writing (too much planning or forcing him to plan his writing first may tank his energy for writing—monitor and support him on this) [NOTE to observers: Please help me know if I recorded the following statement correctly and do I have the right child named here. I was writing quickly as this reflection was voiced during our talking circle on Monday.] *"I've got doors in my ears…"* (brilliant reflections on how he harvests ideas from his imagination)— wow, so self-aware! Honor his think time/ need to have time to formulate this thinking before he can transfer it into writing them down	Drawing ideas from the books she reads; likes to "take the author's ideas and twist it a bit" Mentor: Ask her soon to model her thinking process—especially in identifying and developing her character(s), getting inspiration from favorite authors/texts; staying positive and energized when writing may be/is hard for you
Ian	**Ohruv**	**Anoma**	**Lea**
"…Technology (helps me write) … especially long(er pieces … and when I have lots of thoughts/ideas) … I can write more (when I can use technology as a writer)…" Nurtured his descriptions; monitor and offer more instruction to help his fertile ideas "live on the paper"	Sounds like a really fun and creative story = millionaire and dollar duck is buried; working on crafting in suspense and intrigue I think Seems to have many ideas and details "ready to go"	Daydreaming insights— very mature and effective in helping her generate ideas and stay playful in exploring possibilities for her writing; paying attention to how other authors describe characters in their stories. Draws ideas "dreams and nightmares" Advice to a younger students = "Put pencil on paper … I just get ideas (by writing)." Working on using humor Character = dog	"One idea (is enough) … to tunnel my thinking" (focus is what I think she is going for here—lovely way of describing her thinking—just did not get all of her words written down) Encourage her to mentor classmates in modeling and in peer conferences, too, as I think she would be a compassionate listener and offer constructive feedback to fellow writers

EXHIBIT
7.2
Sample Conference Record Notes (continued)

Keva	Ian	Andy	Leah
"I didn't know I was capable of writing so much ... of writing such a (good) story!"	(My writing ideas ... imagination...) goes inside my body....)	Writing about a monster, people (main characters) are trying to figure out if the monsters is real; encourage him to name and further develop the main character—may be focusing on the action or shock of his story more than character right now.	Talked with her about using cut and paste revision strategies when she needs/wants to change a part of her writing; her revision will most likely involve adding right now.
Vernon	**Arshya**	**Nicole L.**	**Tran**
I/We can turn anything into a story!	*The Monkey in the Market*—incredibly detailed and seems to be a very well developed story line	Worried about her story being boring—may be putting a bit too much pressure on herself that her writing has to/should match her reading—but also her awareness seems to be evidence of mature awareness of fiction elements.	Values daydreaming as a way to generate ideas for writing
	Passion for fiction as reader and writer; trying to use plot in her story(ies)—reads like a library book!	She has lots of ideas; working with great flow—getting her thoughts down, engaged, focused, and able to reflect on her process.	
	Inspired by *Monkey in the Mountain*/her reading and showed me her mentor text, too!		
	Student as teacher/mentor—her energy and enthusiasm in addition to her keen insights about fiction texts would be powerful modeling for her classmates and for younger students, too.		
	Gave me a little book she created as I left —had a dear heart!		
	Well-developed stories (seems like a pattern of performance for A)		

EXHIBIT 7.2   **Sample Conference Record Notes** (continued)

Joshua	Melene	Noma	
Using his background knowledge to inform and shape his writing—football, fighting with his brothers—creating realistic fiction; seems to be visualizing, too; writes with vivid descriptions and really earnest and focused on descriptive writing—again evidence of visualizing, connecting/using his bk, and I think a solid sense of/regard for audience!	Writing about animals—loves to write stories with animals as main characters	"...an author describes..." when asking her about what authors do and think about	

James	Avnar	Sean	Logan
Fishy Crunch (name) One big dog adventure; planning to share with 2nd grade; "You can connect 3 stories..."	Wants to join James & Logan with Big Dog story. "Write about your dreams"—advice to kindergarten buddy (topic generation)	"I wrote more than I often do/thought I could..."	Fiction stories—"make up, get more memories, carry on writing as long as you can..." Big Dog adventure

Nik	Toby	Rhiannon	Chase
"Sister is the main character; make a magic mushroom; (char.) feels kind of weird" Writing parts on a page/paginating well it seems, "You can use your own stuff up ... use (your own) memories..." Reading his writing Character—dog Making up my own movie	"My favorite parts"—seems to reflect thoughtful evaluation of his writing and considering or beginning to consider alternatives and options "It's not about me ... I am not sure about the character (yet)..." Needs think time to formulate and draft his ideas	*Once*—using story language Saving space for drawing /illustrations Using a few words	"not sure" (about character yet)—needed some think time to ponder/ create his character Character ="K.J. He's going to do a lot of exciting things"

EXHIBIT 7.2   **Sample Conference Record Notes** (continued)

CONFERENCE RECORD NOTES from Laura Benson
Canadian Academy, Kobe, Japan

Unit of Inquiry/Student Learning Focus: Monitoring/Checking Understanding with Stop Sign Reading/
Stopping to Think and Self-talk—"I know..." ; Retelling

PD Focus: Managing balanced literacy instruction; small groups; differentiated instruction; running records
and using data to make teaching decisions; high interest in developmental continuums

Teaching Partner Jan B. – KINDERGARTEN STUDENTS   Date: Sept. 23, 27, & 28

Dohyun	Riley	Anu	Kensel
Reading on computer—car racing—From Prompt *"What do you know...? What are you thinking?"* He said—*"Maybe I could make one, too."* Working to understand what he read by using his background knowledge/making connections from his own experiences and what he knows about the world; questioning; and predicting—at a very mature level! Dohyn & Riley are excellent book partners for one another; rare give and take between them →	*"I can read books that are hard for grown-ups"* Using "I know..." statements and working to understand; extraordinarily articulate and advanced in her ability to not only read but in making connections, identifying important ideas, and inferring. Sweetie and gentle with her peers; *"I know sea lions can walk on their back legs..."* Gaining new knowledge from her reading; able to revise earlier thinking when presented with more information; Very confident and self-assured—in a lovely kindergarten way; Really into Table of Contents to guide her nonfiction reading, at least of *Life Size Zoo*, but seems to be something she has been doing for a while	Keep nudging cross checking of cueing systems—including modeling how when using them to problem solve new words and to trigger strong metacognition	
Matthew	**Yuchong**	**Miho**	**Ayane**
Opening up more and more Seems to be drawn to nonfiction and humor texts; *"She has stripes ... She looks funny"* (points to text when responding; seems to return to text to strengthen understanding, especially when prompted);*"Shark opens his jaws..."*	Seems to be using own experiences and background knowledge to understand what is read to him and what he can read from text (pictures; need to follow up on his capacity to read + understand text words)	B-day Tues.; very sweet & friendly & open, esp. 1-1 Understands concepts of grow-doesn't grow; seems to be using her background knowledge well in naming pictures	Reading and naming text pictures/deriving meaning from graphics Figured out "swings" "Think in your mind" (to figure out new words; to understand text)

EXHIBIT 7.2 **Sample Conference Record Notes** (continued)

Hana	Zoe	Nahyun	Ahbay
Friendly & affectionate	Very comfortable sharing her thinking in whole group; seems self-assured and enthusiastic		RR: high percentage of known words (over 95–97%);
Wait time is important in gaining her responses			great book matching;
RR:	Using texts words in developing her responses—good blend of author's words and her own		pointing to text while he reads;
At my School			pat/pater/SC;
(for) In Our Classroom			some repetitions;
Match???	"*Vanish*"—another way to say gone!		predicting, especially with prompt;
Seems to be over using her memory of text and/or background knowledge and not attending to print???	Predicted blocks would be in Toy book		insertions—put "to" in throughout book; encouraged "Let's try that again"
Wait time seems important	"Toys Putting Away"— Syntax???		Using text words for "I know…" up concepts; "…sliding down…" using background knowledge to understand and/or connect with text concepts (text concepts pretty straight forward)
			Seems to be strong at predicting "what next" and connections from his background knowledge to text information/concepts
			Thinking beyond text— "…can't throw trucks in (toy) box…"
			RR: self corrections (self initiated);
			Interesting: He only talked about the boy in the *Playing Outside* even though there is a girl with the boy in all the pictures—"He was going in the tunnel … Next, he's going to play with the swings…"—using his memory in rereading this familiar text

EXHIBIT 7.2	**Sample Conference Record Notes** (continued)

Allysa	Dylan	Andrew	Karina
Using visual cues and grapho-phonic cues to problem solve new words Understands concept of grow–doesn't grow "wave of sand"	"We know (there is a/this is about) a box…:" "We know he cleaned up all by himself"—thinking beyond text and inferring; using his own words such as *playground* Maybe try sticky note flag to note when he understands and when he is confused	Loves to participate in whole group; need to follow up with him in conference to better understanding—some of his responses—some seem way off but he may have a clear reason or connection which he just can't yet clearly articulate "Crocodiles have blue feet…" Seems confident and enthusiastic about learning Writing Ayane's name at writing center	
Issac	**Ricky**		**Small Group Options:**
Oral responses seem to reflect understanding and he was voicing "*I know*…" unprompted	Seems to be making unique connections at a high/mature level, especially when engaged in a collaborative learning experience or read aloud. Becoming more comfortable to share his thinking *Baby*—monitor his und. work/self talk		Abhay, Ayane, Dylan, Zoe, Miho Level 2; Have 1-1; Und. Left to right Gaining & working on basic sight words Need problem solving strategies Riley & Dohyun Level 15/16; retelling but need to work on depth & pers. Connections; have studied nonfiction (TOC; don't have to read every page; index)

EXHIBIT 7.2   **Sample Conference Record Notes** (continued)

CONFERENCE RECORD NOTES from Laura Benson
Canadian Academy, Kobe, Japan

Unit of Inquiry/Student Learning Focus: Connecting & Questioning—"This reminds me of..." & "I wonder..." and "I would connect____ & ____ because..." and (beginning to focus on in small groups) "Somebody wanted but so..." (fiction connections/making connections to key ideas in fiction); Migration & Movement

PD Focus: Management of balanced literacy instruction; small group learning and teaching; differentiation

Teaching Partner: Jenny W. ~ **2nd & 3rd Grade**   Date: September 23, 27, & 28

Jacob P.	Reno	Yujin	Philippa
Using background knowledge Small Group: opposite concepts reflect effective connections & predicting	"On the 1st page, I wonder what's going to happen when he (wondering & predicting what next)..." Connect = so you can think; using self talk; Text to text connections	"This part reminds me of being the fastest..." (self connections & using memory/background knowledge effectively)	"Monsters"—making like/not like connections; able to compare characters Stopping to think & connect—"It said 'It took their breath away...' Pausing really helps me understand, especially when I read mysteries/feels like when I read mysteries..."
Isabella	Aska	Shawronna	Chandrakrit
	"I wonder if...too much gas...spaces." Questioning seems to reflect understanding and disposition to think inferentially; Monitor deep ? Small Group: math patterns to connect; Excellent Connect 2's "the sum + addition" including explaining why/because thinking maturely	"It reminds me of an Indian festival of lights..." Can compare-contrast text concepts in mature ways; Using text words & her own lang. well to describe thinking and develop her under-standing as she reads independently ("zoo" and "grandma's house") and during read alouds ("...our old librarian..." —Miss Brooks)	"My brain told me..." Rereading helps me if I forget something; Summarizing nonfiction reading = reflects understand (nonfiction passion?)
Sofia	Jacob B.	Yutaro	Meena
Spanish speaker Really willing to try and staying engaged; lovely attitude Seems to be understanding some or much of what we were focusing on (worked to convey key concepts by speaking Spanish to her although I wish I knew more!) Can understand pictures of the texts she is reading independently but con-tinue to monitor this closely, especially so that she never feels isolated or left out of our learn-ing studies	Using background knowledge; Suggested books in a series, especially to strengthen his capacity to develop connections before, during, and after he reads and keep him motivated—"I get bored a lot...I like scary stories/book..." We talked about how reading *Goosebumps* might be a good fit for him and discussed some of the questions he could bring to these texts (what to wonder about as one reads scary stories and mysteries)	Small Group	Connected to read aloud of *Miss Brooks* "This reminds me of library time..." Could not name connections as she was reading independently??? Wondering about "Why is there a horse in her room?" Questions make sense but may be a bit literal or straightforward to text illustrations; monitor depth of questions and her metacognition about how she is working to understand what she reads.

EXHIBIT 7.2	Sample Conference Record Notes (continued)

Ema	Karin	Elie	Tristan
Reading *Junie B. Jones* Small Group: *Somebody wanted but so…* Can identify main character/somebody and seems to understand central problem; Enthusiastic and seems to bring positive energy to her reading	Small Group: using background knowledge to determine connections between *Deep in the Woods* to *Goldilocks & The 3 Bears* Inferring *"Mama's bed…"* Syntax? Find out more about her understanding of English grammar and syntax cues	Small Group: "The cover looks like a book I know…" = seems to be making connections between text and using her background knowledge to generate additional connections; Using her knowledge of fiction & knows the language of fiction/ fairy tales "Once upon a time…"	Small Group: "This is kind of like Goldilocks…" Reading nonfiction and using zoo memories/ background knowledge to develop connections as he reads "…sick…" seems to reflect making deeper connections + thinking beyond just literal text information (but find out more about this over time; eval.)
Freesia	**Iljun**	**Young-Ah**	**Innes**
	Small Group: "This reminds me of graphs…" (math text); "Another way to say…" (from our discussion of Connect 2)—brilliant! "…triple…three…" and "…+ and add…" Seems to really love social learning contexts/groups		Small Group: strong connections and seems to be working strategically to understand; support metacognition and reflecting on how he works to understand Enthusiastic, lovely spirit
Ava	**Amelia**	Small Group/Book Club Possibilities	• Migration/Movement Inquiry Clubs (based on common questions students generate about their studies of migration/movement)
"I think it's going to be about learning about hamsters…" connecting to memories of being at friend's house and inferring/predicting "Thinking about Mom & Dad"	"When the book said *whisker curling*, this reminded me of…" Seems to be making strong & effective connections from read alouds and her own indep. reading	• Fiction Reading Club/Fiction Connections • Math Connections Club [IlJun & Aska] • Revisit *Water Hole Waiting* Club	• Innes; Reno; Miho; Ema; & Chandrakrit

EXHIBIT 7.2   **Sample Conference Record Notes** (continued)

CONFERENCE RECORD NOTES from Laura Benson
Canadian Academy, Kobe, Japan

Unit of Inquiry/Student Learning Focus: Inferring with "I bet..." and Identifying Important Ideas (III) with "I learned..." and fiction framework for key ideas—"Somebody wanted but so..." and continuing Jeff's lessons about attending to what person or character say, act, do; PYP Unit—Attitudes; PYP Unit—Electricity

PD Focus: differentiation; nonfiction (biographies, especially)

Teaching Partner: Jeff ~ 4th & 5th Grade   Date: September 23, 27, & 28

Amara	**Oscar**	**Maxine**	**Mika** Tennis player J—
Biography—paying attention to "what changed their lives" (evidence of III)	Using "*I bet...*" Inferring from the title In the habit of writing down his thoughts	III to infer "...this part—I thought he dreamed of walking on the moon and I think he will accomplish that later in the book..." Seems to be in the habit of making "what next" inferences	using her background knowledge to understand explicit & implicit text information "I bet that she wants to play tennis a little more...I bet she's going to win the tournament..." Small Group: "Beds" (predicting in wordless bk); encourage her to expand on her thinking/responses; monitor how and to what detail she is able to identify important ideas; also could not give example of inferring
Sneha	**Prahlaad**	**Maria** Going back to text	**Nathan**
"I bet Phil was very happy...inventing electricity..."	"I wonder what Columbus will dis-cover...where he will sail and find...I think he will find a new island..." Small Group: Dad's chair—attending to the action of the story "I bet..." "(The character faced) many problems (such as) no place to live..."	to develop her response "I bet...since the beginning...whole life, this was his passion..." Water house (concepts? Eval.) "I learned how, if we don't understand (we have to reread or go back to the book)..." Took leadership of small groups in a lovely, compassionate way while still encouraging each member to engage in the required thinking work	Infer—putting himself into character's position/shoes; Helping me understand better = pointing to text "...gets me excited..."

EXHIBIT 7.2	Sample Conference Record Notes (continued)

Yu-en Emily	Hyen	Eugene	Hyeon
"I bet…" = what happened summarizing but also predicting; Duck & Goose—III character and problem	Able to identify character and problem; seems to have gained some important details about character, too	"…inventing…I bet…"	Maybe they're arriving
Robert Advice to kindergarten buddy = listen (so that they really know story/und).	**Daeun** "Looks yummy" (picture of food) Monitor his inferring & III beyond literal text info., especially the visuals	**Fayaz** (I am pretty sure but I have things a bit mixed up) Saying "I bet…" helps us understand what we are reading	**Nagahiro** "I bet…" "I wonder why…" Wait time very important
Konosuke "From what I have read so far, I bet he wouldn't give up…"	**Len** *How does the book need you?* The book needs you to read it! Monitor his meta-cognition for additional insights and ways of understanding Loves adventure books	**Jacqueline**	**Potential Small Group/Guided Reading Collaboratives:** Fiction Book Club Wordless Picture Books Character Development Club Amora, Oscar, Eugene Mika, Prahlaad, Len Len, Daeun, Maria Prahlaad & Mika
			Advice to Kindergarten Buddy from Whole Group: Listen Ask questions about story Stop and think about what's going to happen Teacher should read a book to them and ask the kids what's going to happen next Talk about what they like to do (and read books which reflect their "likes")

| **EXHIBIT 7.2** | **Sample Conference Record Notes** (continued) |

CONFERENCE RECORD NOTES from Laura Benson
Canadian Academy, Kobe, Japan

Unit of Inquiry/Student Learning Focus: Personal Narratives: "Teaching your reader about you" (via Personal Landscape Project/scrapbook writing); understanding the work and thinking of nonfiction writers—"I know why and how to write nonfiction because…" and "I have read a lot of nonfiction and noticed…" (need to continue this focus over time); topic generation (brainstorming, memory writing); revision; going public with your ideas; Humanities

PD Focus: differentiated instruction; texts/book matching; primary sources vs. picture books

Teaching Partner: David ~ **6th Grade**   Date: September 22 & 24

Kaiki	**Lisa C.**	**Nathan**	**Thomas H.**
Skateboard memory/piece; learning/considering how to write to inspire; this text could be a "how to" for other skills Faced with challenges— Keep on going!	Writing about someone who inspired me = Dad…when he went to university in the US "There are many other places that we don't know about…" (open yourself up to learning in new places from new people)	Writing about living in Japan Only here for 6 months (so this will be a wonderful time capsule/ memoir of his time here) Seems to use lists as an effective tool for generating or detailing his topic	Noticed the word "note" in annotated; und. concept
Risa	**Takeharu**	**Alessandro/Alexi**	**Se Gul**
Star = change (reflects thoughtfulness about making piece stronger by adding more detail/s) "…trampoline…" to describe how her dreams grew (Wow!)	Writing piece about Hawaii—learning new stuff…culture is very different in Hawaii (and opening self to another culture); voices and includes vivid detail for his pieces it seems	Landscape = where land is… picture…fields; Writing about ice hockey "First time on the ice…" seems to be using dialogue effectively	
Lisa K.	**Gum Bin**	**Yoshiki**	**Thomas M.**
Adding more details; seems to be doing so effectively (getting specific; supporting readers' visualizing)	Flute lesson writing	Writing about going to Ireland Like my writing (can identify strengths in writing such as working to make piece more clear); feeling excited about clarity of message	

EXHIBIT 7.2	Sample Conference Record Notes (continued)

Jahaku	Jung Yeon	Shina	Jonathan
Then—changed to therefore because thought he was using then too much Asked how he know why/when to make changes and revise his writing = "best word that fits" Help him articulate his thinking and show other examples of revision	Writing about riding a bike; writing about starting to speak English—"I changed my topic" Nudge him to name the places where his writing is clear and where (and why) he needs to work on clarity in his piece	Writing about drawing contest "I was going to quit because I had not won any prizes here at CA…I (stuck with my art) and won a prize…" "My message is don't give up… and you might win a prize…"	I want to teach my reader to never give up!
Mami Writing about cooperation "…teaching through examples—drama…"	**Bobby** Writing about going to/being in England alone Wants to teach his readers "not to be afraid of challenges"	**Karan**	**Key Ideas David is Nurturing:** Writing in the first person Something that happened to you Something that changed you Experience or person who made you what you are Scrapbook + photos Memento Natural features

EXHIBIT 7.2   **Sample Conference Record Notes** (continued)

CONFERENCE RECORD NOTES from Laura Benson
Canadian Academy, Kobe, Japan

Unit of Inquiry/Student Learning Focus: Identifying Important Ideas in Specific Genre—Short Stories (character, problem, setting, solution)—"I learned…"; How to Think as Understanding Readers—self-talk & response to help students be multistrategic readers (connecting, inferring, questioning, and evaluating/identifying important ideas)

PD Focus: Differentiated instruction and groupings; analyze vs. enjoy reading; Using short and spirited texts; Building vocabulary with read-alouds and modeling

Teaching Partner: Lynn ~ **7th Grade**   Date: September 22 & 24

Manhar	Ishaan	Mik	Ray
Bad reputation Thinking about characters and what's happening (now and next) + Identifying Important Idea = character	Rats—"I think the rats will dodge the reef…" (inferring effectively using good combination of text information and background knowledge) + Identifying Important Ideas = climax; twist	I learned that the rats are really furious and angry…haven't eaten in weeks = understanding Going back into text to confirm thinking Seems to be inferring beyond the text, from the text, and make success connections + Identifying Important Ideas	Important to think about what these people need to do—abandon or not… I think it's not true (supporting his because thinking well) Loves twists and seems able to identify them + Identifying Important Ideas = climax; twist
Irene	Katie	Philip	Saifullah
Prologue = reflects understanding "I didn't really like it…" (evaluating text and can explain why) "It's not that strong…not much entertaining (elements)…" + Identifying Important Ideas = fun and inviting piece "Attention passengers" J (written with Tamanna)	See crew coming…trying to board ship = seems to visualizing, connecting, and making logical predictions to understand what she is reading "Short stories are condensed versions!" + Identifying Important Ideas	Thinking about how story will end and considering options—Supply boats? Rats? Someone will help them? Summarizing (but may be retelling too basically or from others—Eval her capacity to identify important ideas in multiple pieces of fiction) Title: Up All Night; seems to be using title to predict and expect text information + Identifying Important Ideas	Inferring and wondering unprompted Rats are very (strong + angry) driving people out like tigers Novel = likes the 2–3 Big problems, keeps her interested HC is main character because… (seems to be drawing logical conclusions and understand most important ideas) + Identifying Important Ideas

EXHIBIT 7.2   **Sample Conference Record Notes** (continued)

Leah	Madeline	Simran	Joseh
Boy thought he was going to die Want more detail; (going to read to find out more); check in with her again to see if she can retell with more details + Identifying Important Idea = character	(Infer)—"They would see skeletons" Predicting twist story from title and rat characters + Identifying Important Ideas	Important ideas or features of fiction stories—morale, climax, anticlimax, "falling off" Details from new novel reading—attending to problem Title—predicting hope—"Building up on each page..." + Identifying Important Ideas	Title = "He thought he was gonna die because in France... temperature..." Seems to be inferring with "what next" predictions well + "...think about moral... predict..."
Preetpal	**Young-Jae**	**Chirag**	**Tamanna**
Rats—"I'm thinking about if these are normal rats vs. ship rats...and if the rats are smart..." Encourage her to use the text to confirm and inform her understanding and support her responses—seems to be relying on memory too much "I remember..." + Identifying Important Ideas = climax; twist	Short story reading = cliff hanger; plot Really likes twist—ending, surprises How do you work to understand fiction? "I really think about and look at words to connect and (think about) details..." Ask Young-Jae to show 2–3 places as evidence of the above (over time) to monitor deep understanding and determine what to teach next Shared some of the "unexpected" ideas from his reading of "A Day's Wait" + Identifying Important Ideas	How did the people get driven off the ship? Wondering in this text and others + Identifying Important Ideas = climax; twist	Probably there's going to be a problem Inferring—what's going to happen next on the island Thinking about the "resolution" "There is a sequel opportunity in novels..." + Identifying Important Ideas = fun and inviting piece "Attention passengers" J (written with Irene)
+ means I received "How to Read Short Stories" advice/ response from student		**Key Ideas Lynn is nurturing:** Main character Plot Beginning, middle, end Events Climax Hook & entertain Information to persuade Visualizing	

EXHIBIT 7.2   **Sample Conference Record Notes** (continued)

CONFERENCE RECORD NOTES from Laura Benson
American School of the Hague, The Netherlands

Kim's First Grade Class   Nov. 28–Dec. 1
Focus: Inferring & Poetry

George	Jean	Tanner	Anastasia	Laurent
implicit inf.—strong BK; R on; encouraged stop sign *I bet*; loved *Zoom*; retell—details; *use pictures to predict; saying I bet...LG; RR 100%*	R *I Want My Tooth*; *Meta: I can feel more confident w/ inf.* *& R...so many things to do w/ it; The Pelican—inf from TOC; stands—LG ?; attention & focus ? IR; RR 99–100%; I bet... Earth is Mostly Ocean; is focusing on predicting*	Inf. what next–"*I bet that something will be little in here.*"	*Whose Shoes*—"*I bet that they his mom asks him to make the shoes*" Inf—pic; detailed retell; becoming more confident to share; SC; RR 97%	ESL; dog—infer; engaged; earnest; meta; some bk; leaving off final consonants; using b.k. to problem solve new words—shawl for scarves; phonics; willing to work hard to problem solve & und.
Giacomo inf—mom from pic.; Vocalizing; has 3 books open ?; repetitions; absent	**Maya** *I bet he's going to pretend...*; pt. to text; *I bet that he's going to get home*; help her reflect & meta.	**Samantha** absent	**Alya** Absent; *The Seed—I bet the seed will grow...* using bk—needs to combine this w/ more phonics dark—darkness; track/rain/sc—train; likes Peter & Jane books; Hop on Pop—did not have *I bet...* T using rhyme to predict what will happen next	
Kai advice to K—*say what you know*; frisky, attentive? Meet 1-1; IR; strong ability to inf. implied messages—magic of *Fred Said*	**Johnny** inf. beyond text info. from RA; frisky; fort of books; holding books upside down; IR; impulsive; meet 1-1; solid bk?	**Maeve** *I bet...I think that he puts stuff...that it over flows...*; pt. to text; strong inf. in GR & solid meta.; growing SC	**Key**: inf = inferring RA = read aloud R = reading LG = large group TOC = table of contents RR = running record SC = self corrections	**Next Steps of Learning:** Continue study of inferring; Build upon students' self talk

EXHIBIT 7.2

Sample Conference Record Notes (continued)

CONFERENCE RECORD NOTES from Laura Benson
American School of the Hague, The Netherlands

David's Third Grade Class   Nov. 27, 2006 to Dec. 1

Student Learning Focus: *Identifying Important Ideas & Synthesizing; Reading & Writing Poetry*

Michael	Macrae	Borja	Miguel	Laura
RR 95–99%; *Popperton I do know this will happen...; predicting; III— poetry—not many words* motivation?— collaboration helps	inf. from cover; *Pigs go to the market—I learned...1st page...returned to* text; title to help predict; nudge III; inf. word meanings: down— sick & light—air = float; monitor confidence? Bubble Map— feeling bad & mad	Contributing LG; III Title—about the book; III poetry some rhyme @ end of line...; W—*blame* describe dog; unusual connections at times?	Advice to K—*R in your head; R to their selves;* meta? M & M— inf. (x) confidence? returned to text; monitor book matching & vocab.	He hates trip—III char.; R = *learning lots of things; poems—don't have to rhyme; speaking more, softly*
Hannah	**Meghan**	**Cecilie**	**Dana**	**Arnold**
...that there is a missing mummy in sci museum— curse; synthesize R fast w/out stopping; swimming poem—symbolic lead	*I learned*—char; pictures; *Whenever you don't know... reread it...;* swimming poem	Arthur—III char; I learned...[Give her sticky flags to make char. III] Advice to K—*stop while R;* II 1 place (text focus)	confident talking in group; good insights; Sabrina; III—repeated words in poems...1 topic & action	R—imagination; III worry = things go wrong; transfers letters/text to pictures; creative & helpful contribu- tions to LG & mature vocab.— "rank" "elderly"
Charlie	**Matthew**			**Key**
Picture III = *It looked like...* predicting; engaged; inferring; using text words & his own to retell; III = hook & fast paced; absent	Text words; think like char. (relating); shy but wait time imp.; pictures; feelings; III— *interesting*—apath etic—pictures III; hopes & dreams			III = identifying important ideas R = reading LG = large group bk = background knowledge
Next Steps of Learning à Continue study of Identifying Important Ideas; add Synthesizing	**Whole Class** Read Alouds Add to Self Talk Concept development - content area vocab. Author Study/Poets Compare "Story" w/ _____	**Small Groups** Student authored texts; nonfiction; Motivation & confidence focused groups Practice creating summaries together Create titles for chap. books	**Individually** Nudge self talk but listen for it to be self-initiated Identify like-minded behaviors & passions for book clubs	

References

Ainsworth, L., and Viegut, D. (2006). *Common formative assessments: How to connect standards-based instruction and assessment.* Thousand Oaks, CA: Corwin Press.

Alber, R. (2010). Letting go in the classroom [blog post]. Retrieved from http://www.edutopia.org/students-guide-learning-constructivism

Allen, D. (1995). *The tuning protocol: A process for reflection.* Providence, RI: Coalition of Essential Schools.

Allen, D. (Ed.). (2007). *Student work, teacher learning.* New York, NY: Teachers College Press.

Allen, D., Blythe, T., & Powell, B. (1996). *A guide to looking collaboratively at student work.* Cambridge, MA: Harvard Project Zero.

Allen, D., Blythe, T., & Powell, B. (2007). *Looking together at student work* (2nd ed.). New York, NY: Teachers College Press.

Allen, D., Blythe, T., & Thompson-Gove, G. (2004). *The facilitator's book of questions: Tools for looking together at student and teacher work.* New York: NY: Teachers College Press.

Allen, P. (2009). *Conferring: The keystone of reader's workshop.* Portsmouth, NH: Stenhouse.

Allison, E., Besser, L., Campsen, L., Cordova, J., Doubek, B., Gregg, L., Kamm, C., Nielsen, K., Peery, A., Pitchford, B., Rose, A., White, S., & Ventura, S. (2010). *Data teams: The big picture—looking at data teams through a collaborative lens.* Englewood, CO: Lead + Learn Press.

Anderson, K. (2010). *Data team success stories.* Englewood, CO: Lead + Learn Press.

Benson, L. (1993). Living a literate life: Strategy apprenticeships for growing readers and writers and their growing teachers. *The Colorado Communicator, 25*(2), 24–38.

Benson, L. (2000). *Colorado reads.* Denver, CO: Colorado Department of Education.

Benson, L. (2001). Living a literate life: Guiding children to books. *The Colorado Communicator, 25*(1), 39–51.

Benson, L. (2002). Going on rounds. *The Colorado Reading Council Journal, 11*(2), 9–14.

Benson, L. (2004). Deep thinking: Sustaining students' strategy learning to cultivate their independence. *The Colorado Communicator, 27*(3), 72–86.

Black, P., Harrison, C., Lee, C., Marshall, B., & Wiliam, D. (2004). Working inside the black box: Assessment for learning in the classroom. *Phi Delta Kappan, 86*(1), 8.

Black, P., & Wiliam, D. (1998). Assessment and classroom learning. *Assessment in Education, 5,* 1.

Blythe, T., Allen, D., & Powell, B. (1999). *Looking together at student work.* New York, NY: Teachers College Press.

Bromley, K. (2009). *Writing for educators: Personal essays and practical advice.* Charlotte, NC: Information Age.

Buchovecky, E. (1996). *Learning from student work.* Newton, MA: Atlas Communities, Education Development Center.

Butler, D., & Winne, P. (1995). Feedback and self-regulated learning: A theoretical synthesis. *Review of Educational Research, 65*(3), 245–281.

Chappuis, S., & Chappuis, J. (2007). The best value in formative assessment. *Educational Leadership, 65,* 14–17.

Clarke, S. (2003). *Enriching feedback in the primary classroom: Oral and written feedback from teachers and children.* London: Hodder Education/Hachette Livre UK.

Clarke, S. (2005). *Formative assessment in action: Weaving the elements together.* London: Hodder Arnold.

Clarke, S. (2008). *Active learning through formative assessment.* London: Hodder Education.

Clay, M. (1991). *Becoming literate: The construction of inner control.* Portsmouth, NH: Heinemann.

Cooper, C., & Boyd, J. (1996). *Mindful learning.* Melbourne, Australia: Routledge.

Czikszentmihalyi, M. (1997). *Finding flow: The psychology of engagement with everyday life.* New York, NY: Basic Books.

Darling-Hammond, L. (2001). *The right to learn: A blueprint for creating schools that work.* San Francisco, CA: Jossey-Bass.

Darling-Hammond, L., Ancess, J., & Falk, B. (1995). *Authentic assessment in action: Studies of schools and students at work.* New York, NY: Teachers College Press.

Davies, A. (2000). *Making assessment work.* Courtenay, BC, Canada: Connections.

Dodge, J. (2009). *25 quick formative assessments for a differentiated classroom: Easy, low-prep assessments that help you pinpoint students' needs and reach all learners.* New York, NY: Scholastic.

Felknor, C., Winterscheidt, V., & Benson, L. (1999). Thoughtful use of individual reading inventories. *Colorado Reading Council Journal, 10,* 10–20.

Fisher, D., & Frey, N. (2007). *Checking for understanding: Formative assessment techniques for your classroom.* Alexandria, VA; ASDC.

Fullan, M., Hill, P., & Crevola, C. (2006). *Breakthrough.* Thousand Oaks, CA: Corwin Press.

Guskey, T. (2005, April). *Formative classroom assessment and Benjamin S. Bloom: Theory, research, and implications.* Paper presented at the annual meeting of the American Educational Research Association, Montreal, Quebec, Canada.

Guskey, T. (Ed.). (2009a). *The principal as assessment leader.* Bloomington, IN: Solution Tree.

Guskey, T. (Ed.). (2009b). *The teacher as assessment leader.* Bloomington, IN: Solution Tree.

Hagerty, P. (2009). *An old story retold.* Denver, CO: Colorado Council of the International Reading Association Conference.

Hattie, J. (1992). Towards a model of schooling: A synthesis of meta-analysis. *Australian Journal of Education, 36,* 5–13.

Hattie, J. (2009). *Visible learning: A synthesis of over 800 meta-analyses relating to achievement.* New York, NY: Routledge.

Hill, B. C. (2001). *Developmental continuums: A framework for literacy instruction and assessment K–8.* Norwood, MA: Christopher-Gordon.

Hill, B. C., & Ekey, C. (2010). *The next step guide to enhancing writing instruction: Rubrics and resources for self-evaluation and goal setting, for literacy coaches, principals, and teacher study groups, K–6.* Portsmouth, NH: Heinemann.

Hill, B. C., Ruptic, C., & Norwick, L. (1998). *Classroom-based assessment.* Norwood, MA: Christopher-Gordon.

Hindley, J. (2000). *In the company of children.* Portsmouth, NH: Stenhouse.

Hodgson, A. R., & Bohning, G. (1997). A five-step guide for developing a writing checklist. *Journal of Adolescent & Adult Literacy, 41,* 138–139.

Johnston, P. (1997). *Knowing literacy: Constructive literacy assessment.* Portland, ME: Stenhouse.

Knipper, S., & Duggan, L. (2006). *Writing to learn across the curriculum.* Alexandria, VA: ASCD.

Kramer, S., & DuBose, L. (2009). Engaging the Nintendo generation. In Thomas Guskey (Ed.), *The teacher as assessment leader.* Bloomington, IN: Solution Tree.

Luntz, F. (2007). *Words that work: It's not what you say, it's what people hear.* New York, NY: Hyperion.

Marzano, R. (2009). *Formative assessment and standards-based grading: Classroom strategies that work.* Bloomington, IN: Solution Tree.

Morrison, T. (2009). The true test of maternal love. Retrieved from http://www.oprah.com

Moss, C., & Brookhart, S. (2009). *Advancing formative assessment in every classroom: A guide for instructional leaders.* Alexandria, VA: ASCD.

Murray, D. (1989). Expecting the unexpected: Teaching myself—and others—to read and write. Portsmouth, NH: Boynton/Cook.

O'Connor, K. (2009). *How to grade for learning.* Thousand Oaks, CA; Corwin Press.

Oliver, B. (2008). Common assessments: Uncommon results. Retrieved from www.justaskpublications.com

Overmeyer, M. (2009). *What student writing teaches us: Formative assessment in the writing workshop.* York, ME: Stenhouse.

Peery, A. (2009). *Writing matters in every classroom.* Englewood, CO: Lead + Learn Press.

Piercy, T. (2006). *Compelling conversations: Connecting leadership to student achievement.* Englewood, CO: Lead + Learn Press.

Piercy, T., & Piercy, W. (2011). *Disciplinary literacy: Redefining deep understanding and leadership for 21st-century demands.* Englewood, CO: Lead + Learn Press.

Popham, J. (2003). *Test better, teach better: The instructional role of assessment.* Alexandria, VA: ASCD.

Popham, J. (2008). *Transformative assessment.* Alexandria, VA: ASCD.

Quate, S., & McDermott, J. (2010). *Clockwatchers: Six steps to motivating and engaging disengaged students across content areas.* Portsmouth, NH: Heinemann.

Reeves, D. (2003). *Making standards work: How to implement standards-based assessments in the classroom, school, and district* (3rd ed.). Englewood, CO: Advanced Learning Press.

Reeves, D. (2004a). *Accountability for learning: How teachers and school leaders can take charge.* Alexandria, VA: ASCD.

Reeves, D. (2004b). The case against the zero. *Phi Delta Kappan, 86*(4).

Reeves, D. (2007). *Ahead of the curve: The power of assessment to transform teaching and learning.* Bloomington, IN: Solution Tree.

Reeves, D. (2010). *Transforming professional development into student results.* Alexandria, VA: ASCD.

Ritchhart, R. (2004). *Intellectual character: What it is, why it matters, and how to get it.* San Francisco, CA: Jossey-Bass.

Ritchhart, R. (2011). Making *thinking visible: How to promote engagement, understanding, and independence for all learners.* San Francisco, CA: Jossey-Bass.

Sadler, D. R. (1989). Formative assessment and the design of instructional systems. *Instructional Science, 18,* 119–144.

Schmoker, M. (2006). *Results now: How we can achieve unprecedented improvements in teaching and learning.* Alexandria, VA: ASCD.

Schmoker, M. (2011). *Focus: Elevating the essentials to radically improve student learning.* Alexandria, VA: ASCD.

Seidel, S. (1991). *Collaborative assessment conferences for the consideration of project work.* Cambridge, MA: Harvard Project Zero.

Seidel, S. (1996). *Learning from looking.* Cambridge, MA: Harvard Project Zero.

Sibberson, F., & Szymusiak, K. (2008). *Day-to-day assessment in the reading workshop: Making informed instructional decisions in grades 3–6.* New York, NY: Scholastic.

Stiggins, R., Arter, J., Chappuis, J., & Chappuis, S. (2004). *Classroom assessment for student learning: Doing it right—using it well.* Portland, OR: Assessment Training.

Stiggins, R., & Guskey, T. (2007). Assessment for learning: An essential foundation of productive instruction. In D. Reeves (Ed.), *Ahead of the curve: The power of assessment to transform teaching and learning.* Bloomington, IN: Solution Tree.

Taberski, S. (2000). *On solid ground.* Portsmouth, NH: Heinemann.

Tomlinson, C. A. (2007/2008). Learning to love assessment. *Educational Leadership, 65*(4), 8–13.

Tomlinson, C. A., and McTighe, J. (2006). *Integrating differentiated instruction and understanding by design: Connecting content and kids.* Alexandria, VA: ASCD.

Wiggins, G. (2003). *Understanding by design: Developing literacy curriculum.* Colorado Council of the International Reading Association Conference.

Wolpert-Gawron, H. (2010). Classroom assessments for a new century: One teacher's quest to move beyond the bubble test. *Education Week, 4* (01), 14–16.

CHAPTER EIGHT

Disciplinary Literacy Redefines Deep Understanding Required for Complex Text

THOMASINA D. PIERCY

"There is no way my students could read such difficult books. The Common Core State Standards must have meant that these books are to be read to students. Expecting teachers to provide instruction with such difficult texts must be a mistake!" Educators expressing similar comments can be heard across the country. The initial realization of the expectations called for in the Common Core State Standards may result in heads looking down while calculating time until retirement.

By raising text complexity expectations for America's students, the Common Core State Standards have disclosed a disturbing truth: education may be considered too big to fail, but without an honest dialogue with teachers and leaders, the literacy gap will become increasingly rocky. The following questions can initiate honest, compelling, and perhaps disturbing conversations necessary to support increased success if students are to be prepared to face their robust futures:

- Why are literacy expectations in the Common Core State Standards significantly increased? Are the expectations unreasonable?

- How can disciplinary literacy instruction contribute to closing the literacy gap between current and new text complexity expectations?

Why Are K–12 Literacy Expectations Significantly Increased in the Common Core State Standards?

High school text readability demands indicate a 265L (lexile) gap between texts read near the end of high school and university texts (Williamson, 2008, p. 618). The 265L (lexile) gap is more than the lexile difference between the end of fourth and seventh grades (MetaMetrics, 2011, p. 2). This alarming concern is addressed in the Common

Core State Standards: "While reading demands in college, workforce training programs, and life in general have held steady or increased over the last half century, K–12 texts have actually declined in sophistication and relatively little attention has been paid to students' ability to read complex texts independently" (CCSSI, 2010, Appendix A, p. 2).

Rigor is vital in the curriculum, as described in *The Condition of College and Career Readiness Report* (ACT, 2010a, p. 20). It explains, "Having appropriate and aligned standards, coupled with a core curriculum, will adequately prepare high school students only if the courses are truly challenging. That is, taking the right kinds of courses matters more than taking the right number of courses." This result corresponds with the findings that additional years of coursework do not have a large impact on student readiness to successfully manage the reading required in college social sciences courses (ACT, 2006, p. 10). Rather than the number of courses being a significant indicator of preparedness, student success is related to "what is being asked of students in these courses" (ACT, 2006, p. 10).

From the Stone Age to the digital age, literacy has experienced dynamic shifts. Looking ahead, it is important to keep in mind that, for the projected 2018 five fastest-growing career fields—education, computer information, management, community services, marketing/sales—more than half of the 2010 high school graduates interested in these areas did not meet the college readiness benchmark in mathematics or science (ACT, 2010a, p. 18). The complexity of information, increased by technology, has intruded into literacy expectations. With this being the case, does it remain the desire of our citizenry to provide a world-class education for each and every student enrolled in public, private, religious, and charter schools across the 50 states and the territories that constitute the United States? If so, what questions, silenced under the cloak of the Reading across the Curriculum comprehension strategies, must be asked?

What Set of Circumstances Resulted in the Current Struggle with Comprehending Complex Texts?

To begin understanding the text complexity concern, we need clarity about its meaning. According the Common Core State Standards (CCSSI, 2010, Appendix A, p. 43), text complexity

> is the inherent difficulty of reading and comprehending a text combined with consideration of reader and task variables; in the Common Core State Standards, a three-part assessment of text difficulty that pairs qualitative and quantitative measures with reader-task considerations is presented.

As this publication goes to press, national leaders and the assessment consortium PARCC (Partnership for the Assessment of Readiness for College and Careers) are focusing on improving the process for measuring text complexity so that it can more readily become a regular part of instruction.

Considering the role of complex text begins with a look at student data. Specifically addressed by ACT was which skills differentiated those students who equaled or exceeded the benchmark score in the reading section of the ACT college admissions test from those who did not (ACT, 2006, p. 16; CCSSI, 2010, Appendix A, p. 2).

What specific reading capacities differentiated students' ability to achieve above and below the ACT benchmark? *Could it have been students' capacity to respond to questions written with Bloom's six cognitive processes associated having higher cognitive demand such as apply, analyze, evaluate, and create?* In a nutshell, with the passage of the No Child Left Behind Act in 2001, educational standards for reading were established with emphasis on K–grade 3 through the Reading First program. As a result, standards led to explicit, aligned instruction based on scaffolded frameworks developed by state and district curricular specialists. Aligned common formative assessments (Almeida & Ainsworth, 2009; Ainsworth & Viegut, 2006; Wiggins & McTighe, 2007) provided timely information for teachers to make instructional changes and identify intervention needs based on students' assessed needs. These strong practices hold true today. Central to the vitality of this accountability cycle were the cognitive processes represented as the verbs in the standards. During the "unwrapping" of the standards process, the verbs indicate the level of instructional rigor, thereby guiding educators to teach students the application of vital cognitive skills. These powerful cognitive processes for teaching students to think deeply and comprehend complex texts are thoroughly integrated into accountability processes. Questions on the ACT assessment require students to reason, draw conclusions, infer, analyze, synthesize, and apply different comprehension strategies. Despite incorporating high levels of cognitive demand in instruction and assessment, this process for alignment was not, in itself, sufficient to differentiate students achieving benchmark and those who did not (ACT, 2006, p. 13). Although these strong, research-based practices have been successful in increasing aligned instruction, what additional actions are needed to increase student achievement?

Should we consider students' capacity to demonstrate understanding of textual elements, including main idea, details, relationships, meaning of words, generalizations, and conclusions, which align with current *state standards? Was this the differentiator between successful students and those who did not achieve benchmark?* A primary factor for learning is for systems to achieve a guaranteed and viable curriculum, a research-based principle. Exactly what does that mean for classroom instruction? An analysis of 35 years of research resulted in "a guaranteed and viable curriculum as the school-level factor with the most impact on student achievement" (Marzano, McNulty, & Waters, 2005, p. 83; Marzano, 2003, p. 22; Schmoker, 2006, p. 128). "Guaranteed" means the curriculum provides clear guidelines regarding the content to be taught. Also, it indicates that disregarding the curriculum is not an option. However, the guaranteed, viable curriculum, too, was not sufficient to avert the gap between K–12 outcomes and college and career expectations. This textual element result is partially due to the fact that although the guaranteed, viable curriculum urgency resulted in horizontal alignment between state and district grade-level standards, assessments, and instruction, *vertical* K–12 state standards were generally not designed at the state level for alignment between middle and high school standards. Having horizontal alignment between standards, assessment, curriculum, and instruction, a vital component for instruction, has not guaranteed the vertical alignment between elementary, middle, and high schools that ensures all student progress can be frequently monitored through graduation and into college and careers.

In many states, the lack of alignment between the elementary/middle school standards and high school standards resulted in reading standards in high school being fragmented—either partially embedded in English standards or simply nonexistent. Without a K–12 curriculum alignment beginning at the state level, district leaders have been left to attempt to identify some congruent standards so instruction could be partially aligned for students when they transitioned to high school. The fractured foundation for student achievement, although having strengths, including providing elementary and middle schools with aligned instruction on text elements, could not support increasing twenty-first-century expectations.

The gap between the end of grade 12 and the beginning of college and career paths has continued to expand. Specifically, more than half of the states "fully define grade-level standards in reading only through the eighth grade" (ACT, 2006, p. 8). Without specific expectations for reading instruction, teachers do not have direction, students are not held to high expectations, and the expansion of the K–12 and college and career path gap continues.

Peering closely at the contents of the gap to grasp understanding, we find that the breakdown in standards alignment between middle and high school resulted in the majority of reading standards actually falling into the gap after middle school, frequently taking textual elements with them, resulting in reduced urgency for explicit, aligned literacy instruction in high school. Communication about literacy instruction between middle schools and high schools was not a priority due to the lack of focus on standards common to all levels. In *Reading Between the Lines*, these problems are described as students "not being asked to meet specific, rigorous reading standards during their high school years—a time when it is crucial for them to continue their reading skills" (ACT, 2006, p. 7). The terrain within the K–12 and college and career gap has become rugged. Yet, these concerns still were not the main differentiator between students achieving above and below the ACT benchmark for reading. Fortunately, the vertical misalignment has been resolved by the Common Core State Standards, which provide solid K–12 alignment that includes college and career readiness.

Pursuing the main differentiator of the student success question further, the indicator aligned with student success on reading benchmarks was their ability to read, understand, and respond to questions about complex texts (CCSSI, Appendix A, 2010, p. 2; ACT, 2006, p. 16). While text demands became less challenging within K–12 curricula, college and career expectations did not decrease; instead, they became increasingly difficult. All the while, Reading across the Curriculum strategies became the instructional focus for adolescent reading improvement. During this time, heavy doses of instructional *scaffolding* were being provided, including KWL charts, graphic organizers, and reciprocal teaching. Typically, the strategies remained in concrete form, as with the comprehension strategy, reciprocal teaching. For example, the goal for incorporating reciprocal teaching as a Reading across the Curriculum comprehension strategy typically did not evolve into its potential—a metacognitive process for students to use during independent reading as they self-monitored. Generally, reciprocal teaching remained a small-group discussion strategy, having minimal transfer outside the classroom, which limited its potential to impact independent reading outside the classroom.

While these instructional practices were occurring, *students were experiencing difficulty reading expository texts.* Shanahan and Shanahan (2008, p. 45) explained, "Although most students manage to master basic and even intermediate literacy skills, many never gain proficiency with the more advanced skills that would enable them to read challenging texts in science, history, literature, mathematics, or technology." This problem is exacerbated by students' limited access to informational texts of higher complexity due to the focus on narrative texts during elementary and early middle school.

How Well Are High School Graduates Able to Understand Complex Texts Today?

A gap with a rocky terrain now exists between skills possessed by high school graduates and those required for college and career demands. Students who are unable to read complex texts with understanding read those texts less often at a time when twenty-first-century life's complexities are growing. Increasing the gap in students' ability to comprehend complex text is the adolescent and adult interest in social media and its typically minimal demands for deeply developed concepts. As students' lives increasingly include being "adolescent citizen-journalists" by default, these *literacy surfers* are making impulsive decisions while skimming electronic texts and responding immediately to large audiences. Not only is this reality promoting surface-level thinking but also it can have grave impact on the lives of others.

How *Reasonable* Are the Increased Demands for Text Complexity?

In response to the urgency created by the text complexity gap, the Common Core State Standards have woven text complexity expectations into the fiber of every grade, beginning with grade 2, through the progression of standard 10, which defines grade-by-grade student progress in reading complex texts. In fact, the Common Core State Standards have made *increased text complexity one of the key requirements* in its document (CCSSI, 2010, Appendix A, p. 2). The document's appendixes, the anchor standards, together with the staircase format build student progress between grades and across school levels. Aligned curriculum and assessments for kindergarten through grade 12 will eventually support increased accountability for student proficiency with complex texts, transforming the vital, gradual changes in the Common Core State Standards into reasonable expectations.

How Can Disciplinary Literacy Instruction Redefine Deep Understanding to Close the Text Complexity Gap?

Students need to hit the ground running in middle and high school, being equipped with the informational knowledge and text know-how required to read complex texts with understanding. One day while walking through high school, students stopped me to say, "Remember how shy I was?" "I'm on the football team now." "Look at my new tattoo!" Later, walking through a class for at-risk readers, these students were not so happy to see me. Eyes lowered, hoods went up. A few days later, I returned to talk with these students. I asked them one question: "If you had one reading wish for children in elementary school today, what would that wish be?"

> Read MORE! Actually read. Teachers reading to you is not the same.

> Read more books because you'll need it. **I tell you this!**

> Read interesting books so you will not think that reading is boring.

A powerful dialogue continued. Listening carefully, it became clear that none of these suggestions requires new line items in our budgets. Adolescents simply need to read. Imagine if these students had been prepared to read discipline-specific texts as experts would: as you will see, when adolescents read as historians, scientists, mathematicians, literary critics, and musicians, they find their voice and eagerly partake in passionate dialogue with confidence.

Disciplinary literacy is a key to unlocking critical reading skills. McConachie and Petrosky (2010, p. 16) state, "Disciplinary literacy involves the use of reading, reasoning, investigating, speaking, and writing required to learn and form complex content knowledge appropriate to a particular discipline." As discussed previously, with text complexity being the "biggest issue" to resolve, especially for informational texts, disciplinary literacy provides teachers instructional procedures to guide informational learning while their students read a variety of complex texts. Not only did ACT (2006, p. 16) report that "performance on complex texts is the clearest differentiator in reading between students who are likely to be ready for college and those who are not," but it also later explained (ACT, 2010b, p. 5) that for *all students to achieve literacy skills in history/social studies, science, and technical subjects, as well as English language arts, states must ensure teachers use specific content knowledge to support students' ability to read, write, and communicate in different disciplines.*

In conjunction with the Common Core State Standards increasing text complexity expectations, recent disciplinary literacy studies and literature call for disciplinary-specific instruction to support increased adolescents' success with complex texts. But how are complex texts *different* from what students typically read for instruction? The three-part model for determining text difficulty and grade specifications for increasing text complexity, provided as a Common Core State Standards initial model to begin addressing text complexity, includes a qualitative dimension measurable by a human reader, a quantitative dimension measured by computer software, and considerations to match readers and tasks. Of these, the disciplinary literacy instructional model in this chapter incorporates two of the three aspects of text complexity: the *qualitative dimension* and the *reader and task considerations* (as indicated in the preceding text, the quantitative dimension of text complexity is typically measured with computer software and thus not discussed in detail here).

- **Qualitative dimensions** of text complexity include using informational texts that have an implicit purpose, written with norms of the discipline, including graphics providing information not conveyed in the text, and discipline-specific vocabulary. The text complexity expectations include knowledge demands such as providing a different perspective and a need for use of literacy actions, including synthesis, to understand specialized intertextuality.

- **Reader and task considerations** incorporate the teacher's professional judgment to match texts to students. It is important to note that highly motivated readers are willing to put effort into trying harder to read a text for understanding when it is about information they are excited to learn (CCSSI, 2010, Appendix A, p. 7). In English language arts classes, complex texts include literary nonfiction such as essays, speeches, memoirs, and biographies to read for the literary experience, not just for information. Rigor and complexity are offered in longer, informational texts across the disciplines.

The disciplinary literacy model described in this chapter is an instructional framework with discipline-specific processes for deep understanding of complex texts. It makes the statement that adolescents can no longer *not* be provided literacy instruction just because they are in high school—or because they are in science class, math class, history class, or music class. At a time when students are soon to be responsible for learning with texts of increasing complexity, teachers are being provided essentials for instruction to help them achieve that learning: the K–12 English language arts Common Core State Standards, including the 6–12 reading standards for literacy in history/social studies, science, and technical subjects; formative assessments aligned with the standards; and an instructional model aligned with the high expectations posed by the Common Core State Standards for literacy that is discipline specific. With the general comprehension strategies for Reading in the Content Areas, or Reading across the Curriculum, *being insufficient* to improve adolescents' comprehension of discipline-specific complex texts through middle and high school, as described later in this chapter, the qualitative study by researchers Shanahan and Shanahan (2008) explains that, for adolescents to read with deep understanding in different content areas, they need to be taught how to read and think in the ways experts read. The increasing information in the literature, including the Council of

Advancing Adolescent Literacy's (2010a) final report, *Reading in the Disciplines*, provides a strong foundation for discipline-specific instruction, which begs some fundamental questions on how studies in the literature can leap off policy pages and into the classroom:

- What does a model of disciplinary literacy instruction *look like?*

- In what ways are disciplinary literacy instruction and Reading across the Curriculum strategies *different?*

- What are specific *connections* between disciplinary literacy instruction and the Common Core State Standards?

What Does a Model of Disciplinary Literacy Instruction Look Like?

The seeds of disciplinary literacy instruction are widespread. Adolescent literacy achievement was identified as an area requiring intense attention as a priority goal (Council of Advancing Adolescent Literacy, 2010b, p. viii), and for good reason. While students' scores in grade 4 are among the world's best, grade 10 students fall to among the lowest. The No Child Left Behind legislation's focus on "reading first" for primary students had a positive impact, but it was not an inoculation against adolescent failure. Strong readers and communicators are vital for providing society with future scientists, engineers, and inventors. The constructs of disciplinary literacy are based on the premise that "skills taught in English…aren't sufficient to help students study math, science, history, or literature. Texts in these content areas have different structures, language conventions, vocabularies, and criteria for comprehension. Adolescents benefit from being let in on the secret" (Snow & Moje, 2010, p. 67). This chapter provides an overview of a process for disciplinary literacy instruction that lets the secret out.

The processes stem from recent, urgent research results: outcries voiced in *Time to Act* (Council of Advancing Adolescent Literacy, 2010b); and the Common Core State Standards' expectations to increase adolescent literacy achievement. They incorporate the premise provided in the literature that Reading across the Curriculum strategies have proven less successful than expected. Strategies once considered a cure for weak comprehension have provided mediocre results—and that was *before* the new expectations emerged for students to read texts of increased complexity. Yes, adolescents need increased rigor. But models of how to provide rigorous literacy instruction are needed. Demands for text complexity need direct, explicit instruction that can stand up to the increased expectations. Recently, the congruency between the demands of content-specific texts and the capacity of general strategies to support comprehension for adolescent readers has been questioned.

A study on the unique demand of content reading at the secondary level, compared to the instructional preparation provided to middle school students, has produced disconcerting results (Shanahan & Shanahan, 2008). The depth of this study was represented simply in the form of a pyramid that depicts the increasing specialization of literacy. Divided into three sections, the pyramid's segments include the following (Shanahan & Shanahan, 2008, p. 44):

Basic literacy—"Literacy skills represented here include decoding and knowledge of high-frequency words that underlie virtually all reading tasks." This segment is located at the wide bottom third of the pyramid. It represents the skills and abilities you use in every activity involved in literacy, such as sounding out words and reading words as a sentence.

Intermediate literacy—"Literacy skills represented in this section are common to many tasks, including generic comprehension strategies, common word meanings, and basic fluency." This section, which spans approximately grades 4 through 8, is represented in the middle of the pyramid and includes skills that are frequently used, such as reading complicated sentences.

Disciplinary literacy—"Literacy skills in this segment are specialized to history, science, mathematics, literature, or some other subject." This section is represented by the top of the pyramid. At this level, adolescents must know how to read not only a literature book but also a science book. The focus is on how to make meaning in a discipline and how to partake in the discipline-specific understanding and communication.

For the average student, disciplinary literacy instruction should begin at the middle level and continue through high school, although students in grades 4 through 12 are included in the changing literacy demands (Council of Advancing Adolescent Literacy, 2010b, p. 1). This promising model of instruction has been enriched by the contributions of Elizabeth Moje. Moje explains that teachers "need to engage in a set of practices. One is *drawing from the knowledge that kids have* and developing necessary knowledge. The second is *talking about text*. There's just not enough of that in our middle and high school classrooms. We don't talk about texts, with texts in front of kids' eyes. That's absolutely critical. A third is *synthesizing across text*. We don't come back around very well" (Moje, 2010, p. 74). The profound perceptions in the research and literature about current limitations of adolescent literacy compared with the potential of disciplinary literacy have provided reasons to reconsider adolescent literacy instruction. What instructional approach can enable adolescents to read a science text, or any text, as a scientist would? As a historian, a mathematician, a literary critic, a musician?

This chapter describes the four-stage text-investigation components of context, text, and two subtexts as they apply to discipline-specific text. This instructional model, designed to generate deep understanding in each discipline, may be used with standard curricular materials. However, incorporating authentic texts, such as those available on National Public Radio's (NPR, n.d.) Web site accompanying its "This I Believe" feature (http://thisibelieve.org/essay/), expands opportunities for students to comprehend complex texts that support the Common Core State Standards' expectations, state-level curricula documents, and district curricula. Documents similar to those available from NPR can be found at Our Documents (http://www.ourdocuments.gov/), USA.gov (www.USA.gov/Topics/Reference_Shelf/Documents.shtml), and the Library of Congress Digital Collections & Services (http://www.loc.gov/library/libarch-digital.html). These resources provide experiences with comprehending complex texts adolescents will encounter outside of school, during college, and throughout their careers and personal lives.

Each discipline's model contains four stages. The text-investigation questions *are specific for each discipline*, as they arose *from* the discipline. This chapter describes the text-investigation model for one discipline, history. The discipline models for reading as a scientist, a mathematician, a literary critic, and a musician are included in *Disciplinary Literacy: Redefining Deep Understanding and Leadership for 21st-Century Demands"* (Piercy & Piercy, 2011).

With a focus on literacy, it is important to question what information historians look for when reading texts, what information they question, and how they use what they find out from the text to shape their understanding and to contribute to historical interpretations. For example, when students read a history text, they generally see it as gathering factual information. Historians reading the same text do not see it as factual, but as an argument, so they recognize the author's perspective (Wineburg, 2001, p. 76). Historians, according to Wineburg, view a "text" (first stage) as a "speech act" rather than a series of words on a page. Therefore, a speech act is a communication created by a person(s) at a specific time in history. It is executed within a "context" (second stage) and fulfills a specific purpose or achieves a plan, such as an "impersonal subtext" (third stage) or a "personal subtext" (fourth stage), which arises from particular personal motives and intentions and which may have an impact on people and society.

These four stages provide meaningful interpretations of the text, the context of the text, and the two subtexts within texts of impersonal and personal. However, to read the subtext for understanding, students have to know there is one. As Wineburg's (2001, p. 80) seminal work explains, "When we abandon the controlled vocabulary of the comprehension passage and look not at schoolchildren but at people who read for a living, we wind up with a different image of comprehension." How might students incorporate specific questions generated by each stage of text investigation to develop sound interpretations? The four stages, broken down as Stages A, B, C, and D of the text investigation model that follows, provide a framework for reading as a historian, scientist, mathematician, literary critic, and musician. As mentioned earlier, history is used as the example throughout the chapter.

- **Context—Stage A:** Context is the situation that surrounds, influences, and clarifies the meaning in the text. When adolescents are able to consider the important background of a text, they are contextualizing, or acquiring information to generate a frame for understanding (Exhibit 8.1). Questions about the context provide details that may not have been overtly stated, which can lead to a more thorough understanding. The context of what is said impacts how we view the text. The questions in this stage include *When was this text made?* For example, when reading classes of high school at-risk readers read the primary document "Address to a Joint Session of Congress and the American People," by President George W. Bush (2001), they saw the date was September, 20, 2001. *What was happening that was important to society in that time frame?* Corroboration guided students as they read as historians to recognize that authoring a text does not always ascertain credibility, as with textbooks. *What was happening that was historically important? Who is the speaker? Why is he or she important?* For this text, September 20, 2001, was just days after the 9/11 terrorist attacks, and the president was addressing the U.S. Congress. Adolescents responded to the text-investigation questions by thinking critically, and dialogue unfolded about Americans realizing they were vulnerable on their own soil. The students passionately discussed that idea that not only were innocent American people targeted but also freedom was under attack. It is important to minimize/balance prior knowledge development so it

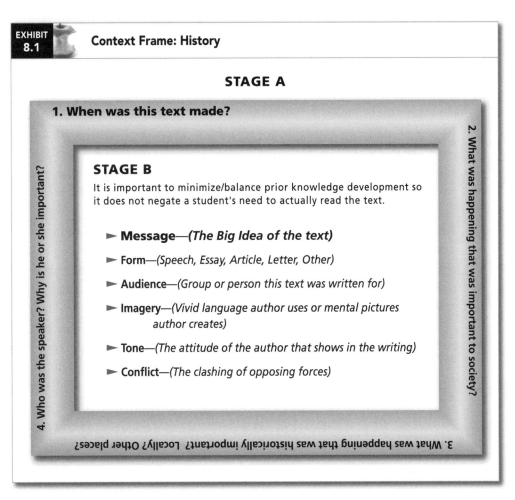

EXHIBIT 8.1

Context Frame: History

STAGE A

1. When was this text made?

2. What was happening that was important to society?

STAGE B

It is important to minimize/balance prior knowledge development so it does not negate a student's need to actually read the text.

- ▶ **Message**—*(The Big Idea of the text)*

- ▶ **Form**—*(Speech, Essay, Article, Letter, Other)*

- ▶ **Audience**—*(Group or person this text was written for)*

- ▶ **Imagery**—*(Vivid language author uses or mental pictures author creates)*

- ▶ **Tone**—*(The attitude of the author that shows in the writing)*

- ▶ **Conflict**—*(The clashing of opposing forces)*

4. Who was the speaker? Why is he or she important?

3. What was happening that was historically important? Locally? Other places?

does not negate a student's need to actually read the text. (At this point, you may need to remind yourself, as I did while in the classrooms, that these were at-risk readers now reading as historians.)

- **Text—Stage B:** Text refers to a writing that is composed of sentences linked together from thoughts. In this stage of the text-investigation model, questions must include an alignment between the purpose for the lesson as determined by the specific standard and objective, the complexity of the text, and questions that rigorously expect high cognitive demand of the student.

  The process of "unwrapping" the standards provides clarity about the level of cognitive demand needed in the questions and tasks. <u>Expecting cognitive demand of the reader through discipline-specific questions, including textual evidence, increases student capacity to demonstrate deeper understanding of increasingly complex texts.</u>

  Examples of Stage B questions about the text include requiring students to analyze conflict evident in the text by providing three points of conflict relevant to the time period. Request textual evidence for Stage B questions. Proceeding with additional questions about the Address to Congress, examples include: *What is the author's message?* In essence, *what is the Big Idea?* Considering this question alone requires much critical thinking. Lines blur between the four stages, as when students characterized the president's message as being intended to give hope. The message of the text is determined by the ways the author prefers to communicate. *What form did the writer choose to present the message? Who is the intended audience?* The students were able to dig deeper into the text by understanding that although this speech was given to Congress, the audience included all Americans so they would know to stand strong in their beliefs that the United States would not collapse. The students discussed the idea that the intended audience also included the terrorists. *What imagery has been included to engage the reader and depict the author's less obvious ideas? What was the author's tone, or attitude, revealed in the writing?* The elements are all connected to achieve the author's message, and they must be analyzed together to describe the *conflict* with understanding (Exhibit 8.1). Too frequently, adolescent readers' understanding is cut short by ending their ride of the text at the end of the written word highway, missing the side roads filled with deeper understanding beyond their view. It is through specific textual evidence combined within the curves of subtle, unwritten thoughts that compelling aspects of the text are revealed. After the meaning of the text and the details of the context are considered, comprehension is enhanced by looking closely at what is beneath the surface of the text, in the subtext.

- **Impersonal subtext—Stage C:** Reading between the lines occurs during Stage C in the disciplinary literacy's text-investigation model. It is impersonal because the reader deduces the plan and purpose of the author based on support from the context and text while trying to maintain a neutral stance. During this stage, while the reader determines the author's *purpose* and *plan,* he then digs further to look behind the lines for the motives and intentions of the author. Understanding subtext allows the reader to achieve this type of close reading. With the impersonal subtext, the reader incorporates *inferring* and *evaluating* to uncover the unstated messages by using the subtext guide (Exhibit 8.2) to glean the implications beyond the written text. Investigation questions at the impersonal subtext level include, *What does the author plan to do or gain?* In the case of President Bush, what students heard in his address was that he wanted retaliation, or "to get back." *What larger plan might the author have?* The speech to Congress was a request to the world. *What purpose did the author have in writing this text? Was it achieved?* The rich dialogue the students engaged in about the president's speech led to achieving the instructional goal of comprehending complex text with deep understanding.

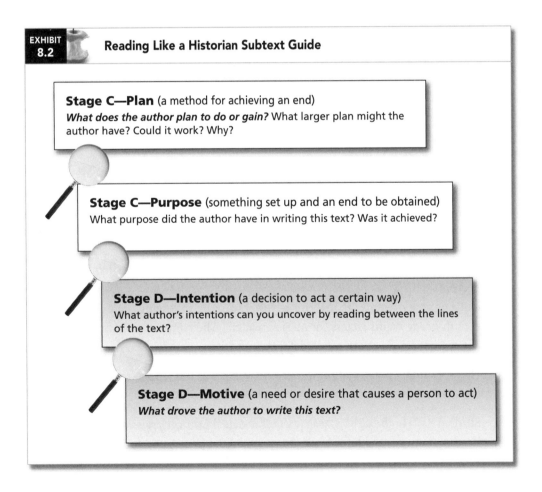

EXHIBIT 8.2

Reading Like a Historian Subtext Guide

Stage C—Plan (a method for achieving an end)
What does the author plan to do or gain? What larger plan might the author have? Could it work? Why?

Stage C—Purpose (something set up and an end to be obtained)
What purpose did the author have in writing this text? Was it achieved?

Stage D—Intention (a decision to act a certain way)
What author's intentions can you uncover by reading between the lines of the text?

Stage D—Motive (a need or desire that causes a person to act)
What drove the author to write this text?

- **Personal subtext—Stage D**: The deepest level of the disciplinary literacy's text-investigation model is the investigation of the subtext at the personal level. Meaning can be uncovered that the author did not intend to reveal. Having inadvertently become woven within the text, the reader takes on attributes of an archaeologist while *synthesizing* and *judging* to reconstruct bits of meaning that portray the author's *motives,* desires that cause someone to act, and *intentions,* determinations to act in a particular way. Continuing with the example of the president's speech to Congress, students understood that threatening terrorists was a primary intention of the speech. The motives beneath the words may center on the author, revealing bias, or center on the reader, acting as a catalyst for shifts in personal views, enlightened understanding, or highlighted issues that may impact society or lead to further research. Whatever the author's target, motive gives way to intention, the desire to act. Investigation questions at the personal subtext level include, *What author's intentions can you uncover by reading between the lines of the text? What drove the author to write this text?*

The components of the impersonal subtext, plan and purpose (Stage C), together with the personal subtext, motive and intention (Stage D), establish an interlocking scaffold surrounding the text. Although there is a relationship between the author's motive and intention and the purpose that fuels the plan of their writing, there is not a linear order in how students address these four elements of the subtext. Think of the depth our students are empowered to comprehend when they frame the author's message in the text by examining the context, trace the specific purpose and detect the plan (impersonal subtext), disclose the author's intention for writing (personal subtext), and reconstruct the motive behind it all.

The key to success is the noticeable, engaging student dialogue as teachers and students become learners together. As called for by Moje (2010, p. 74), talking about text is absolutely critical. We need to increase talking about texts with students while the text is in front of their eyes. Whether the context for learning was an urban setting or a suburban classroom, and despite the varied capacities of students, they enthusiastically participated in classroom discourse when instruction was connected to their capacity to think deeply.

As an example of students reading as *historians,* the following dialogue excerpt is from a ninth-grade reading class for at-risk readers. The complex text they were reading was a current article about a foiled Taliban attack.

History subtext investigation (Stage D): "What was the reporter's intention for writing?"

Student 1: "He thought it was a shocking deal and others should know. Reading between the lines, the author is scared. He is scared for the kids."

Student 2: "I do not think he cares about the kids. He wants to make a difference and get more people in the army to help, by making us aware. If he really cared, he would do more for kids."

A dynamic level of dialogue is possible when discussion stems from understanding. Classroom investigations of complex texts, including authentic documents with discipline-specific text-investigation questions, stir passion in adolescents, including those identified as at-risk learners. Disciplinary literacy instruction results in adolescents becoming "self-determining" (Pink, 2009, p. 71) in their literacy lives and beyond.

In What Ways Are Disciplinary Literacy Instruction and Reading across the Curriculum Strategies Different?

The preceding text-investigation model provides adolescents with direct connections to text during reading. It does not require an additional layer of comprehension strategies, which can deter students' focus from the text. Walking through classrooms with walls covered with posters of strategy checklists such as "FATP-P," "Stop-Ask-Fix" word attack strategies, and "Strategies for During Reading," it is difficult to not be distracted. Researchers McKeown, Beck, and Blake (2009), in fact, recommend that strategy teaching be coupled with attending directly to the text. Snow and Moje (2010, p. 67) concur: "Making readers aware of skills they automatically employ or strategies they don't need may actually interfere with comprehension." Is this stance a departure from decades of focus on comprehension strategy instruction? Yes, but it does not imply that strategy instruction is not valuable in any situation but rather that strategy instruction is not generalizable to learning content-specific material, as is the current practice. Additionally, an article in *Education Week* proposes that pedagogical approaches typically preferred by English teachers are not close, analytical readings of assigned works but rather nonanalytical approaches such as a personal response, including when interpreting literary nonfiction (Stotsky, 2010, p. 25).

Explaining the differences between content strategies and disciplinary literacy instruction, Shanahan (2010, p. 43) said, "If you go into most content area reading texts, they are full of strategies and techniques—the Frayer model, how to brainstorm, QAR, three-level guides, and so on," yet generalizable strategies do not support reading that needs to be tailored to a specific discipline. Traditional strategies and disciplinary literacy processes are different approaches. When adolescents' eyes meet text, those children need to be *engaged* in the text. Hattie (2009, p. 36) agrees: "It is not the knowledge or ideas, but the learner's construction of the knowledge and the ideas that is critical." Literacy actions including *summarizing* or *evaluating* while also *questioning* lead to deeper thinking about what the author is saying. The following overview for literacy actions provides an instructional framework for how skills, strategies, and processes support twenty-first-century learning needs.

Typically, reading instruction has emphasized comprehension skills. *Skills* involve a single step intended to be used automatically without conscious intention, as in the literal recall of information. On the other hand, *strategies* are composed of multiple steps applied intentionally and megacognitively (Shanahan, 2007). Yet, skills, as viewed by the Partnership for 21st Century Skills (P-21, 2009), incorporate creativity, innovation, critical thinking, and problem solving plus communication and collaboration. These skills, as defined under the organization's 21st Century Rainbow Framework for Student Outcomes, are substantially different from the traditional single-step concept of skills. *Process* is another concept involved in reading comprehension. David Hyerle (2009, p. xiii) explains that process is "the highest form of learning and the most appropriate base for curriculum change." He continues, "It is through process that we can employ knowledge not merely as a composite of information, but as a system for continuous learning." Notice how *different* the various definitions of skills are, while the definitions for processes and skills, as defined by P-21, are similar.

Even when defining skills, strategies, and processes, why do edges of meaning remain fuzzy? In many cases, definitions and labels arose from past twentieth-century expectations. So where does that leave us today? Wineburg (2001, p. viii) explains that complex meaning is acquired not through labels but through *a depth of understanding*. He proposes that the act of labeling is not an attempt to understand the concepts behind the label but instead leads to discussions of pedagogy. While our quest for understanding literacy must accept complexity, beginning with the fundamental definitions, the lack of agreed-upon literacy definitions should not render us bewildered. Accepting complexity means literacy must be grounded in *common understandings*, unlike simple labeling. Therefore, rather than entering into the pedagogical debate over the correct labeling of specific skills, strategies, or process categories, this chapter refers to the literacy components identified here as literacy actions (Piercy & Piercy, 2011). Each skill, strategy, and process serves a variety of important purposes for the reader, but the concept of literacy actions respects complexity by focusing on a *depth of understanding*.

Which literacy actions must be taught to provide our students capacity for engaging in and understanding such rapidly evolving complexities of life? The literacy action frameworks present sets of specific actions used to increase understanding. Such actions, or verbs, are used in ACT questions, the Common Core State Standards, and assessments. Combining these actions into sets of actions leads to deeper understanding, and they have proven successful in taxonomies and research. For each action, the following questions are addressed:

- *What does the literary action of ___ look like? Why is it an important twenty-first-century skill?* Here, the literary action is first presented not as a definition but as a relevant true story example of a real-life application. In this way, students can actively construct their own understanding.

- *What is ___?* Definitions are provided after the real-life account, including "student-friendly" versions for differentiation.

- *As a result of ___, what will learners understand, be able to do, and explore to improve the quality of their twenty-first-century lives?* Examples of how to naturally integrate each literacy action into instruction are included.

- *As a result of ___, what will twenty-first-century leaders understand, be able to do, and explore?*

Literacy Action Frameworks

EVALUATING

What Does *Evaluating* Look Like?

Why is evaluating a twenty-first-century literacy life skill?

Learning objective: *You will be able to identify and use evaluating to read complex text and specific words and phrases with independence and confidence.*

From the raging Shenandoah River 600 feet below, young voices could be heard yelling "9-1-1." Hearing the faint pleas, we dialed the now universal crisis number. Soon, our deck became a command post for coordinating communication among the fire and rescue squad, Hostage and Evacuation Assistance Team, CSX Railroad, and medivac helicopters. Ten children's lives grasped the last particles of hope from the edges of river rocks as the powerful river pulled their weakened bodies from the rocks protruding toward the nighttime sky. What composed the survival lifeline connecting panicked voices and the helicopter's rescue baskets that saved the children from slowly slipping into the darkness of the river? The decision of the children to simultaneously yell "9-1-1" rather than the less discriminate call of "help" allowed this crisis number to permeate the thunderous sound of the waterfalls and cross the distance up the mountain into the consciousness of our quiet Sunday evening on the deck.

Headlines read, "Shenandoah Rescue" as the article described "a miracle rescue." The miracle of this rescue stemmed from the evaluation skills of the helicopter pilot. Though being the person in the most precarious situation of all emergency personnel that evening, the pilot provided the only voice of reason, as he became the one mitigating the situation to provide necessary information for appropriate actions. "We need to be accountable," he calmly said through the speaker for all standing in the safety of the command post to hear. "How many people need to be rescued? Let me be perfectly clear. Did the child who was hanging from the rock make it to safety?" While operating the treacherous nighttime rescue just above the falls between the Blue Ridge Mountains, the pilot's voice equaled the power of his searchlight as he calmly and steadfastly demonstrated evaluation elements that appraised the situation and selected next steps that would result in the safe rescue of all 10 children.

1. **In what ways did the pilot's ability to *evaluate* the precarious nighttime rescue contribute to saving all the children?**

2. **Describe the importance of the evaluation skills displayed by the children and the pilot. How do they compare?**

3. **Explain how *you* use evaluating in your daily life.**

What is evaluating?

To evaluate is to take a stand or make a decision. It is the learner's or leader's ability to appraise a situation and then make a choice based on standards. Evaluating is an attempt to increase understanding. Evaluation is applied to research. Evaluating includes being able to argue, appraise, assess, conclude, coordinate, critique, discriminate, justify, prioritize, rank, recommend, value, make a judgment, fix a value, weigh evidence.

Student-friendly terms for differentiating meaning of evaluating: check, support, understand, question

---

As a result of evaluating, what will *learners* understand, be able to do, and explore to improve the quality of their twenty-first-century lives?

To evaluate is to consider criteria to make a decision. Evaluation includes being able to justify the decision by providing solid support for and/or a defense of the decision. Examples of evaluating include participating in a debate, determining appropriate information to include in a composition, and designing a plan for a project. Also, evaluating is a particularly vital life skill for adolescents because they are faced with personal, potentially life-threatening choices from peer pressure.

As a result of evaluating, what will twenty-first-century *leaders* understand, be able to do, and explore?

A leader who incorporates evaluating into his disciplined practice will be able to appraise any situation after collecting all appropriate information. Determining appropriate steps, the leader will make decisions by selecting actions that support the intended outcome and result in satisfactory resolutions. Leaders possess the capacity to act. During the four-hour Shenandoah River rescue, leadership changed hands many times as the situation evolved and more information was gathered. Yet, it was the pilot's capacity to evaluate that provided the strongest leadership among the collective brave group. The ability to lead is demonstrated by a person's ability to evaluate the situation by stepping up and assuming command or standing down and accepting directions. Leaders evaluate situations and take personal actions that demonstrate their ability to lead, follow, or step out of the way as dictated by the situation.

When providing instruction on literacy actions within the context of life, adolescents recognize and make connections that transfer into decisions.

What Are Specific Connections between Disciplinary Literacy Instruction and the Common Core State Standards?

There are three dynamic connections between disciplinary literacy instruction and the Common Core State Standards' intended outcomes for student learning (Exhibit 8.3).

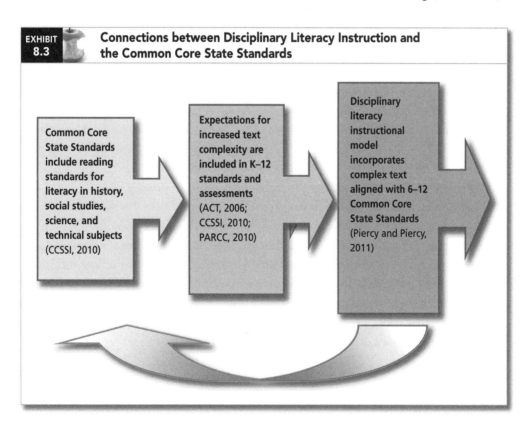

EXHIBIT 8.3   Connections between Disciplinary Literacy Instruction and the Common Core State Standards

Common Core State Standards include reading standards for literacy in history, social studies, science, and technical subjects (CCSSI, 2010)

Expectations for increased text complexity are included in K–12 standards and assessments (ACT, 2006; CCSSI, 2010; PARCC, 2010)

Disciplinary literacy instructional model incorporates complex text aligned with 6–12 Common Core State Standards (Piercy and Piercy, 2011)

As shown in Exhibit 8.3, the three connections between disciplinary literacy and the Common Core State Standards are the following:

- The Common Core Standards include reading standards for literacy in the contents of history/social studies, science, and technical subjects.

- Specific text complexity expectations for grade 2 through grade 12 are established in the Common Core State Standards. These are depicted in the anchor standards and standard 10 at every grade level. Text complexity expectations are "a fundamental aspect" of PARCC's (2010) literacy component.

- Disciplinary literacy instruction incorporates complex text with questions of high cognitive demand in the four-stage text-investigation model.

The body of literature studying text complexity is enticing to read (maybe not quite to the James Patterson level, but if you're reading this text, chances are you agree). The following descriptions synthesize the literature with emphasis on Shanahan and Shanahan's (2008) study to support adolescents in reading discipline-specific complex text, including primary documents. The purpose of guiding adolescents to read and think as experts is not to have them focus on specific content but to ensure they understand how to explore text, including everyday text, through the lens of an expert. The text-investigation questions, also discipline specific, tailor students' focus on each discipline so they are able to grasp the content. Overviews of instructional models for reading as a historian, scientist, and mathematician follow.

Reading as a historian. For historians, contextualizing is important, but it is a difficult skill for students because background knowledge in history is limited. That being the case, it is becoming an important life skill for students to filter the large amounts of information available to them for reading and responding quickly. Previewing the text using specific questions for each discipline provides historians with information about the author or source regarding credibility and bias to inform them of how to best approach the text. The existence of history textbooks makes the expert history skill of contextualizing difficult because of the large scope of history being compiled into one text, which may present a limited or perhaps only one perspective. Errors of fact in textbooks are also a concern in a field dependent on actual events. In one state, dozens of errors were identified in two history textbooks (Sieff, 2011). It seems the need for critical text-investigation questions is increasing. Historians use literacy action skills such as *judging* to interpret history and *analyzing* while reading documents. They consider purpose and the subtext to determine the author's perspective so it can be weighted among the factors considered when reading between the lines to determine the intention and motive of the source or author, and thus his credibility.

Examples of aligned connections between the reading as a historian instructional model (offered in this chapter) and the English language arts (ELA) Common Core State Standards are depicted in Exhibit 8.4.

Reading as a scientist. Because science is one of the disciplines highlighted in the 2010a ACT report for having more than half of the 2010 high school graduates interested in the discipline (science) *not* meet the college readiness benchmark, suggestions for increased literacy for science complex texts are described here. In the case of scientists, reading is a process of transforming information into deeper understanding and scientific questions worthy of further research. This *analysis* leads to full understanding and stems from scientists' confidence in being able to read and comprehend scientific text.

| EXHIBIT 8.4 | Redefining Deep Understanding for Text Complexity Demands: History |

Reading as a Historian Text-Investigation Questions for Adolescent Learners	Examples of Common Core State Standards Literacy Connections in History/Social Studies
Context and Text Investigations What was happening that was important to society? What was happening that was historically important? When was this text written? Who is the speaker, author, or source, and why is he or she important? Corroborate evidence from at least two other texts to support the Big Idea within this text. Analyze conflict evident in the text by providing three points of conflict relevant to the time period. Integrate data to visually support three points cited in the text. After reading an original speech, evaluate how the outcome of the message was changed by analyzing two or more edits made by the author. What is the Big Idea? How does this text compare with, or corroborate, others I have read, and with my prior knowledge? Who is the audience? Describe the conflict or argument. What is the tone? What is the form of the text? How is it integrated with digital texts? **Subtext Investigations** What does the author plan to do or gain? What is his or her point of view? What larger plan might the author have? What purpose did the author have in writing this text? Was it achieved? What author intentions can you uncover by reading between the lines of the text? What drove the author to write this text?	**ELA Literacy in History/Social Studies 6-12** 6-8: Distinguish among fact, *opinion, and reasoned **judgment*** in a text. 9-10: Cite specific textual evidence to support **analysis** of primary and secondary sources, *attending to such features as the date and origin* of the information. 11-12: Cite specific textual evidence to support **analysis** of primary and secondary sources, *connecting insights gained from specific details to an understanding of the text as a whole.* 6-8: Identify aspects of a text that reveal an author's point of view or purpose (e.g. loaded language, inclusion or avoidance of particular facts). 6-8: Integrate visual information (e.g. in charts, graphs, photographs, videos, or maps) with other information in print and digital texts. *6-12 Anchor: Range and Level of Text Complexity* *Read and comprehend complex literary and information texts independently and proficiently.*

Despite the occasional emergence of questionable texts, such as the recent assertion that a medical journal report associating autism with vaccinations was inaccurate, scientists do not typically focus on bias or motive. Scientists visualize while reading and may *create* thought experiments. They generalize experimental findings to other experiments based on hard facts, not empathy and inference as does a literary critic. Scientist literacy is based on "truth," unlike that of historians, who accept that "historical truth" requires interpretation. Scientists also generalize their knowledge to news of the day, such as when reading an article on the greenhouse gas effect. Research is transformed into facts, which prompt further scientific prediction and questions. Science educators may promote the detailed pursuit of science alone, without focusing on the elements of scientific literacy, resulting in a void in adolescents' perception of science and its connection with their lives. Scientists "do" science daily by *applying* it to their daily thinking. Likewise, adolescents need to do scientific thinking daily, just as they do math. When students read a text, they raise a question and may create a thought experiment on the computer, which can yield data. This data can become a response to a scientific question or dilemma.

Examples of aligned connections between the reading as a scientist instructional model and the ELA Common Core State Standards are depicted in Exhibit 8.5.

Reading as a mathematician. With math being one of the two disciplines highlighted in the 2010a ACT report for having more than half of the 2010 high school graduates interested in the discipline (mathematics) *not* meet the college readiness benchmark, suggestions for increasing math literacy are provided. Reading, for mathematicians, is fundamentally different than it is for historians. How could a mathematician be concerned about author bias if (1) the truth is in the text —it just is—and (2) mathematicians may not know or really care who wrote the text. Mathematicians read for the truth, yet error detection is key. As a universal language, mathematics and its equations and formulas are as clear to its readers in Seoul as they are in New York. Mathematicians look for meaning and connections to *analyze* and tell the "number story" residing beneath the surface. New questions arise from meaningful number stories. Mathematicians read closely—that is, they read the text again and again. Specific meanings of words are understood—and if not, resources are used, because it is important to "get it right"—every word.

Math is about accuracy, not about an author's opinion. Mathematical proofs can provide pleasure when an intriguing idea connects to the formula leading to completion, just as a measure of music can add completeness to a beautiful melody. Not merely a process to plug in numbers, math is a way of thinking.

Say you are conducting a walk-through of a ninth-grade lesson. The focus for the lesson is "reading math!" Do you ask, "reading what?" Teaching literacy in math requires an understanding of how to think about discipline-specific texts. Questions needing to be considered include, *Who will likely struggle with this text? What are the special demands*

EXHIBIT 8.5	Redefining Deep Understanding for Text Complexity Demands: Science

Reading as a Scientist Text-Investigation Questions for Adolescent Learners	Examples of Common Core State Standards Literacy Connections in Science and Technical Subjects
Context and Text Investigations What area of scientific research forms the backdrop for the text? What scientific facts were transformed from the research? Cite specific textual evidence. Who is the author? What scientific expertise does he have? How might the message transform into further research? What scientific questions are raised by this text? Provide three examples by integrating data and charts. What scientific dilemma is raised by the text? Incorporating intertexuality, provide data from three additional sources to confirm accuracy. **Subtext Investigations** What scientific question or dilemma should be explored further? Visualize and describe a thought experiment that could be developed to answer the question or resolve the dilemma. How is the answer to this scientific question likely to change my life or generalize to the lives of others? How might the resolution of this scientific dilemma impact my life or the lives others?	**ELA Literacy in Science and Technical Subjects 6-12** 6-8: Cite specific *textual evidence to support* **analysis** *of science and technical texts.* 9-10: Cite specific *textual evidence to support* **analysis** of science and technical text, attending to the precise *details of explanation of descriptions.* 11-12: Cite specific textual evidence to support **analysis** of science and technical texts, attending to important distinctions the author makes and *to any gaps or inconsistencies in the account.* 6-8: **Analyze** the author's purpose in providing an explanation, describing a procedure, or discussing an experiment in a text. 9-10: **Analyze** the author's purpose in providing an explanation, describing a procedure, or discussing an experiment in a text, defining the question the author seeks to address. 11-12: **Analyze** the author's purpose in providing an explanation, describing a procedure, or discussing an experiment in a text, identifying important issues that remain unresolved. *6-12 Anchor: Range and Level of Text Complexity* *Read and comprehend complex literary and information texts independently and proficiently.*

of this discipline? As the literature explains, reading math requires the student to read differently than for any other discipline. Students need to incorporate close reading, an intense consideration of each word, because error detection and precision of understanding result in correct answers. Reading as a mathematician, students read and reread math passages. They reread math frequently compared to reading a novel.

Examples of aligned connections between the reading as a mathematician instructional model and the ELA Common Core State Standards are depicted in Exhibit 8.6.

The disciplinary literacy instruction model offered in this chapter incorporates text complexity considerations. By providing an instructional model for literacy in five disciplines, teachers will be able to begin to transfer recent research into the classroom. This model is designed to be used with informational primary documents, essays, speeches, memoirs, and biographies in different disciplines. These texts provide opportunities for intertexuality instruction.

Conclusion

The pace of change during the first decade of the twenty-first century altered traditional understanding of reading comprehension. Today, reading comprehension skills are blending into a Web-hosted database with access to unlimited data points and suggested literacy processes, practices, interventions, and models. The Carnegie Corporation report *Time to Act* (Council of Advancing Adolescent Literacy, 2010b) recommends that state standards in all subject areas ensure their content standards make explicit the challenges of reading and writing within each discipline. This recommendation is supported by P-21 (2009), demonstrating how twenty-first-century skills can be integrated into the core subjects. Also, the Common Core State Standards Initiative for K–12 English language arts (2010) includes a companion document, "Reading Standards for Literacy in History/Social Studies and Science and Technical Subjects 6–12," that explicitly requires "shared responsibility for literacy." No longer can instruction of reading, writing, and speaking be disaggregated and segregated to one specific curricular area or identified as the responsibility of a sole source provider of specific content knowledge.

Literacy is under the urgency spotlight; school and system leaders must provide clarity and direction. Scientifically based, reading-researched strategies published by the National Reading Panel (2000) were developed to produce efficient adequate yearly progress results. They made significant contributions to the field of reading. Today, as reading adapts to numerous cultures, migrates between populations, and resides on multimedia platforms, it merges with the richly blended components of literacy. In short, world changes outside of the school world are raising expectations for student achievement within the school. However, as Reeves (2009, p. 116) explains, instructional leadership "does not mean very much if the leaders and teachers hold vague and inconsistent views of the most essential elements of effective instruction in literacy."

| EXHIBIT 8.6 | Redefining Deep Understanding for Text Complexity Demands: Mathematics |

Reading as a Mathematician Text-Investigation Questions for Adolescent Learners	Common Core State Standards for Mathematics
Context and Text Investigations What areas of mathematics are connected to this text? What deeper meaning is revealed in the text? What do I predict will be the author's message? What ideas or claims in the text can be explored mathematically? What is the number story? What does the math reveal or tell me about connections and relationships between the text and the number story? **Subtext Investigations** How does the mathematical analysis, or the number story, support or refute the author's ideas? How does the number story deepen your understanding of this text? Based on your understanding of this point, should this text be changed? How would you summarize the concepts presented? What new questions does the number story raise? How might these be investigated mathematically?	**Mathematics Standards—Grade 6–High School** Gr. 6-The Number System-8. Solve real-world and mathematical problems by graphing points in all four quadrants of the coordinate plane. Include use of coordinates and absolute value to find distances between points with the same first coordinate or the same second coordinate (p. 43). Gr. 6-Expressions and Equations-2. Write, read, and **evaluate** expressions in which letters stand for numbers (p. 43). Gr. 6-Expressions and Equations-2-b. Identify parts of an expression using mathematical terms, (sum, term product, factor, quotient, coefficient) (p. 44). Gr. 6-Statistics and Probablility-5. Summarize numerical data sets in relation to their context such as by: a. Reporting the number of observations (p. 45). Gr. 8-Geometry-3. Describe the effect of dilations, translations, rotations, and reflections on two-dimensional figures using coordinates (p. 56). Gr. 8-Geometry-5. Use information arguments to establish facts about the angle sum and exterior angle of triangles, about the angles created when parallel lines are cut by a transversal, and the angle-angle criterion for similarity of triangles (p. 56). High School-Making Inferences and Justifying Conclusions-3. Recognize the purposes of and differences among sample surveys, experiments, and observational studies; explain how randomization relates to each (p. 81).

Therefore, returning to the question that began this literacy journey, what begs to be asked must extend beyond reading comprehension performance on assessments to indicators of success as evidenced in learners and leaders *understanding, applying, and exploring* literacy actions to address the needs of complex twenty-first-century lives. The urgent questions that must be asked to improve today's students' comprehension requirements are as follows.

Literacy Questions for Twenty-first-Century Lives

1. *To increase student capacity* (compared to proficiency) *to understand and apply* (compared to just answer) *the evolving* (compared to fixed, scientifically based, previously identified) *complexities of literacy* (compared to isolated skills) *throughout their twenty-first-century lives, how can literacy be taught for understanding?*

2. *How can instruction honor unique disciplinary literacy demands of specific content?*

Notice how these questions build on current expectations while expanding connections. Questions asked by leaders during compelling conversations with teachers and Data Teams, and questions generated from these conversations, have a profound impact on teachers' decisions and their students' learning. Honest and sometimes disconcerting conversations about expectations for adolescents have been initiated by the Common Core State Standards. The Common Core have pointed out that a serious gap exists between K–12 reading ability and college and career reading requirements and that the current text complexity measurement tools are imperfect, and they call for improvements to make text complexity considerations a part of everyday classroom instruction. While current measurements of complexity are challenging, the closure of the gap has begun. We must now develop awareness of the importance of text complexity and begin to include it as part of the professional conversation and instructional planning process.

Fortunately, the adolescent literacy research, literature, national reports, and policies are opening minds and hearts to a different future for instruction. Yet, the questions posed by Wineburg (2001, p. 81), "the questions we most need to answer—what would teachers have to do differently to create history classrooms, where real learning takes place? How would teachers learn to teach in these different ways?" are rarely addressed by these reports. These questions hold true for all content areas. The instructional models discussed in this chapter can provide explicit instructional direction through their focus on the unique qualities of content-specific text, which incorporate considerations of knowledge demands and the matching of text with readers' motivation. Reducing scaffolding at the end of grade bands while expanding students' capacity to apply text-investigation questions increases students' deep understanding. Text-investigation questions complement students' use of literacy actions, such as synthesizing and reasoning. As adolescents enthusiastically read as scientists, historians, mathematicians, literary critics, and musicians, they are able to deeply understand and make connections in all complexities—whether within text or throughout life.

Educational direction has reached a juncture once again. Are we prepared to acknowledge the approaching literacy crisis stemming from the need to educate students in two languages—those of the pre- and the postdigital worlds? Can K–12 educators wait another 20 years to address the gap that exists between the status quo and providing students with literacy qualities essential for living in a transparent, connected world? Let's listen to our teachers' voices as we approach this rocky gap so we can encourage them to lift their heads with confidence.

Acknowledgments

Excerpts included in this chapter are from *Disciplinary Literacy: Redefining Deep Understanding and Leadership for 21st-Century Demands* (Lead + Learn Press, 2011), coauthored by William Piercy. Brian Wienholt and Lori Thompson were contributors to that book.

References

ACT. (2006). *Reading between the lines: What the ACT reveals about college readiness in reading.* Iowa City, IA: ACT.

ACT. (2010a). *The condition of college and career readiness report.* Iowa City, IA: ACT.

ACT. (2010b). *A first look at the Common Core and college and career readiness report.* Iowa City, IA: ACT.

Ainsworth, L., & Viegut, D. (2006). *Common formative assessments: How to connect standards-based instruction and assessment.* Thousand Oaks, CA: Corwin.

Almeida, L., & Ainsworth, A. (2009). *Engaging classroom assessments: The making standards work series.* Englewood, CO: The Leadership and Learning Center.

Bush, G. W. (2001). Address to a joint session of Congress and the American people. Retrieved from http://www.law.ou.edu/ushistory/bush-addr-jsc-nation-9-20-01.shtml

Common Core State Standards Initiative (CCSSI). (2010). *Common Core State Standards for English language arts & literacy, mathematics, history/social studies, science, and technical subjects.* Washington, DC: Council of Chief State School Officers & National Governors Association.

Council of Advancing Adolescent Literacy. (2010a). *Reading in the disciplines: The challenges of adolescent literacy.* New York, NY: Carnegie Corporation of New York.

Council of Advancing Adolescent Literacy. (2010b). *Time to act: An agenda for advancing adolescent literacy for college and career success.* New York, NY: Carnegie Corporation of New York.

Hattie, J. (2009). *Visible learning: A synthesis of over 800 meta-analyses relating to achievement.* New York, NY: Routledge.

Hyerle, D. (2009). *Visual tools for transforming information into knowledge* (2nd ed.). Thousand Oaks CA: Corwin Press.

Jacobs, V., Shanahan, T., Shanahan, J., Draper, R., Conley, M., Moje, E., Overby, M., Tysvaer, N., ... Lewis, W. (2008). Various articles. *Harvard Educational Review, 78*(1).

Library of Congress Digital Collection & Services. (n.d.). Retrieved from http://www.loc.gov/index.html

Marzano, R. (2003). *What works in schools: Translating research into action.* Alexandria, VA: ASCD.

Marzano, R., McNulty, B., & Waters, T. (2005). *School leadership that works: From research to results.* Alexandria, VA: ASCD; Aurora, CO: Mid-Continent Research for Education and Learning.

McConachie, S., & Petrosky, A. (2010). *Content matters: A disciplinary literacy approach to improving student learning.* San Francisco, CA: Jossey-Bass.

McKeown, M. G., Beck, I. L., & Blake, R. G. (2009). Rethinking reading comprehension instruction: A comparison of instruction for strategies and content approaches. *Reading Research Quarterly, 44*(3), 218–253.

MetaMetrics, Inc. (2011). The lexile framework for reading. Retrieved from http://lexile.com/about-lexile/grade-equivalent/grade-equivalent-chart/

Moje, E. (2010). "But my English teacher said...": Supporting students in how to read and write in the natural and social sciences. In Y. Lyons, A. R. Marri, and A. Rivet (Eds.), *Proceedings of the Content Area Literacy Conference 2010: Teachers College Columbia University: Program in Reading Specialist, Social Studies Education, and Science Education.* New York, NY: Teachers College, Columbia University and Carnegie Corporation of New York.

National Public Radio. (n.d.). This I believe. Retrieved from http://thisibelieve.org/essays/featured/

National Reading Panel. (2000, December). *Report of the National Reading Panel: Teaching children to read: An evidence-based assessment of the scientific research literature on reading and its implications for reading instruction.* Jessup, MD: National Institute for Literacy.

Our Documents. (n.d.). Retrieved from http://www.ourdocuments.gov/index.php?flash=true&

Partnership for the Assessment of Readiness for College and Careers. (2010, September). *PARCC Consortium awarded Race to the Top assessment funds.* Washington, DC: Achieve.

Partnership for 21st Century Skills (P-21). (2009). *The mile guide: Milestones for improving learning and education.* Tucson, AZ: Partnership for 21st Century Skills.

Piercy, T., & Piercy, W. (2011). *Disciplinary literacy: Redefining deep understanding and leadership for 21st-century demands.* Englewood, CO: Lead + Learn Press.

Pink, D. (2009). *Drive.* New York, NY: Riverhead Books.

Reeves, D. B. (2009). *Leading change in your school: How to conquer myths, build commitment, and get results.* Alexandria, VA: ASCD.

Schmoker, M. (2006). *Results now: How we can achieve unprecedented improvement in teaching and learning.* Alexandria, VA: ASCD.

Schmoker, M. (2011). *Focus: Elevating the essentials to radically improve student learning.* Alexandria, VA: ASCD.

Shanahan, T. (2007, December 7). Teaching reading comprehension [PowerPoint slide presentation on blog]. Retrieved from http://www.shanahanonliteracy.com/

Shanahan, T. (2010). What it means to teach disciplinary literacy. In Y. Lyons, A. R. Marri, and A. Rivet (Eds.), *Proceedings of the Content Area Literacy Conference 2010: Teachers College Columbia University: Program in Reading Specialist, Social Studies Education, and Science Education.* New York, NY: Teachers College, Columbia University and Carnegie Corporation of New York.

Shanahan, T., & Shanahan, C. (2008). Teaching disciplinary literacy to adolescents: Rethinking content-area literacy. *Harvard Educational Review, 78*(1), 40–50.

Sieff, K. (2011, January 13). Virginia Board of Education withdraws approval of two history textbooks. Retrieved from http://www.washingtonpost.com/wp-dyn/content/article/2011/01/13/AR2011011307050.html

Snow, C., & Moje, E. (2010). Why is everyone talking about adolescent literacy. *Phi Delta Kappan, 91*(6): 66–69.

Stotsky, S. (2010, December 8). Let's spread the blame for reading underachievement. *Education Week, 30* (14), 24–25.

USA.gov. (n.d.). Retrieved from http://www.usa.gov/Citizen/Topics/History_American.shtml

Wiggins, G., & McTighe, J. (2007). *Schooling by design: Mission, action, and achievement.* Alexandria, VA: ASCD.

Williamson, G. (2008). A text readability continuum for postsecondary readiness. *Journal of Advanced Academics, 19*(4), 602–632.

Wineburg, S. (2001). *Historical thinking: And other unnatural acts charting the future of teaching the past.* Philadelphia, PA: Temple University.

Living the Impact of Standards and Assessment

Change is difficult. Change takes time and effort. While our educational system is not necessarily designed for change, some of our systems need to transform—right now—to help our students. Grading and twenty-first-century learning are current hot topics in education. These are also the issues that are frequently avoided due to time, energy, and policies. This section exposes some of the holes in our system and at the same time provides practical solutions for quick change.

Are you using grades to improve student achievement? If so, you should know that the most powerful way to improve student achievement is to provide feedback. Most of our grading policies are designed to report, assign, and rank. Those purposes are not always amenable to providing feedback. Stephen Ventura shows us how to make improvements to our current grading policies. He opens the chapter by acknowledging that changing a grading policy takes time and dedication but assures us that the rewards are immense. Steve provides specific strategies and possible solutions to address the most frequently asked questions about student grading. He takes us through activities that require reflection and planning. Most importantly, Steve shows us how to design a grading policy that will reduce failures, improve discipline, and increase faculty morale. Are you ready to change? Do you need to change? This chapter will help you to take those first steps toward using grading as a powerful form of feedback for your students.

Gabriel Rshaid provides conclusion to this book by encouraging us to change—and to change by preparing our students for today's world and tomorrow's future. The phrase "lifelong learning" continues to be a buzzword in education and is something that most of us strive to achieve; our schools of today aren't always structured to encourage learning beyond a calendar year. Our aim is to teach toward academic targets, measure achievement levels, and increase student achievement. He helps us to see that our goals and beliefs about learning are slightly mismatched. Gabriel encourages us to view twenty-first-century learning standards as transdisciplinary, dynamic and customized, related to age and timeliness, and inclusive of content standards. He also recommends the creation of an assessment system that is flexible, is authentic, and uses technology and self-assessment as a few guiding principles. Gabriel provides multiple examples as well as strategies that will help schools build a system of standards and assessment that reflects the needs of the twenty-first century. Some changes are more easily made than others; all the solutions offered will help to support lifelong learning in our schools. Change is hard, but it is a moral imperative if we want to help our students become meaningful contributors to our society.

CHAPTER NINE

Effective Grading Practices: Creating a Compelling Case for Improvement

STEPHEN VENTURA

Without question, grading is one of the most emotional topics in all of education. Don't believe me? Conduct an Internet search for "grading policies," and you will find countless articles about controversial grading initiatives combined with strong sentiment among community members, teachers, and administrators. The problem with creating grading systems is more than just implementing a new scale of progression. To demonstrate professional respect for educators, it is important to first ask "why" before we implement a new strategy or grading initiative. Making an initial case for change is absolutely essential when adjusting grading practices and policies, as any effort to suggest that grading systems should be changed requires a considerable degree of justification. The tradition of common practices is deep, and therefore many common practices are continued, even when we know that they are not effective.

So, think about these three questions:

1. Are you right now enjoying record high levels of homework completion/compliance?

2. Are you enjoying record high levels of student engagement?

3. Are you enjoying record low levels of student failures?

If you answered yes to each question, then your grading policies are probably working. But if you are like thousands of educators who say kids are not finishing homework, not engaged, and not succeeding, *then please do not continue the same practices and expect different results.* Changing classroom grading policies requires a notable degree of schoolwide dedication and consistency. When we can greatly reduce the variation in teacher grading practices, we will improve student achievement.

Grades need to be accurate while supporting learning. This chapter focuses on creating a compelling case for improvement while providing examples of grading practices that will have the greatest impact on student achievement. You will have an opportunity to identify your most urgent needs in terms of grading, feedback, and accuracy while looking at ways to implement some of the best alternatives to the zero and other toxic grading practices. After all, if we can improve our grading practices, we can reduce student failures, improve discipline, and increase faculty morale.

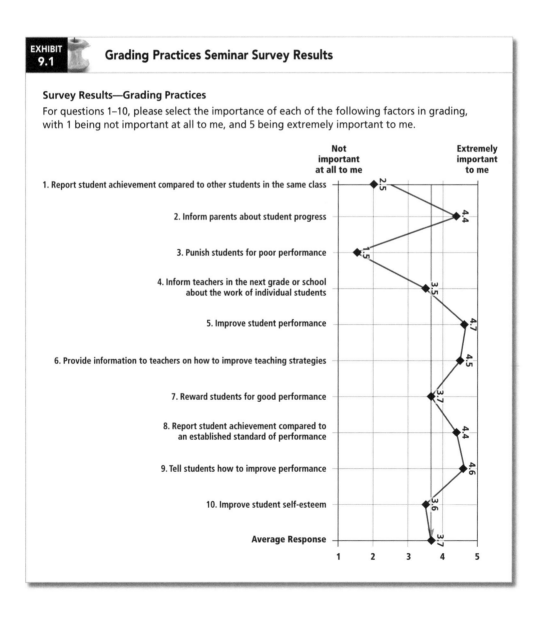

EXHIBIT 9.1

Grading Practices Seminar Survey Results

Survey Results—Grading Practices

For questions 1–10, please select the importance of each of the following factors in grading, with 1 being not important at all to me, and 5 being extremely important to me.

	Not important at all to me			Extremely important to me
1. Report student achievement compared to other students in the same class		2.5		
2. Inform parents about student progress				4.4
3. Punish students for poor performance	1.5			
4. Inform teachers in the next grade or school about the work of individual students			3.5	
5. Improve student performance				4.7
6. Provide information to teachers on how to improve teaching strategies				4.5
7. Reward students for good performance			3.7	
8. Report student achievement compared to an established standard of performance				4.4
9. Tell students how to improve performance				4.6
10. Improve student self-esteem			3.6	
Average Response			3.7	
	1 2 3 4 5			

Survey Results—Grading Practices

The Leadership and Learning Center conducts several Effective Grading Practices seminars throughout the country. These seminars attract a wide variety of participants, including school board members, central office leaders, administrators, and teachers. The purpose of these seminars is to help attendees identify ineffective grading practices and to offer alternatives that lead to better feedback, accuracy, and timeliness.

Exhibit 9.1 illustrates combined survey results completed by attendees from several grading practices seminars. As you can see, most people reject the statement that grades should be used as punishment for poor performance (statement 3). Additionally, statements 5 through 9 show strong levels of agreement that grades should be used to increase student achievement. The question is, are our grading practices really working? Furthermore, do we really rebuff the statement that grades are not to be used as punishment? Do we really use grades to improve achievement?

If these beliefs are indeed true, then why do so many educators believe that awarding a grade of zero will motivate students? I hope to sensitively challenge readers by suggesting that grades are largely influenced by personal judgment and that the same student with the same work can receive wildly different feedback based on the grading policies of the teacher.

Consider the views of leading experts in grading and assessment that follow.

> [G]rades are so imprecise that they are almost meaningless. This straightforward but depressing fact is usually painfully obvious when one examines the research and practice regarding grades with a critical eye.
> —Robert Marzano, *Transforming Classroom Grading*, 2000, p. 1

> [O]ur work over the past several years has convinced us that a lot of current practice in grading and reporting is shamefully inadequate. We persist in the use of particular practices not because we've thought about them in any depth but, rather, because they are part of a tradition that has remained unquestioned for years.
> —Thomas Guskey and Jane Bailey,
> *Developing Grading and Reporting Systems for Student Learning*, 2001, p. 1

> Although teaching has become increasingly standards based, and we know more than we ever knew about how people learn, traditional grading practices persist, especially in middle and high schools. These practices often not only result in ineffective communication about student achievement, but also may actually harm students and misrepresent their learning.
> —Ken O'Connor, *A Repair Kit for Grading*, 2007, p. xiv

Simply put, letter grades do not reflect student achievement in an astonishing number of cases. The situation has long been tolerated because of the pervasive belief that teaching is a private endeavor and grading policies are the exclusive domain of those private practitioners.
—Douglas B. Reeves, *The Learning Leader*, 2006, p. 113

Regarding grades, Reeves (2004) believes schools should set policies to ensure that grades in all classrooms are:

- *Accurate*—The same piece of student work receives the same grade regardless of who the teacher is.

- *Fair*—Differences in grades should reflect variations in the quality of work, not differences in gender, ethnicity, or social class.

- *Timely*—Students and parents should be told about grades early enough to correct problems.

EXHIBIT 9.2   **Effective-Grading Worksheet**

Criterion for Effective Grading*	Description of Grading Practice that Meets this Criterion	Description of Grading Practice that Violates this Criterion

*Choose ONE of the following criteria: accurate, fair, timely, or understandable.

• *Understandable*—Students should get detailed information about how to improve, not just a summative grade or comment.

Think about your current grading systems and consider whether those systems meet the criteria listed in Exhibit 9.2. In fact, choose one of the criteria listed and describe in rich detail a grading practice that meets this criterion and another example of a grading practice that violates this criterion.

The Zero Dialogue

"What happens to a student who doesn't turn in the work?" This a fair question that arises time after time, particularly when we make the case against the zero. The zero on a 100-point grading scale represents mathematical inaccuracies because failing grades cover a disproportionate 3/5s of the scale while passing grades cover 2/5s. Giving zeros on a 100-point scale exceedingly distorts students' grades because the zero is six times worse than the D. The evidence is that eliminating zeros improves homework completion, reduces failures, and improves student discipline. Questions about consequences for missing assignments stem from a desire to teach personal responsibility and a good work ethic, traits that we all agree are desirable. The only question is, does the zero improve achievement and motivation?

We should not be asking what to do if students fail to turn in work; the question should be how we can ensure that our assignments guarantee the highest rate of return, motivation, and achievement. It is less costly, on a number of different levels, to think of ways to reduce student failures first, as opposed to reacting to them later. Schools always find the resources and teaching staff for students who fail. We always find the money for extra programs after students drop out. It is far less expensive to prevent failure and dropouts than to endure them, and that is precisely why the zero should be eliminated. This approach should not be confused with holding lower expectations for students, nor am I advocating that we go easy on kids. There are consequences for not submitting work; we just need to make sure that those consequences actually improve achievement, that they are the kinds of consequences that help kids overcome failure with resilience.

I usually respond to the "missed assignment" inquiry by asking some clarifying questions to achieve an honest conversation about avoiding high-stakes consequences.

Is your school using the early final exam option? Many middle and high schools have incorporated a student incentive program that rewards students with the priceless commodity of time. The early final exam option is designed to reduce failures while increasing student achievement. The premise is simple: students who have completed all of the work and maintain a letter grade of A or B can take the semester final one to two weeks early. To prevent academic dishonesty, this is not the same final exam students will take at the end of the semester. If they pass the "form B" early final, their semester is over.

Some educators believe the disadvantages of the early final exam outweigh the advantages. The misconception here is that a number of students may become a disruption because they have completed the final and have nowhere to report. What typically happens, in fact, is that many of these students wind up tutoring other students who still need to attend class until the end of the semester. They often continue to report to the same classroom with the satisfaction of knowing that they have completed the semester work with a week to spare. Some students are assigned office duty or other tasks on campus. Schools that use this strategy create a list of predetermined activities for students to take part in if they pass the early final exam.

The consequences of students earning an A or a B before the end of the semester under the early final option are far less damaging than the more likely scenario of students who never engage deeply in learning the material at all.

Think of the psychological advantages of the early final. Students learn that their control over their semester depends on effort and motivation. If they maintain above-average grades with no missed assignments, they get back what they want most—*time and freedom*. Adults get back what they want most—a reduction in missed assignments, higher levels of homework completion, and students who are engaged and focused.

Can the student make up the work before, during, or after school? This strategy can significantly reduce the number of failures by teaching students personal responsibility. Many schools and districts assign same-day after-school suspension for students who fail to turn in work on time. What do students do during this time? They complete the work. The consequence for missing assignments is not a zero. The consequence is doing the work before, during, or after school. In most instances, the work is completed by the end of the day. Of course, it would have been better had the work been submitted on time and students had been perfectly organized, but at least the work is getting done. Students don't fear zeros. *What they fear is doing the work*. This is one of the best strategies in response to missing assignments.

Are assignments overly weighted, thereby contributing to higher levels of failure? Critics of eliminating the zero should consider giving regular and timely feedback designed to improve performance. Assignments that make up a third of the letter grade increase the probability of missed work while decreasing higher levels of student success. It is far better to employ more assignments that require less time rather than fewer assignments requiring more time. The rationale is simple: Frequent, incremental assignments provide a source of feedback that is applicable and timely. However, if assignments are disproportionately weighted, the probability of failure is magnified. If a student fails to submit one assignment, or if the assignment is done poorly, that's one-third of the grade already scuttled. These "semester killer" assignments typically include projects that must be completed over a three- to four-week period. In the example that follows, we use 200 points as the weight of the assignment. Of course, many students will, four weeks after receiving the assignment, deliver it on time. But what about the student who already lacks motivation and may not start the work? If we do not provide incremental levels of feedback, by the time the third week rolls around, it is too late for that student to adequately complete the project. Starting with a baseline of the 200-point weighted assignment, here we consider some alternatives to the "semester killer."

The big project
(or, the "semester killer"):

Four weeks—200 points

Option 1: Assign four, 50-point projects. The student performs the same amount of work, and often more, and he receives feedback throughout the course of the assignment (Exhibit 9.3).

EXHIBIT 9.3   Breakdown of Four 50-Point Assignments

Week One	Week Two	Week Three	Week Four
50 points	50 points	50 points	50 points

Some students require *very fast* incremental feedback (Exhibit 9.4):

EXHIBIT 9.4   Breakdown of 10, 20-Point Assignments

Four-week Assignment									
20 Points	20 Points	20 Points	20 Points	20 Points	20 Points	20 Points	20 Points	20 Points	20 Points

Option 2: Assign 10, 20-point projects. The purpose here is simple—as educators, we talk a very good game about differentiated instruction. It makes sense, then, to provide differentiated levels of feedback as well.

What happens to students who fail one or two assignments worth two-thirds of the letter grade? They realize that their semester is functionally over. Your worst discipline problems are from students who do not see that any effort will change their course; they become a source of stress for the teacher and a disruption to the class.

Have you considered using a menu system? The menu system permits students to choose another assignment from a predetermined list that is of equal value to the missed assignment. The quantity and quality of the work remains the same. For example, if a student scores low or fails a 100-point test, the student can either choose another 100-point item from the menu or do four 25-point items. This is a viable alternative to one-size-fits-all assignments, and students are still responsible for getting the work done, not getting a zero.

Are students who fail being enrolled in extracurricular activities? At first glance this suggestion may seem counterintuitive. Shouldn't we be denying students access to extracurricular activities until they can improve their grades? One study suggests just the opposite. In an article that appeared in *Educational Leadership*, Doug Reeves (2008) writes about Woodstock (Ill.) High School, which serves almost 2,000 students. The data suggests that when students took part in three or four extracurricular activities throughout the year they earned dramatically better grades than those who participated in no extracurricular activities (Exhibit 9.5). These activities include athletics, academics, ethnic identity clubs, cultural groups, and many others.

Based on these surprising results, what might be a response to a student who fails algebra? *Welcome to the drama club!*

Have you considered assigning a score of "50" rather than a zero? The recommendation to abandon the zero, or to use a minimal grading system, yields emotional reaction and confusion. But consider the case for dropping the zero.

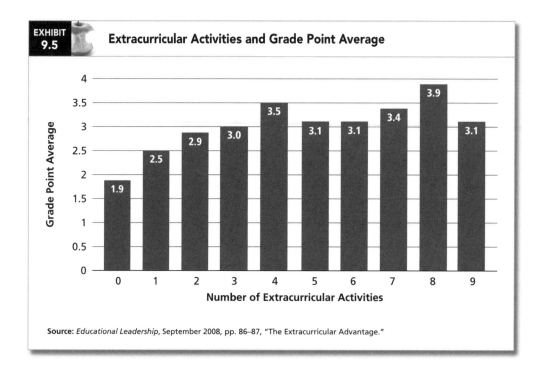

EXHIBIT 9.5

Extracurricular Activities and Grade Point Average

Source: *Educational Leadership*, September 2008, pp. 86–87, "The Extracurricular Advantage."

EXHIBIT 9.6	Demonstration of the Effect of a Zero Grade

Assign-ments	1	2	3	4	5	6	Total Percent	Final Grade
Scores	100	100	0	100	100	100	83%	B
Scores	100	100	100	50	100	100	92%	A

Many educators have come to the conclusion that assigning zeros for grades is no longer an acceptable practice because of mathematical errors. To be clear, the 50 percent should be assigned to student work that is completed but not of passing quality, and for work that is not completed.

In some schools, students receive a score of no lower than 50 percent (because the 50 is 10 points lower than the D grade) for completed work that is not of passing quality and for work that is not completed. Remember that a 50 is an F, and an F is not a "gift," as some would suggest. This process merely incorporates equal intervals between each grade. The rationale is that assigned zeros have an undeserved and devastating influence, so much so that no matter what the student does, a single zero can distort the final grade and any true indication of proficiency or mastery. If students act irresponsibly and/or do not learn, we fail as teachers, and failure is failure, no matter the degree (Wormelli, 2006, p. 140). Consider the grading scenario shown in Exhibit 9.6.

Should a string of perfect papers for a grading period be combined with one missing assignment? What would happen if we did not count the lowest grade?

Many educators claim that assigning zeros represents real-world responsibility and application, but I'm not sure we would want to average the zero into the very real world of weather forecasting.

Imagine that your local area's meteorologist collected temperatures for the entire workweek but forgot to record Friday's temperature (Exhibit 9.7).

Like all forecasters, he is interested is displaying the average temperature for the week. In this example, I am not suggesting that we replace Friday's temperature with a "50," but rather demonstrating that the average temperature would be 67 degrees without accounting for Friday's temperature, a figure that does not accurately show the weather from that week, unless, of course, the actual temperature on Friday was indeed zero degrees.

EXHIBIT 9.7	Demonstration of Zero in Weather Forecasting			
Monday	Tuesday	Wednesday	Thursday	Friday
82	84	86	83	0?

If you must assign a zero, use a four-point grading scale. I just described six strategies to reduce student failures, improve discipline, and increase faculty morale. However, even after I propose several different options for reducing missing assignments and poor grades, some people still believe that it is helpful to teachers to have more students fail. These systems are not perfect, but the prevailing attitude is that if they cannot work for all students then we should not try any of them. Do we really rebuff the statement that grades are not to be used as punishment if we go out of our way to maintain policies that do not positively influence achievement and reduce the failure rate?

Take a look at the economic impact of improved educational results (Alliance for Excellent Education, 2010):

- In 2010, 1.3 million students dropped out of school nationwide. That figure translates to $337 billion in lost wages and productivity for *one class.*

- The United States would save more than $17 billion in health care costs over the course of the lifetimes of each class of dropouts had they earned their diplomas.

- American households would accumulate more than $74 billion in additional wealth if all heads of households had graduated from high school.

- The American economy would see a combined savings and revenue of about $8 billion in reduced crime spending and increased earnings each year if the male high school graduation rate increased by just *5 percent.*

The two most common causes of course failures are missing homework and poor performance on a single major assignment. Adjusting grading policies would have a huge impact on student failures. Think about it: just two or three zeros are sufficient to cause failure for an entire semester, and just a few course failures lead to high school dropouts. Based on the economic impact of dropping out, it is easy to conclude that the best economic stimulus is a high school diploma.

EXHIBIT 9.8	100-Point Grading Scale Versus Four-Point Grading Scale

100-Point Scale	4-Point Scale
A = 100	A = 4
B = 89	B = 3
C = 79	C = 2
D = 69	D = 1

On a typical 100-point grading scale, an A is a 90, a B is an 80, a C is a 70, and a D is a 60. But what happens when a student does not turn in work? He receives a zero. The D (60) would be considered near failing, but the zero is six times worse than near failing—this scenario does not make sense, as there are equal increments (10) between the A, B, C, and D. When students receive zeros based on a 100-point grading scale, recovery is difficult because the zero carries inappropriate weighting and distorts the calculated grade. The application of a minimum grading system is criticized because of the obvious reward a student receives when no reward has been earned. If this is true, then we must also evaluate grading policies that over-punish students—a result that they have equally not earned.

On a four-point grading scale, an A is a four, a B is a three, a C is a two, and a D is a one. The stark difference between these two grading scales is that there is a one-point increment between the D and the zero.

To illustrate, let's use a set of grades and apply both grading scales to the same work, completed by the same student (Exhibit 9.8).

Your task: determine the final grade for a student who received the scores shown in Exhibit 9.9. Each score represents an assignment—an activity the teacher regarded as important; it may have been homework, a project, a quiz, or a test.

How does a single missed assignment distort the grade based on a 100-point grading scale?

Evaluation of Common Grading Practices

Consider the following common grading systems and, either alone or in a group, analyze the advantages and disadvantages of each policy (Exhibit 9.10). Take into account the criteria for effective feedback that we have already established (accurate, fair, timely,

EXHIBIT 9.9	Final Grade Worksheet

Assignment #	Grade
1	B
2	D
3	C
4	Missing assignment
5	A

and understandable). As you brainstorm, see how common these systems are among colleagues and then begin to determine a better list of common practices. This activity is not designed to change an entire grading policy. Select just one element that is not consistent with the criteria presented and think of one way that we can improve just that one grading practice.

Personal Reflection

After you have analyzed the grading policies in Exhibit 9.10, take time to reflect about a grading practice you may be using and determine if the disadvantages outweigh the advantages. If they do, you may want to eliminate that particular policy.

Guiding Principles for an Effective District Grading Policy

Following is a list of suggestions that can help jump-start your new district grading policy. Remember that we want to provide feedback that is accurate, timely, and understandable. Doing so permits students to use feedback right away and apply it accordingly. In fact, classroom and district grading policies should be so clear that the student ought to be able to tell you what his grade will be even before you calculate it.

| EXHIBIT 9.10 | Advantages and Disadvantages of Common Grading Practices | | |

Grading Practices	Advantages	Disadvantages
Average to compute final grade		
Final exam that is 20% of the final grade		
Refusal to accept late work		
Reduction in grade for late work		
Use of zero for missing work		
Reduction in grades for poor attitude		
Reduction in grades for poor behavior		
Reduction in grades for unexcused absences		

1. Grades Should Only Represent Individual Student Achievement

Perhaps the most common misuse of grading is combining other nonacademic behaviors with student achievement. These variables typically consist of behavior, effort, participation, improvement, attitude, attendance, group work, work ethic, and organizational skills. To be sure, these are important traits, but they must be recorded and reported separately.

Exhibit 9.11 is an example of participation grades that are combined with other scores to determine overall achievement. Even the new Common Core State Standards do not reference the importance of textbooks that must be covered. How many other nonacademic behaviors are included in this report?

EXHIBIT 9.11	Example of Nonacademic Grade Book Entries

Participation

Date	Assignment	Weight	Mark
8/24/2009	Textbook Scavenger Hunt	1	40/40
8/25/2009	Book Covers	1	8/15
9/11/2009	Notebook Check 1	1	23/50
9/15/2009	Misplaced Modifiers, p650	1	10/10
9/16/2009	OGT p. 33–38 #11–14	1	10/10
9/16/2009	Challenge Word Practice 3	1	5/5
9/16/2009	Vocabulary List #3 Crossword	1	5/5
9/18/2009	Participation Week Ending 9/18/09	1	13/25
9/24/2009	Finalized Topic	1	10/10

2. Appropriate Implementation of (Common) Formative Assessment

We often use formative assessment to assign a letter grade, when the purpose of these assessments is to provide feedback to both the student and the teacher about what the student did well, what the student did poorly, and how to improve. Therefore, letter grades for practice assignments, homework, and quizzes should not be factored into the overall course grade. Should the student receive feedback on these types of assignments? Absolutely. *Often students respond better to timely feedback when it is not attached to a letter grade.*

3. Appropriate Implementation of Summative Assessment

Summative assessments should only be given following learning and formative assessments. Grades should be determined based primarily on a variety of end-of-unit assessment and course/grade-level assessment that is completed more toward the end of the unit or grading period. In other words, use the average less while evaluating the best work. If learning were truly developmental, then it would make no sense to factor in early assessment results toward the end of a grading period. We should expect students to grow with time and frequent, repeated opportunities.

4. Use Grading Policies to Prepare Students

The reason grading policies are difficult to change is because of the tradition of individual policies by individual teachers. Although there is a sincere desire to motivate students and prepare them for the next grade, we often assume that preparing students means replicating expectations for college preparation or entry into the workforce. The question is, are those assumptions correct? Sometimes people use a model of resistance to change. Change depends on their own goodwill in helping to get kids ready.

Grading procedures should not focus on replicating the "real world" of college and the workforce. Many real-world professionals, including doctors, teachers, and lawyers, have multiple opportunities to obtain mastery/certification. The school or district's goal should be to fully *prepare* students for college and the workforce, not to *replicate* college and the workforce in K–12 settings. Over time, grading procedures become more stringent and student accountability gradually increases with every grade level.

Synthesis

Think about the following questions and how you might answer them to shape your grading practices and policies:

1. What are new ideas, research, and insights that you have gained?

2. What will be your greatest challenges in implementing improved grading practices?

3. What will be your greatest rewards in implementing improved grading practices?

Use the fishbone diagram shown in Exhibit 9.12 to brainstorm for possible causes of the effect or problem. The purpose of this activity is to find the most effective solution that will permit you to achieve your goals.

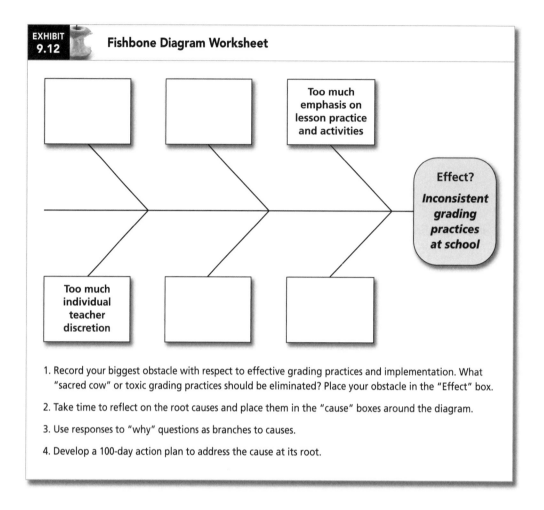

EXHIBIT 9.12   Fishbone Diagram Worksheet

Too much emphasis on lesson practice and activities

Effect?
Inconsistent grading practices at school

Too much individual teacher discretion

1. Record your biggest obstacle with respect to effective grading practices and implementation. What "sacred cow" or toxic grading practices should be eliminated? Place your obstacle in the "Effect" box.

2. Take time to reflect on the root causes and place them in the "cause" boxes around the diagram.

3. Use responses to "why" questions as branches to causes.

4. Develop a 100-day action plan to address the cause at its root.

The 100-Day Implementation Plan

To create a 100-day effective grading practices leadership plan, select a grading policy or strategy that could make the greatest difference in your organization if you accomplish it. Identify why this project really matters over the long haul for all stakeholders. What will the accomplishment of this project really mean in terms of motivation, achievement, and professional practice? You can quickly organize your plan by considering the following five steps:

1. Select a project that will have the greatest impact on student achievement. For example, if all students become proficient or better in priority standards, what would this allow them to do and be? What difference would that make?

2. Identify in advance when you will measure and report on indicators that show short-term wins. Populate those actions first on your 100-day project plan.

3. Once you have your actions for measuring and reporting on indicators in place, fill in with other high-powered actions. Use the LEAD tool to help you do this:

- LEARN: Actions that require you and others to learn
- EVIDENCE: Actions that require you to collect, analyze, and use data to guide decisions
- ATTITUDE: Actions that challenge unhelpful attitudes (yours and others') and that support emotions and attitudes that help the project
- DECISIONS: Actions that put you at a decision point

4. Build in actions that require you to learn and try new, helpful leadership behaviors as you roll out your project. Look for ways to overcome your personal leadership Achilles heel.

5. Update your project weekly. Your 100-day project plan allows you to premediate the most powerful actions needed to move your project forward in the first 100 days. Review and revise these actions promptly and as needed. Do not let a week go by without doing this.

Some grading policies and practices are determined at the district level; some are determined at the school level; some are determined at the classroom level. Identify the specific role for making policies or making policy recommendations that applies to you. It is imperative that this activity, the implementation plan, be personally and professionally relevant for you. Based on the context of The Leadership and Learning Center's own national research, you are most likely to implement changes if they take place within 100 days from the time you consider them. Although some changes may take many years to accomplish in full, you are now focused on changes that you can make immediately, within the next 100 days.

Exhibit 9.13 is an example of a 100-day action plan template that helps address the following:

1. The most critical grading policy needed in my school/district/organization: **To reduce inconsistent and toxic grading practices**

2. Project title: **Guiding Principles for an Effective Grading Policy**

3. My high-impact grading strategies/tactics (**Day one:** 1/03/2011–**Day 100:** 4/12/2011):
   a. **Eliminate the zero for missed or late work**
   b. **Eliminate the use of the average**
   c. **Eliminate "semester killer" assignments**

| EXHIBIT 9.13 | 100-Day Action Plan |

Date	Actions	People and Networks to Work With	Date Completed
1/03/2011	Start of 100-Day Effective Grading Practices Leadership Plan		
1/05/2011	Team Reports: What's wrong with present policy?		
1/05/2011	Team Reports: Best practices—what's working?		
1/15/2011	Communicate to board, staff, and community		
2/21/2011	Identify research questions and action research methods		
3/01/2011	Written reports from action research teams with a focus on evidence		

Conclusion

Improving grading policies is not easy, but the opportunities for more student accomplishment, better grading practices, fewer discipline problems, and greater professional enjoyment all are worth the effort.

The best grading practices I have seen have a laser-like focus on improving student achievement and motivation. These policies create student respect for teacher feedback because students have the opportunity to use teacher feedback on a consistent and regular basis. When students do not take into account teacher feedback it is often because there is little or no opportunity to apply that feedback for improved performance. The grading practices described in this chapter help to create more incentive not only for improved student performance but also for greater student respect for teachers.

I am hopeful that you have a better understanding about the importance of effective grading practices and that the evidence presented is convincing and informative. Grading is one of the best ways to provide feedback to students. When teachers and school leaders make specific improvements in grading practices, they provide a fair and accurate method of grading, which, in turn, has a positive effect on every subject and every grade level. Additionally, when schools implement effective grading practices, they reap the unexpected benefit of improved engagement by students, faculty, and parents.

References

Alliance for Excellent Education. (2010). About the crisis. Retrieved from http://www.all4ed .org/about_the_crisis

Reeves, D. (2004). *Accountability in action* (2nd ed.). Englewood, CO: Lead + Learn Press.

Reeves, D. (2008, September). The extracurricular advantage. *Educational Leadership, 66*(1), 86–87.

Wormelli, R. (2006). *Fair isn't always equal: Assessing & grading in the differentiated classroom.* Portland, ME: Stenhouse.

CHAPTER TEN

Assessing the
Twenty-First-Century Learner

GABRIEL RSHAID

In a classic and often-cited scene of the movie *The Bells of St. Mary's* (1945), the fictional easygoing Father O'Malley, played by Bing Crosby, confronts the no-nonsense school principal, Sister Mary Benedict, portrayed by Ingrid Bergman, about the situation of Patsy, a troubled child whom he has taken under his wing and whose grades will prevent her from graduating with her own class. Father O'Malley is trying to find a way to see that this girl does not fail and wants to know why the passing grade is set at 75.

The principal bluntly faces him, asking, "Do you believe in just passing everybody, Father?"

He answers, "Maybe I do," and then goes on to pose the eternal assessment-related question: "Are we here to give children a helping hand—or are we here to measure their brains with a yardstick?"

And, although at first glance it seems paradoxical that so many years later this debate is still relevant, if anything, the twenty-first-century scenario that puts to the test most accepted educational axioms is acknowledgment of the tension between measurements and learner progress that is almost intrinsic to any model of schooling.

It is, by now, universally accepted that the whole world of education was turned upside down by the advent of the Internet and the possibility of accessing infinite knowledge. This access results in a series of complex technical challenges related to assessment that we attempt to analyze in this chapter. However, and parallel to the limitless possibilities that emerge out of the new knowledge paradigm, there is a growing awareness of the need to cater to each and every learner in ways that ensure that schooling will help and not hinder them from rising up to their full potential. The question posed by Bing Crosby's fictional character acquires, then, on both counts, increased significance when thinking of assessment for the future learner.

The Twenty-First-Century Scenario Meets Assessment Models

Despite the fact that speakers, thinkers, authors, and modern-day gurus have dealt extensively with issues related to the new educational scenario, the twenty-first-century challenge to educators remains elusive in its definition and scope. Already on the threshold of its second decade, the twenty-first century, in the views of educators, continues to be associated with a far and distant future, whereas, in sharp contrast, the students, whose education is occurring today, intuitively perceive the disconnect between current educational practice and the prevailing model.

Regardless of an almost inevitable confusion that stems from the fast-paced changes and an inherently dynamic scenario, the main characteristics of the twenty-first-century challenge can be identified in the context of analyzing the evolution of assessment for today's learners.

A New Knowledge Paradigm

Perhaps second only to the invention of the printing press by Gutenberg, which allowed access to knowledge to common people as opposed to it being restricted to manuscripts found only in centers of learning, the unplanned explosive growth and expansion of the Internet resulted in a dramatic shift in the knowledge paradigm. We—all people who are engaged in learning—are the first generation in history to have full access to all accumulated human knowledge, and the consequences on the schooling model are direct and immediate: we have seamlessly transitioned from a pedagogy of poverty, in which the teacher concentrated and dispensed knowledge with the aid of, at the most, textbooks, to one of infinite abundance.

These fundamental changes, which have led to what is known as the knowledge era, have a direct impact on assessment and standards. The traditional focus of evaluation, as many of us adults have painfully experienced, was based on factual recall and memorization and sit-down, written-test–dominated assessment instruments. Standards were written with specific content mastery objectives in mind, many of which were associated with apprehending, rather than understanding or using effectively those contents.

The renewed knowledge paradigm challenges some of the most fundamental conceptions of assessment instruments in their focus, which should now target some goal other than facts or storage of information. Of course, memorization and developing a solid knowledge base are still relevant in the new paradigm, to an extent that needs to be determined, but those activities certainly will be less emphasized than in the past.

Focus on Lifelong Learning

Another fundamental tenet of the old model of education was that learning occurred specifically in the physical spaces destined and conceived intentionally for a mostly passive model of learning. Formal schooling was almost synonymous with education, and only through journal subscriptions or the purchase of books could individuals continue learning outside of schools or universities.

In the new scenario, where knowledge is only a few keystrokes away, learning can continue for life, and that long-honored principle of lifelong learning can finally descend from its wishful habitat in mission statements down to reality. The possibility of continuing the learning process beyond formal education acquires, then, fundamental importance and should constitute the overarching goal of the educational system as a whole. Once again, assessment has largely been geared to evaluate how much learning occurred during the formal schooling years, and not to how learners have developed skills that enable them to transcend their learning experience in school throughout the rest of their lives. If lifelong learning is the global objective, then both assessment and related standards must reflect this goal and attempt to measure whether learners have acquired the desired skills.

Every Child Can Learn

The truly revolutionary enlightenment of the twenty-first-century scenario is the acceptance by educators that every child can learn and that it is desirable, even if difficult, to develop an educational system that caters, inasmuch as possible, to each and every child's abilities and learning style.

The one-size-fits-all model of education that grew out of the industrialized school constitutes an ill-fitting match for the nonuniform and overwhelmingly complex twenty-first-century scenario, and, as such, related assessment models that expect the same (standard) outcomes from all students are doomed to be counterintuitive to the principle of a customized education. The ensuing challenge to rethink assessment and standards in the face of the need for personalization is inextricably linked to system constraints that include the teacher-to-student ratio, size of classrooms, and other characteristics of the current model.

Collaboration

The development of technological tools that have shortened distances has not only enabled communication between people for social purposes but also provided a platform that allows unlimited possibilities for collaboration. Regardless of their physical location, people from all over the world can stay in touch with one another and work cooperatively on projects, share working documents, and interact on- and off-line at all times. This connectivity has resulted in numerous benefits to productivity, and the seamless collaborative model has enabled the pooling of diverse talents and a general improvement over the individual model. The prevailing paradigm in all workplaces is now collaboration.

It is not surprising that collaboration, once again, presents a challenge when confronted with the existing assessment schemes, which are overwhelmingly geared toward individual efforts for the sake of accountability. A major driver for reform of the current assessment model can also be identified in terms of the need to focus on collaboration as an essential skill in the learners' toolbox, and any twenty-first-century models must be oriented not only to individual contributions but also to the learning of this paramount skill in today's context.

New Skills

It is an almost inevitable consequence of any such drastic changes in the underlying paradigm that, in order for students to emerge with the capabilities required to be functional and productive in the new environment, many new skills will emerge that need to be taught and subsequently assessed.

Because students will have to do things that they have never done before, and deal with a sometimes mind-boggling, completely changed scenario that accompanies their growth and their learning, it is important to rethink the focus of traditional skills, as well as the relative emphasis on skills and contents in terms of assessment.

In effect, and just as one example, one key skill that the twenty-first-century learners must develop throughout their schooling is what is often called filtering, that is, going through extensive material and information until they find whatever is relevant to the problem at hand. Assessment of filtering, and determining standards of proficiency in the attainment of such a new skill, can clearly be a challenge, and one that takes educators well out of their comfort zone. Irrespective of the taxonomies for these skills, there are and will be many new twenty-first-century skills, as well as other skills (i.e., associated with creativity and imagination) that have not formed part of the formal curriculum and now need to be accounted for.

Standards and Assessment in the Pre-Internet World

In order to elucidate how standards and assessments may evolve within the leveled playing field for education, it is pertinent to try to take a step back and view the big picture in terms of the meaning of assessment and standards, and why they have acquired such a strong role in today's school systems and the current model.

The primary role of assessments is, of course, to evaluate and ensure that students are effectively learning what the curriculum stipulates. In turn, standards themselves intend to prescribe contents and skills that guarantee that all learners, regardless of their schools or districts, acquire mastery over contents and skills that have been determined to be adequate, essential, or desirable by some team of experts who, over the years, have compiled their expectations to generalize them to all learners at the age in question.

Even though teachers have their own criteria and attempt to customize their programs to what best suits their students, curricula and assessment are still dominated by these standards, mostly by virtue of their influence on accountability: many teachers are judged by the results their students achieve in standardized tests, and, for example, under the much maligned No Child Left Behind legislation, the collective effect of these scores has a decisive influence on schools.

It is a fair assumption to say that standards and assessment drive instruction. This assumption has become blatant travesty in that the basic premise is that assessment should measure and account for learning, and not determine the learning itself. Sufficient proof of this statement is the eternal battle cry of students anywhere when confronted with a topic: "Will this be on the test?"

Similarly, when planning what and how to teach, given the test-score–dominated environment under which they operate, teachers perforce ask themselves a similar question, this time related to whether the contents or skills are included in the standardized test. It is not by chance that these evaluations are known as high-stakes tests.

Assessment as Ranking

As Sir Ken Robinson repeatedly says in his presentations, the problem with taking things for granted in education is that we do not realize that we take them for granted—because we take them for granted. And one of the trademarks of assessment and standards in our schools that is taken for granted and never questioned is the fact that, rather than serving the preeminent role of providing constructive feedback to help students learn, assessment also explicitly ranks the students by assigning the much-coveted numeric grade. Whether in the all-time classic 0–100 scale or other more or less sophisticated incarnations, numeric assessment ultimately ranks students according to their ability to meet the goals and standards in the prevailing model. The use of assessment as a measuring stick results in what we all witness in classrooms: students who over the years become not great learners but very proficient and skilled test takers. Thomas Guskey (2008) once said in a keynote address on assessment: "As long as assessment is secret, learning becomes a guessing game. Some of us get very successful at it."

Within the twenty-first-century scenario, with its premises of customized learning and individualized instruction and the realization that learning is not uniquely geared to fixed standards but is instead dynamic, such a rigid numeric model falls flat in the face of the underlying principles of the new knowledge era. It is clearly counterintuitive to rank students based on the limited dimensions that these tests can measure, and experienced educators are painfully aware of the indelible damaging effects that can be inflicted on students' fragile self-esteem as a consequence of these high-stakes failures.

Formative versus Summative

Another negative mutation of assessments away from their primeval function of gauging student learning with the goal of helping them in the instructional process is the fact that, for reasons that have to do with the very nature of standardized tests, and also because the implicit premise is that the responsibility to learn is mostly on students' shoulders, assessment occurs at the end of the unit, period, or year. This scheduling is also viewed as an enticement for students to actively study (and remember) contents so as to, it is hoped, consolidate and secure learning. End-of-unit tests are, by far, the dominant species in assessment instruments. Furthermore, I have yet to work in a school where students do not complain that all teachers tend to concentrate their tests toward the end of the marking period and that, consequently, they are forced to cram and study under high-pressure conditions that are obviously not conducive to learning.

Even though much more is said than done in this respect, in recent years the evident flaws of summative assessment have been pointed out by writers and educators. In addition, there is a trend to gradually switch to formative assessments, or assessment for learning, that is, evaluations that are frequent and continuous and that include relevant feedback during the instructional process and not at the end, when there is no time for students to discover what learning they have missed once they get their test back. In that respect, summative assessment has been graphically compared to an autopsy: you get to know the cause of death when nothing can be done to treat the patient.

Who's Who?

In my presentations I often use an exercise that I have found to be a great example of the disconnect between the prevailing models and the twenty-first-century scenario. I hand participants a clicker (handheld interactive response system) and I project on the screen the images of four people who are relatively well known but who are not necessarily readily identifiable to everyone. I give the attendees a couple of minutes to work on the problem on their own and then ask them to send the four names by means of the clickers. Once this is done I paste on screen their answers; I give the group some time to read them, still in silence; and then I show them the four faces again, asking participants once more to supply me with a new answer. Repeating the procedure, they text in their responses; I project the responses on screen; and, almost invariably, the second time many more people submit correct answers.

The reason for increased success is self-evident: by reading what other people have answered, participants have a far better chance of getting the answer right themselves. Following the first exercise, I ask the audience to reflect on what happened and why we do not take advantage of the obvious, that pooling talents and collaboration yield better results and improved learning. Participants often find the exercise counterintuitive, and many in the audience share that they were reluctant to look at other people's answers, feeling that they were cheating.

What is wrong with the whole exercise? It defies our perceptions to think that the second time students are tested on material we award better "grades," and our instincts seem to rebel against this idea of getting help from other participants. However, the benefits are there for everybody to see, and more significant learning occurs.

The problem is not the model of collaboration, but the assessment instrument itself. Because the identification of the faces is mere factual recall, the twenty-first-century scenario of having access to fellow participants' answers makes no sense. The issue is not the interaction, but rather the question, and the example serves to identify the main problem with the current model of assessment, that attempting to gain proficiency in learning in a different paradigm with an outdated assessment model can only be a self-defeating process.

Standards and Assessments in the Twenty-First Century

Clearly, major changes need to be introduced in assessment systems and a greater scope of accountability must be evident through standardized tests or other forms of determining whether learners at schools have achieved the desired learning outcomes. However, as often occurs, there is not necessarily a linear connection between what should not be and what should be, and it is much easier to pinpoint the shortcomings of a system than to develop a new one that addresses them.

Going from the general to the particular, then, we seek to lay out the foundations of a new system of standards and assessment and identify some current assessment practices that point to what assessment might look like in the future, practices that may help to gradually reshape the current system toward meeting the needs of twenty-first-century learners.

Nonstandardized Standards?

If schools could give only one guarantee about students' education in the twenty-first century, it should be that all graduates will have the tools, skills, and motivation to truly embrace lifelong learning as a way of life, as a guiding mind-set.

Standards, and ultimately assessment instruments, must then, first and foremost, ensure that this global, overarching objective is met. How can we define standards that measure the progress of attaining lifelong learning at different age levels?

Two inhibiting factors come to mind immediately in the face of such a question. First, most educators do not know enough about the thinking process itself and related higher-order skills. We feel comfortable defining skills and contents in our respective areas of expertise, and, more or less, we can write standards and design evaluations geared to measure the proficiency in subject mastery, and even , after years of experience, determine what can be expected of students in that respect at different ages.

But what does success look like for skills such as lifelong learning? How can students expect to evolve in their ability to learn how to learn? When we enter the realm that goes beyond technique, of motivation, of developing a new mind-set about learning, what does mastery in those fields look like?

So the first driver is that a more scientific approach to the teaching of the new skills needs to be developed, including technical learning about thinking processes, clearly tied to advances in neurocognition that promise to shed a completely new light on pedagogical efforts.

The second alarm bell that rings internally has to do with the need to completely reassess the way we think of standards. So far, most standards are fixed, timed, and based on agreed-upon clear success outcomes. Come the twenty-first century and an intrinsically dynamic and changing environment, where the previous linear analytical approach fails, it could be argued that even in content-based standards the approach needs to be completely different. When confronted with a higher-order skill like metacognition, lifelong learning, or critical thinking, the standards and subsequently related assessment instruments must be more geared to what students are expected to do, in terms of tasks, in ways that are not uniform. The development of such a skill also validates what educators have long known and whispered in informal settings: that no two children are alike, that their development is unique, and that mastery of any skill may not be fixed in time and expected to be the same for all learners.

So we are confronted with almost an oxymoron: nonstandardized standards? But this seemingly contradictory idea can be thought of not in terms of universal and time-fixed outcomes for all students but as a road map with tasks that have to be ticked off. We can imagine a list of competencies that define the standards, that is, that students are able to perform certain tasks that shall be defined in the context of the skills that need to be acquired, and the tasks themselves, in various forms that reflect the twenty-first-century environment and the evolving demands of the workplace.

The Nature of Standards for Twenty-First Century Skills

The problem we have to deal with is how to translate the school's mission statement to the reality of the classroom. Mission statements have forever adorned the walls of schools and been reproachfully featured in administrative offices, whose occupants knew that, in most cases, they represented semi-utopian expressions of wishful thinking. But how do we know whether they are actually being fulfilled in schools? Or even worse, how do we measure whether the virtues extolled in them are being embodied by students—and staff?

Now the traits that are contained in these mission statements come alive in that critical thinking, lifelong learning, and other higher-order skills are now achievable thanks to the renewed knowledge paradigm and the infinite knowledge scenario.

In that environment, then, standards for lifelong learning and other twenty-first-century skills (content-based or subject area standards are discussed later) would be of a very different nature from those we know today, and themselves embody some of the principles of twenty-first-century education. Some of the essential characteristics of those standards would be that they are based on principles, dynamic and customized, task oriented, not solely individualized, transdisciplinary, and geared to age level and timed.

Based on Principles

As counterintuitive as it may seem as related to the subsequent possibility of measuring them, standards must focus on basic principles like learning itself, respect, academic integrity, creativity, and other basic tenets of twenty-first-century education. Because the definition of successful outcomes is increasingly elusive, it is hard to determine exactly which very specific skills need to be prescribed. Thus, a suggested principle for the writing of twenty-first-century standards would be to operate in two levels, a general one that outlines clear expectations about principles, virtues, and traits that must be acquired by all students throughout the schooling process, and a second tier of standards, probably determined at the school or district level, that focuses on observable skills that eventually can be measured through assessment.

Dynamic and Customized

Especially at the second level, in drawing up the skills that represent the attainment of these principles, each school or district must have a say in how to best embody the learning of these general-level standards. We can imagine a centrally suggested list of skills, for instance, that illustrate how lifelong learning or critical thinking looks in real life, based on state-of-the-art research for that particular principle of twenty-first-century education. Perhaps even supplementing that suggested list with what is known to work best in that particular environment would be possible. Due to the transient nature of everything in our time, these standards would need to be updated and revised periodically in order to incorporate new ideas and advances in research and pedagogy.

Task Oriented

In all likelihood, in order to define standards—expectations that need to be fulfilled by all students alike—they will be written in terms of what students should be able to do and competencies that they need to acquire and define certain manners of conduct that will be expected. Again, as an example, if it is accepted that creativity is a paramount skill in the twenty-first-century scenario, one of these twenty-first-century standards may read, "Students will be able to come up with various original solutions to open-ended problems," which in turn poses an even greater challenge in how we teach, assess, and measure the completion of such a task.

Not Solely Individualized

Another completely outdated feature of current standards is that they are almost exclusively geared toward describing individual performances. In a world that has already embraced the collaborative model as the default setting for any productive work, expectations that are solely individualized are out of sync with one of the most salient characteristics of the present and future work environment. Once again, this leads us to determine how to assess and measure effective collaboration throughout schooling and to define expectations according to age level as to how students may progress in these associated skills (i.e., moving from contributing to the group to collaborating effectively in producing a joint document to self-assessment of group performance). Here again, these hitherto marginalized skills must gain mainstream focus in defining and better understanding from a technical point of view how they are to be taught and learned. In this particular category, standards may include the use of tools that foster collaboration and that involve software or technology.

Transdisciplinary

It is clear that the nature of twenty-first-century standards cannot be artificially compartmentalized through aseptic separation in subject areas. One fundamental shift in thinking about school curriculum is that, within the previous underlying paradigm, skills emanated out of the content areas, and teachers drew out these desired capabilities what could be learned in terms of skills out of that particular subject matter. That is, the primary consideration was centered on the contents to be taught, and as almost an afterthought what skills could be derived from the teaching of those contents.

In a new paradigm where, once and for all, skills and an underlying mind-set take precedence over the contents that drive instruction, the sequence is inverse. At this point, the question that needs to be raised is which contents better suit the skills that need to be acquired. For example, which subject area and particular contents are best suited to teach critical thinking, or lifelong learning?

One interesting thought in that respect is what Seymour Papert, the well-known researcher and creator of the LEGO programming system, is reported to have stated: that the teaching of computer programming, for many years considered to be anathematic to learning IT, is one of the best conduits for learning how to learn, because programming involves a critical stage known as debugging, in which the programmer needs to revise the source code of the program to spot the errors once the program is run.

Similarly, other contents need to be reexamined in the light of how they can contribute to the development of critical twenty-first-century skills. As another example, art, typically relegated to elective status in many high schools, is now considered to be one of the best ways to develop a sense of appreciation that serves the twenty-first-century learner well in the overwhelming amount of data that he is confronted with on a daily basis. On the other hand, math, sitting atop the pyramid of subjects, was rightly regarded as the prime vehicle for fostering analytical skills that are no longer so important in the future context. This notion does not conclude that more art and less math should be taught, but when standards are conceived primarily through these principle-based skills, the contents have to be reassessed as to how they are suited to the skills and not the other way around.

Geared to Age Level, and Timed

Another long-accepted truth about education is that not all students develop alike. Robinson (2006) humorously refers to the current educational system's greatest commonality, that it groups students exclusively by date of manufacture. The pre-Industrial Age schools where many students of different age groups converged by default within the same classroom and the teacher had to divide time among them forced the embodiment of what is now a desirable postmodern trait: personalized instruction and, often, older students tutoring/mentoring younger ones.

Some jokes can sometimes become almost paradigmatic metaphors of reality. A shepherd is lazily dozing under a tree while his sheep are grazing, and a tourist comes by and scolds him for being indolent. The tourist suggests that the shepherd should be on top of his sheep, getting them to produce more. "What for?" asks the shepherd, and the tourist gives him the full-blown story of how he can create a globalized wool industry, make lots of money, and so on. At each stage, the shepherd dutifully asks, "What for?" until finally the well-meaning tourist says to him, exasperated, "When you have a lot of money, other people will do the job and you don't need to work and can rest." As expected, the shepherd replies laconically, "And what am I doing now?"

In a way, education has also come full circle. After endless evolutionary cycles, personalized instruction and differentiation have taken us back to where it all started. We acknowledge the developmental differences in the students, which questions the validity of standards by age group and in turn provide ideological justification to fixed-time assessments. It can be conceived that standards will cover a more extensive period than the one-year academic unit of time and allow leeway for students to be ticking off these tasks or skill-oriented standards throughout a longer period.

We can think of standards that students will be completing, in terms of twenty-first-century and other related skills, via an individualized road map, an approach that may also determine the projects or tasks they will be engaged in. You can imagine a group of teachers/counselors deciding, based on what tasks have been accomplished so far, to assign students to certain projects and teams for the period at stake, taking into account the standards that remain to be met and that even may be carried on to a subsequent cycle.

Subject-Area Standards

While recognizing that subject standards should not precede skills but rather the other way around, students will not become empty repositories of data that they will forget the moment they switch off their portable Internet connection. The call for a new pedagogy that teaches twenty-first-century and other new skills does not preclude some of the traditional instruction and, especially, the teaching of contents, which, in turn, will lead to new, related standards.

The big difference, when planning a true twenty-first-century curriculum, is that contents will now serve two purposes, both of which have not been analyzed enough. On the one hand, students need to learn, and remember, certain information to ensure that they are cultured enough to be conversant citizens, and that they are able to build on that knowledge to develop higher-order skills, which are built on the prerequisite basic skills. And, subsequently, as previously suggested, the choice of subject matters that will constitute the standards that all students in that school or district are to learn should be made in terms of how well they can contribute to the development of the skills that need to be taught.

Curriculum developers should be asking themselves these difficult questions. What threshold knowledge is essential to build up the culture and the identity of that particular community? Which subjects are better suited to deliver twenty-first-century skills? Needless to say, there are no right or wrong answers, and probably the accumulated collective knowledge of the teaching profession is not ripe yet to provide answers, but serious and systematic research must be undertaken in order to start to unearth clues to the answers of these essential questions.

Principles of Twenty-First-Century Assessment

In his book *Education Nation*, Milton Chen (2010, p. 26) shares a story that can be related to the current state of affairs regarding assessment. An educator from India, speaking with an American colleague, questions the American obsession with testing. "In India," he says, "when we want to grow the elephant, we feed the elephant, we don't measure the elephant."

Thus, when defining principles for twenty-first-century assessment, a good starting point is to confront some of the harder underlying truths: the current assessment system, with its focus on evaluation rather than on education, is originated in the assumption that assessment must be used as a coercive incentive to get students, who otherwise would be disinclined to do so, to study and learn through fear of failure. In turn, this underlying assumption takes us to one of the basic needed mind-set changes of twenty-first-century education: to shift responsibility of learning from the shoulders of the students to those of the educators. The true fundamental insight of the new model is that we can move from expecting that every student must learn to sharing the burden and accepting that each and every student should learn.

If we gradually disenthrall ourselves from teaching to our self-image and accept that it is our moral imperative to engage students and to attempt, inasmuch as possible, to cater to each learner's styles and abilities, we can see the whole concept of assessment in a completely different light and lay out principles for the evolution of evaluation so that it can also feed the elephant and not just measure it.

Formative—for Learning

The first principle, almost self-evident at this point, has been amply discussed in recent years: that assessment must be formative and foster learning as opposed to the traditional end-of-unit summative evaluation system that still largely predominates in schools world-wide. Formative assessment, assessment for learning, or any other incarnation of the same principle has been discussed extensively by a multitude of authors and writers, and the virtues of providing timely feedback that helps the learning process are, at this point, irrefutable. Formative assessment is also well tailored for twenty-first-century skills, and, in particular, to lifelong learning. A presentation at the OECD/CERI International Conference, *Learning in the 21st Century: Research, Innovation and Policy*, stated (OECD/CERI International, 2008):

> Formative assessment builds students' "learning to learn" skills by:
>
> • Placing emphasis on the process of teaching and learning, and actively involving students in that process.
>
> • Building students' skills for peer- and self-assessment.
>
> • Helping students understand their own learning, and develop appropriate strategies for learning.

Diagnostic

The key to being able to make good on the promise of individualized and customized assessments that cater to a diverse range of capabilities and learning styles is being able to make ongoing, accurate diagnostics for each learner. The groundbreaking advances in the understanding of the inner workings of the brain and their application to technology are further providing a scientific basis for improvements in the instructional process and, further, in understanding learning so that adequate assessment instruments can be devised.

In this respect, technology can provide tools and mechanisms to start a diagnostic and categorize learning styles, constantly match the level of ability with increasingly challenging questions from a database or repository, and keep track of the progress and data generated by these evaluations.

Meaningful/Authentic

Again, the quest for assessments to become more authentic has been an ongoing battle for educators who have tried to add significance and meaning to evaluations that often are disconnected from reality. Within the twenty-first-century scenario, the need for authenticity becomes more stringent in that students are no longer isolated in their own reality but have access to the entire globalized, networked world through the Internet, so their degree of connectedness to reality and subsequent requirement for relevance is probably at an all-time high.

Implicit/Embedded

The concept of the test, and especially the end-of-unit evaluation, is so deeply ingrained in the students that any attempts to innovate or stray from this ageless form of assessment invariably meet skepticism for purported lack of rigor. But the artificiality of this ritual assessment method is so flagrant that it becomes self-defeating if the ultimate goal is to help learning. Formative assessment and other more modern forms of assessment instruments attempt not only to provide more continuous feedback but also to become more implicit or embedded within the learning process.

The test scenario sends out the clear message that learning stops to allow for evaluation to take place, whereas any other situation in which assessment progressively occurs throughout the learning process can be viewed as an integral part of the process itself. In that respect, a great example is found in gaming. When using games for learning, teachers can trust that feedback is given instantaneously (characters can even die); students will continue attempting to achieve success, and the log, score, or any other software feature that allows monitoring of the gamer's progress is enough assessment to determine proficiency—and all without the students even realizing that they have been assessed or, for that matter, even that they have learned.

Flexible

The current model of assessment, with some of its retrograde features, has not been the product of the collective malevolent minds of successive generations of educators wishing harm to their students. Rather, it has evolved through a sort of Darwinian natural selection process, mostly shaped by constraints faced by schools, such as the number of students in each classroom and external demands that required very specific outcomes from schools.

With the acceptance that learning is nonuniform and that the road to success is not one-dimensional, educators can now act on the long-held belief that assessment must be as flexible as needed to accommodate learning. There are only very few examples of "do right or die" activities (surgeons and perhaps test pilots or astronauts), and even those occupations train their professionals not by administering sit-down written tests but by drilling them endlessly through simulations. So any twenty-first-century assessment system must be flexible, allowed to be redone as many times as necessary, and non-threatening in terms of time. Easier said than done, and the internal constraints are still in place, but schools need to find a way to stray from such a narrowly defined focus of success through evaluation. It may prove to be an elusive equilibrium, but very much worth the effort in terms of the influence that assessment has on the learning itself.

De-penalize Failure

Once again, thinkers and authors have been vocal in advocating the need to reform a system that stigmatizes failure and, as such, is such a powerful inhibitor of creativity. Robinson and Aronica (2009), most notably, have argued persuasively in favor of creating a completely new system that allows for mistakes and failures as part of the learning process, thereby encouraging people to find their true call so that they can "find themselves within the element." One of the reasons Robinson's talks on the TED series of conferences have gone viral and attracted so many people (I get more e-mails suggesting I view these talks than on any other topic in my professional life) is that when he calls out for a completely new system that de-penalizes failure he resonates deeply with so many traumatic school experiences of the current generation (Robinson, n.d.).

Redefining assessment in the twenty-first century in such a way that mistakes are seen as a part of the learning process is a pending assignment, albeit an essential one in a world with increasing open-ended problems that require creativity and innovative thinking as almost survival alphabetization skills.

Twenty-First-Century Assessment Practices

The task ahead may seem daunting and even insurmountable, and many experts call for a complete, but certainly unrealistic, overhaul of the whole educational system. The truth is that, with the notable exceptions of charter schools or independent schools that have purposefully been created with that end in sight, no school administrator can overthrow the system and compromise test scores for the sake of introducing innovative practices.

And despite the many studies that painstakingly correlate the introduction of certain initiatives with raises in test scores, not all new projects necessarily will result in improved results, for the simple reason that, as we have already analyzed, these stan-dardized tests only measure certain dimensions of learning, and if these innovative ini-tiatives are attempting to address some of the newer skills, they will not always be reflected in better performances in the tests themselves.

However, assessment practices can be a great starter for curriculum reform. Because students and teachers alike will respond to the drivers set by assessment instruments, reforming assessment practices can provide an important initial catalyst toward a twenty-first-century curriculum. Even though it may seem that, in a way, it is like starting from back to front, the nature of some of these innovations is inextricably linked to the instructional process and will result in direct changes in the teaching and learn-ing process.

The following sections discuss a noncomprehensive list of examples of innovative assessment practices that are addressing the learning within the new knowledge paradigm, tackling several of the characteristics and principles of twenty-first-century education.

Rich Tasks

Rich tasks are just one embodiment of project-based learning (PBL), the ageless model of learning that teachers have used forever and that reemerges in the twenty-first cen-tury with its renewed promise of relevance and learning by doing.

An initiative of Queensland, Australia's Department of Education and Training (2001) that applies to all schools in that province, rich tasks are systematically inter-spersed throughout the curriculum and comprise a series of transdisciplinary tasks that constitute "a reconceptualisation of the notion of outcome as demonstration or display of mastery; that is, students display their understandings, knowledges and skills through performance on transdisciplinary activities that have an obvious connection to the wide world."

For each of the suites of tasks, grouped into three-year periods, there are explicit descriptions of the tasks, expected curriculum expectations, and resources to assist in the development of each. Also included are so-called targeted repertoires of practice, quasi-standards that describe what students should be able to accomplish as a consequence of the realization of these tasks.

Beyond the catchy name, which captures the essence of PBL, rich tasks and their extensive and systematic associated documentation are hailed as one of the best frame-works for PBL and exemplify how learning by doing these inter- or transdisciplinary projects can be rigorous and target the development of higher-order skills by exposing students to the intricacies of collaborative work in an environment that relates to real life.

Digital Portfolios

An interesting application of technology toward a more holistic form of assessment, digital portfolios attempt to provide evidence of accomplishment in various forms via the use of technological devices that allow storage of these files in a network or another medium that facilitates review by instructors.

The simplest form is to document accomplishment of a task by using personalized devices (palmtop computers, cell phones, netbook computers) so that students can take photographs, record short audio snippets and videos, and submit texts throughout the development of a project. Even in this first, unpretentious incarnation, digital portfolios present advantages related to assessment, in that they can easily record the whole process, not just the final product, and provide searchable access to teachers for future reference and storage of various forms of evidence of student accomplishment.

However, the use of digital portfolios can be taken one step further. When working on a project students can be explicitly asked to document via their digital device each stage of the development of the process, and provide feedback to their peers in the same way. Working with short-duration audio and video clips recorded by the students, with which they reflect on their own project or assess those of their peers, is a good way to prevent the "politically correct" mode into which students seem to lapse when asked to provide judgment. The regular use of these snippets promotes spontaneous answers and provides a natural medium in which students may reflect.

Digital portfolios can also be used to showcase student work online, providing a seamless transition toward the sharing or publication of student samples.

Goldsmiths (n.d.), a traditional and prestigious technical institute within the University of London, has been working on Project e-scape, an electronic-portfolio initiative that uses handheld devices and specialized software to collect data in multimedia form immediately as activities are performed, allowing learners to build a dynamic online portfolio that reflects their performance. Assessment is based on comparative pair judgment, which eventually results in a ranking of projects that substitutes the grade. The system also includes built-in checks to ensure fair and accurate evaluation of the portfolios.

Computerized Adaptive Testing

When I went to college, there was an old and legendary professor there who used to say, "Some teachers are good at asking students what they don't know. I am good at asking students what they know." This timeless dichotomy related to assessment, which is at the root of many of the conflicts that teachers experience who are intent on designing the killer evaluations that probe deep into the perceived weaknesses of students, is particularly relevant in the context of an education that, as we have repeatedly stated, needs to provide for each learner's needs and learning styles.

When testing takes place, wishful thinking dies a slow implementation death; it is obviously impractical to think that teachers can design individualized evaluations that try to bring out the best in each and every student when dealing with current class sizes. But this is where the sometimes vilified technology can come to the rescue.

Computerized adaptive testing (CAT) is a well-known and fast-developing computer-based testing system that uses software to continually assess the test taker's ability and select the best fit from a question bank to match that ability.

In an iterative process, the software incorporates this extensive bank of questions and problems and estimates an initial ability for the student taking the test (typically, for example, within the 50th percentile) and, after each response, reevaluates the ability of the test taker, consequently selecting the best-suited question among those that have not been used yet to match the level of ability estimated. In that way, test takers are evenly matched with respect to not only their level of ability but also, in more sophisticated versions of the software, their learning styles and even the topics that need to be covered.

Computerized adaptive testing is being increasingly adopted in numerous testing services, including, most notably, GMAT (Graduate Management Admission Test, used for admission to postgraduate degree programs in management and related fields), GRE (Graduate Record Examination, another general-purpose test used for admission to other graduate programs), AICPA (the American Institute of Certified Public Accountants), and many other organizations.

An evolution in CAT involves more user-friendly graphical interfaces and is even entering the realm of gaming, with different scenarios and challenges posed based on each learner's styles and abilities.

Self-Assessment and Creating Assessment Instruments

Once more coming full circle, another often used practice by teachers consists in students administering some form of self-assessment of their own learning. In the light of the new knowledge paradigm and the primary stated goal of lifelong learning, self-assessment becomes the ultimate skill.

If we are able to learn through life and beyond school and the teachers who evaluate that learning, it is absolutely essential to develop internal criteria that allow each person to assess whether a topic or skill has been learned or not, and, as such, it becomes one of the main drivers of twenty-first-century assessment.

The reasons that our goals do not match the current technical knowledge for most educators become self-explanatory in the need to deepen research on some of these forms of assessment. A much more scientific approach needs to be taken toward self-evaluation. As with any skill, it needs to be progressively fostered and developed in students from a very early age, and the habit of evaluating whether one has learned or not should be ingrained in them all throughout the schooling process until it becomes almost second nature.

Another related skill that promotes reflection and metacognition is developed when students create their own assessment instruments and write related rubrics. Because the knowledge era requires a much higher general level of consciousness with regard to one's own learning, all of the alternatives to traditional assessment that involve thinking about the learning process itself are undoubtedly beneficial to the effort of creating this mindset of heightened awareness about learning.

Gaming

Although still considered almost educational blasphemy in some more conservative environments, the introduction of educational games in the classroom is vastly underrated in terms of the benefits to be gained by students. At a lecture in 2007, Douglas Reeves summed up the many advantages of using games in the classroom: students do not complain about injustice every time they lose in the game, which more often than not gets them literally killed, but they try over and over again until they learn from their mistakes and succeed.

In effect, the video game environment genuinely embodies many of the desired traits of assessment: students are engaged, they are given unlimited opportunities to progress and achieve the learning objectives, feedback is instantaneous and relevant, and the experience is customized in that most games feature the ability to choose characters or earn new capabilities that players can select from to improve their avatar's abilities. One of the great advantages from the teacher's point of view is that assessment is implicit and embedded in the game. We can imagine a rubric that simply correlates a numeric grade with the number of points that have to be attained in the game, or how many stages have to be cleared. Many of these games also include logs that keep tabs on gamers' activities and allow the instructor to gauge the accomplishments of and dedication by students, so as not to just rely on how skilled they could eventually become at playing the game.

Marc Prensky (2006), the long-time technology pioneer, has written a well-read book on the topic, aptly named *Don't Bother Me Mom—I'm Learning!* and is one of the recognized leaders of the Serious Games movement, which advocates for the use of educational games for learning. It could be argued that not enough realistic games can be found on the market that cater to educational needs, and it is a fair comment. However, as an Internet search will yield, there are many more free resources for educational games than one would imagine. Every year I have my junior year students scout for games on the Web and persuade teachers to use them in their lessons. I thought that after so many years in the classroom I had exhausted my capacity for astonishment at excuses by students, but after assigning this project for a couple of years I am amazed at the reasons many adults give for not breaking out of their comfort zone.

Creativity, Imagination, and Nonconventional Skills

Even though the twenty-first century is full of promise, and we have explicitly and implicitly highlighted the many benefits of having access to unlimited information, the shortcomings of the model are also evident in the loss of some capacities by students, which consequently become very important skills.

The fact that there is no need to project or visualize concepts and that, from Google Earth all the way down, the younger generation is able to transform the www into whatever, wherever, whenever, may threaten some capacities like visualization, imagination, and creativity at an age when the battle cry is to not reinvent the wheel.

Consequently, schools need to incorporate the teaching of these skills and abilities within the curriculum, and, yes, also assess them.

Once again we are technically at a loss in that assessment instruments have overwhelmingly been geared to gauge content acquisition and, in the best of cases, some subject-related skills. A good way to start addressing the issue of twenty-first-century skills is to challenge teachers to develop specific rubrics to assess creativity, originality, and imagination, just to cite a few skills, as well as the other dimensions of learning that are continually assessed.

Despite the lack of a solid volume of technical expertise in the matter, some simple solutions can start paving the way by rewarding students for, as an example, suggesting multiple approaches to solve a problem or awarding credit not just for right or wrong answers but also for the process itself. Could we conceive of an evaluation by which students are forced to present more than one answer or solution to a problem (which, of course, needs to be construed in such a way that it allows for multiple perspectives)?

Imagination, creativity, and other high-order skills can be taught and evaluated, and there is consensus that gone are the days in which a person could be considered to be born with these traits or not have them at all. In that respect, Carol Dweck's (2007) groundbreaking work on looking beyond a fixed definition of intelligence and prevailing upon students to accept that thinking skills can be learned is a pending assignment in schools, where, if anything, the focus on judgmental assessment has reinforced a deterministic, fixed view of intelligence to the detriment of talent development of many a generation of learners.

Assessing Unlearning?

Another apparent oxymoron would be to try to think of how to assess unlearning. One of the basic tenets of the new paradigm is that flexibility, lifelong learning, and a general learner mind-set are not enough to achieve success in the future. In order to be truly open to changes and learning what is new, the twenty-first-century learner must also be ready to unlearn the old ways, as preconceptions and locking ourselves into the way we have done things is, undoubtedly, one of the greatest inhibitors of change—so much so that the American futurist and writer Alvin Toffler is famously quoted as saying: "The illiterate of the 21st century will not be those who cannot read and write, but those who cannot learn, unlearn, and relearn."

But how can we assess unlearning? If we want to act on this principle of twenty-first-century learning, we should be able to evaluate the degree of unlearning, or openness to new solutions and nonattachment to solutions of the past.

Beyond the obvious joke that some poorly performing students would get top grades at unlearning because they never learned the previous stuff anyway, specific assessment can be geared toward evaluating readiness for change and the ability to unlearn and relearn. Breaking away again from conventional wisdom, the instructional process may include stages in which students learn to perform activities one way and are then taught alternative methods that are intentionally far more efficient. The evaluation can then pose a problem without prescribing the application of one method over the other and assess how students are able to discern the most conducive method for the solution.

The Tipping Point for Standards and Assessment

I once saw in a presentation a cartoon that portrayed a mother traveling down a road with her child. The mother says to the boy, "Stop asking 'when are we getting there?' I told you, we are nomads!"

And, in a way, that is what happens with education in the twenty-first century. Like the child in the cartoon, we need to acknowledge that we will never find one-size-fits-all definitive solutions that cater to every school and district, and that the very dynamic changes that are the norm in this particular time in history will force us to continually—playing on words—reassess assessment, as well as associated standards.

It is commonly said that many of the jobs that the current generation of school students will perform in the future have not been invented yet, and, as the workplace scenario evolves, new skills will emerge and standards and assessment will have to be subjected to an ongoing revision process that will become almost intrinsic to educational planning.

Educational reform is an inherently complex process. Education is one of the most traditional professions that exist, mostly for the reason that it has remained almost unchanged throughout history. The changes that are now affecting it are so radical and widespread that they are hard to fathom, and it is almost inevitable that we, the current teachers, will, for all purposes, become a transitional generation of educators. It is understandable, in terms of implementation, that there is such a big difference between what is known and what is done, but, as Peter Drucker reportedly said, the tipping point happens when remaining as we are is more risky than changing. I think that we have arrived at that point in education today. Change is not a trend or a sign of the times but rather a moral imperative for educators who want to serve their students well. And assessment and related standards may well prove to be the best and easiest catalyst to change in education these days.

References

Bellanca, J., & Brandt, R. (2010). *21st century skills: Rethinking how students learn* (Leading Edge). Bloomington, IN: Solution Tree.

Chen, M. (2010). *Education nation: Six leading edges of innovation in our schools.* San Francisco: Jossey-Bass.

Dweck, C. (2007). *Mindset: The new psychology of success.* New York, NY: Ballantine Books.

Goldsmiths. (n.d.). Project e-scape. Retrieved from http://www.gold.ac.uk/teru/projectinfo/ projecttitle,12370,en.php

Guskey, T. (2008). *Enhancing and evaluating the effectiveness of professional development.* Paper presented at the English Speaking Scholastic Association of the River Plate Conference, San Miguel del Monte, Argentina.

OECD/CERI International. (2008, May). *Learning in the 21st century: Research, innovation and policy. Summary report.* Paris: OECD/CERI International Conference.

Prensky, M. (2006). *Don't bother me Mom—I'm learning!* St. Paul, MN: Paragon House.

Reeves, D. (2007). *Closing the implementation gap.* Paper presented at the English Speaking Scholastic Association of the River Plate Conference, Buenos Aires, Argentina.

Robinson, K. (n.d.). Various presentations. Retrieved from www.TED.com.

Robinson, K. (2006). *Ken Robinson says schools kill creativity.* TED Talks [video]. Retrieved from http://www.ted.com/talks/lang/eng/ken_robinson_says_schools_kill_creativity.html

Robinson, K., & Aronica, L. (2009). *The element: How finding your passion changes everything.* New York, NY: Penguin.

State of Queensland Department of Education and Training. (2001). *The rich tasks.* Retrieved from http://education.qld.gov.au/corporate/newbasics/html/richtasks/richtasks.html

Index